M000103099

初級日本語
〔げんき〕

AN INTEGRATED COURSE IN
ELEMENTARY JAPANESE

GENKI

I

Eri Banno 坂野永理
Yutaka Ohno 大野裕
Yoko Sakane 坂根庸子
Chikako Shinagawa 品川恭子

The Japan Times

First edition: May 1999
60th printing: June 2011

Editorial assistance: guild
Illustrations: Noriko Udagawa and Reiko Maruyama
Cover art and Editorial design: Nakayama Design Office
                         Gin-o Nakayama, Mutsumi Satoh, and Masataka Muramatsu
Published by The Japan Times, Ltd.
5-4, Shibaura 4-chome, Minato-ku, Tokyo 108-0023, Japan
Phone: 03-3453-2013
http://bookclub.japantimes.co.jp/
http://genki.japantimes.co.jp/

ISBN4-7890-0963-7

Printed in Japan

はじめに

　本書は学生へのニーズ調査に始まり、実際にくり返し使用し、学生の反応や意見、感想を受けて、細部にわたる改訂を重ねて作成しました。本書をこのような形で出版するまでに4年余りという時間を要しましたが、そのかいがあり理想の教材に近づくことができたと感じています。この教材によって、学習者は絵やゲームなどを通して楽しく、無理なく日本語の力をつけることができると確信しています。

　本書が完成したのは多くの方々のおかげです。特に出版にあたり、ジャパンタイムズ出版部の関戸千明さんには大変お世話になりました。また、11課以降の作成に加わってくださった渡嘉敷恭子さん、本書を試用し助言をくれた関西外国語大学留学生別科の同僚、実習生、試用版のイラスト担当の田嶋香織さん、翻訳面でご協力いただいた大川ジュディさん、今まで私たちをご指導してくださった先生方に心からお礼を申し上げます。そして、最後に本書作成の出発点であり、原動力でもあった関西外国語大学の留学生に感謝の意を表したいと思います。

Preface

Producing the materials for this textbook involved a long process of surveying students' needs, writing up the results, making detailed revisions to the material based on the surveys, and responding to the reactions and comments of students who used a trial version of this text. It has taken more than four years to complete this project. Our labor has been rewarded, however, because this book is based on our original plan to produce the ideal textbook——one that will enable students to learn Japanese smoothly, while also enjoying lively games and helpful illustrations.

We have an extensive list of people to thank for the completion of this textbook. First, our sincere thanks to Chiaki Sekido of the Publications Department of The Japan Times for seeing this book through the publishing process. Particular acknowledgment goes to Kyoko Tokashiki who helped in the production of Lesson 11 and following, to our colleagues and trainees in the Asian Studies Program of Kansai Gaidai University who attempted the trial version and made invaluable suggestions, to Kaori Tajima for her illustrations in the trial version, to Judy Okawa for translating, and to the teachers whose heartfelt guidance encouraged us throughout the process. Finally, we would also like to express our gratitude to the foreign students at Kansai Gaidai University for providing us with the opportunity to write this book.

初級日本語 [げんき] I

もくじ

▶ 会話・文法編
かい わ ぶん ぽう へん

▶ 読み書き編
よ か へん

▶ 巻末
かん まつ

本書について

Ⅰ 対象とねらい

　『初級日本語 げんき』は初めて日本語を学ぶ人のための教材です。第Ⅰ巻・第Ⅱ巻の2冊、全23課で初級日本語の学習を修了します。大学生はもとより、高校生や社会人、日本語を独習しようとしている人も、効果的に日本語が習得できます。文法の説明などは英語で書いてあるので、英語がある程度わかることを前提としています。

　『初級日本語 げんき』は総合教材として、日本語の四技能（聞く・話す・読む・書く）を伸ばし、総合的な日本語の能力を高めていくことを目標としています。正確に文を作ることができても流暢さがなかったり、流暢ではあっても簡単なことしか言えないということがないように、言語の習得の目標とすべき「正確さ」「流暢さ」「複雑さ」がバランスよく高められるように配慮してあります。

Ⅱ テキストの構成

　テキストは大きく「会話・文法編」「読み書き編」「巻末」から構成されています。以下、順番に説明します。

A ▶会話・文法編

　「会話・文法編」では、基本的な文法を学び、語彙を増やしながら、「話すこと」「聞くこと」について学習します。「会話・文法編」の各課は以下の部分から構成されています。

●会話

　「会話」は、日本に来た留学生とその友人・家族を中心に展開し、学習者が日常生活で経験しそうなさまざまな場面から成っています。会話文を通して、学習者は「あいづち」などを含めた自然なやりとりに触れ、会話の中で文と文がどのようにつながっていくか、どのような部分が省略されたりするかなどを学ぶことができます。「会話」には、その課で学ぶ新しい学習項目が多く含まれているため、課の初めに学習者がこれを読むと非常に難しいと感じるかもしれません。これらの項目は練習を通して定着が図られるので、初めは難しくてもあまり心配しないようにしてください。

　また、「会話」は別売の CD に録音されています。学習者にはこの CD を聞いて、発音やイントネーションなどに気をつけながら、くり返して言う練習をすることを勧めます。

●単語

　「単語」には、その課の「会話」と「練習」に出てくる新しい単語がまとめてあります。この中で、「会話」に出てくる単語には＊印が付けてあります。第 1 課と第 2 課では機能別に単語を提示し、第 3 課からは品詞別に提示してあります。また、巻末には全課の単語を収録した「さくいん」があります。

　「単語」の中の言葉はその後の課でもくり返し出てきますから、学習者は毎日少しずつ覚えるようにしたほうがいいでしょう。第 3 課から、常用漢字で書ける単語にはすべて漢字を併記してありますが、この漢字は覚える必要はありません。

　なお、このテキストでは語のアクセント（拍の高低）を示していません。日本語のアクセントは地域差や個人差（世代間の差など）が激しい上に、語形変化や単語の連結などによる変化も複雑です。ですから、アクセントにはあまり神経質にならず、文のイントネーションなども含め、できるだけ CD の音声を模倣するように心掛けてください。

●文法

　文法説明は、かなり詳しく書いてありますので、独習している人も容易に理解できます。また、教室で学んでいる学習者はあらかじめ文法説明を読んでから授業に臨んでください。

　後の「練習」で取りあげられている項目はすべて「文法」の中で説明してあります。練習はしないが説明が必要な文法や語彙については、「文法」の最後の「表現ノート」に随時まとめてあります。

●練習

　「練習」は、各学習項目に関して基本練習から応用練習へと段階的に配列してあり、学習者がこれらの練習を順番にこなしていくことによって、無理なく日本語が習得できるように配慮してあります。

　答えが一つに決められるような基本練習は CD に録音されており、［🔊］の印がついています。CD には解答も録音されていますから、学習者は各自で自習することが可能です。

　また、「練習」の最後には「まとめの練習」があります。これは複数の学習項目を組み合わせた練習や「会話」を応用して別の会話を作る練習など、その課の学習の仕上げとなる練習です。

●コラム

　課の最後に必要に応じてコラムを設けてあります。このコラムには、第 1 課の「じかん・とし」のようにその課のトピックに関連した表現や、第10課の「駅で」のように場面ごとに使わ

れる表現がまとめてあります。これらの単語も、巻末の「さくいん」に載せてあります。

B ▶ 読み書き編

「読み書き編」では、日本語の文字を学び、文章を読んだり書いたりすることによって、読解力と書く力を伸ばします。第1課でひらがな、第2課でカタカナを学習した後、第3課以降で漢字を学習します。第3課以降の各課は、以下のような構成です。

●漢字表

漢字表には、その課で学ぶ新出漢字が掲載されています。各課で約15の漢字を学びますが、一度に覚えるのには無理があるので、毎日少しずつ覚えていくようにしてください。漢字表は以下のようになっています。

①と⑤に示された漢字や単語の読み方で、ひらがなで書かれたものは「訓読み」、つまり日本語古来の読みです。カタカナで書かれたものは「音読み」、つまり昔の中国語の発音を輸入したものです。訓読みも音読みも、単語の中で使われた時、音が変化する場合があります。(たとえば、「学」という漢字は「ガク」と読みますが、「学校」という単語の中では「ガッ」と読みます。)そのような派生的な読み方もこの部分に表記されています。

なお、漢字の中には多くの読み方を持っているものもありますが、漢字表には、初級レベルにふさわしい読みが挙げられています。

④と⑤で　　の中に入っている読み方や単語は、その課で覚えるべきものです。一方、　　以外のものは参考として挙げたもので、覚えなくてもかまいません。

それぞれの漢字は、ワークブックの読み書き編の中に練習シートがありますので、テキストの漢字表に示された筆順を見ながら何度も練習してください。

●練習

　『げんきⅠ』には、漢字の練習、読解本文と内容についての質問、そして書く練習が載せてあります。漢字の練習は、漢字を分解してできる部品から漢字を再構築する問題や漢字から単語を作る問題など、さまざまな形式の練習を通じて漢字に慣れていくことを目標としています。読解本文は、短く、親しみやすいものを中心に構成しています。それまでに「会話・文法編」で学んだ文法や単語の知識が前提とされており、新出単語はその都度、単語表を掲載しています。練習の最後には、書く練習として作文トピックが提示されています。

　『げんきⅡ』には、読解本文と内容についての質問、そして書く練習が載せてあります。読解本文は、手紙、物語、エッセイ、広告など、さまざまな分野の日本語を取り上げています。その課までに学んだ単語や文法、漢字の知識が前提とされており、課を追うごとに、長さや難易度などが増していきます。新出単語も本文での提出順に掲載されています。練習の最後には、作文トピックが提示されています。

C ▶巻末

　第Ⅰ巻・第Ⅱ巻それぞれの巻末に「さくいん」を準備しました。一つは和英さくいんで、各課の単語表やコラムに掲載されている単語を五十音順に再録しました。単語に付された数字は、その単語が導入された課の番号を示しています。英和さくいんでは、各課の単語が訳語のアルファベット順に再録されています。

　その他に、動詞の活用表と助数詞の音の変化をまとめた表を掲載しました。

Ⅲ　表記と書体について

　本文は基本的に、漢字仮名交じりで表記しています。漢字表記は、基本的に常用漢字表に従いましたが、常用漢字に含まれている漢字でも、初級の学習者には無縁であるようなものは、ひらがな表記にしてあります。

　また、「会話・文法編」のみを学習することも可能なように、「会話・文法編」では漢字にはすべてふりがなが振ってあります。

　ただし、「会話・文法編」冒頭の「あいさつ」と第1課、第2課は、学習者の負担を軽減し自習を容易にするため、ひらがな・カタカナ表記とし、ローマ字を併記しました。このローマ字併記はあくまでも補助的なものですから、最初から頼りすぎないように心掛けてください。ひらがなは「読み書き編」の第1課で、カタカナは第2課で、それぞれ学習します。

　なお、「読み書き編」では、漢字を第3課以降に学習していきますが、学習の定着が図れるよう、既習の漢字にはふりがなが振ってありません。

　本文の日本語は、ほとんどが「教科書体」の書体で組まれています。教科書体は手書き文字に近い書体ですから、学習者は自分が書く文字のモデルとすることができます。ただし、実際に印刷された日本語文では、さまざまな書体を見ることがあります。文字によっては、書体によってかなり形が異なります。特に、離れた二つの線が筆づかいによって一つにつながる場合があるので、注意が必要です。

例：	教科書体	明朝体	ゴシック体	手書き文字
	さ	さ	さ	さ
	き	き	き	き
	り	り	り	り
	ら	ら	ら	ら
	こ	こ	こ	こ
	や	や	や	や

Introduction

I Aim and purpose

GENKI: An Integrated Course in Elementary Japanese is a textbook for beginners in the study of the Japanese language. Students can complete the elementary-level study of Japanese in the 23 lessons of this text, which is divided into two volumes. The book is designed mainly for use in university and college courses, but it is also effective for high school students and adults who are beginning to learn Japanese either at school or on their own. Hopefully, students will have at least a basic knowledge of English, because grammar explanations are given in English.

    GENKI: An Integrated Course in Elementary Japanese is a comprehensive approach to developing the four basic language skills (listening, speaking, reading, and writing) in order to cultivate overall Japanese-language ability. Much emphasis has been placed on balancing accuracy, fluency, and complexity so that students using the material would not end up speaking accurately yet in a stilted manner, nor fluently yet employing only simple grammatical structures.

II Structure of the textbook

This textbook basically consists of three sections: Dialogue and Grammar, Reading and Writing, and the Appendix. A detailed explanation of each part follows.

A▶ Dialogue and Grammar
The Dialogue and Grammar section aims at improving students' speaking and listening abilities by learning basic grammar and increasing vocabulary. The Dialogue and Grammar section of each lesson is comprised of the following components:

●Dialogue
The dialogues revolve around the lives of foreign students living in Japan, their friends, and their families, presenting various scenes that students are likely to face in their daily lives. By practicing natural expressions and *aizuchi* (responses that make conversations go smoothly), students are able to understand how sentences are connected and how some phrases are shortened in daily conversation. Because the Dialogue section of each lesson covers a lot of new grammar and vocabulary, students may feel it is too difficult

to understand at first. Don't be overly concerned, however, because the grammar and vocabulary will gradually take root with practice.

Dialogues are recorded on the accompanying CD. Students are encouraged to practice regularly by listening to the CD and carefully noting pronunciation and intonation.

●Vocabulary

The Vocabulary section presents all the new words encountered in both the Dialogue and Practice sections of each lesson. Words that appear in the Dialogue are marked with an asterisk (*). Words are listed according to their function in Lessons 1 and 2, and by parts of speech in Lesson 3 and following. In addition, all words presented in the text are also found in the Index at the end of each volume.

Words found in the Vocabulary section of each lesson appear frequently in subsequent lessons, thus students are encouraged to learn them little by little each day. After Lesson 2, commonly used kanji equivalents of some words (Joyo Kanji) are also listed, but students are not required to memorize them.

This textbook does not indicate a word's accents. The accent of a Japanese word varies considerably, depending on the region, the speaker's age (including the generation gap between speakers), the word's paradigmatic form, and its connection with other words. Therefore, don't be overly concerned about the accent, but try to imitate as closely as possible the intonation heard on the accompanying CD.

●Grammar

Grammar explanations are detailed, so that students can easily study them on their own. Students at school are expected to read the grammar explanations before each class.

This section also fully explains the items found in the Practice section that follows. Necessary explanations for the grammar and vocabulary that are not found in the Practice section can be found in the Expression Notes at the end of each Grammar section.

●Practice

This section includes questions related to what was taught in each section of the lesson, providing students with both basic practice and application. By answering the questions sequentially, students can naturally build up their Japanese-language ability. The exercises with only one answer are marked with 🔊 and recorded on the CD, allowing students the opportunity to practice on their own.

The last part of the Practice section contains Review Exercises, which incorporate aspects of the lesson as a whole. For example, some questions combine various topics covered in the lesson, and some call for the creation of new phrases based on what was learned in the Dialogue section.

●Supplement

Finally, some lessons include additional or supplementary information. This includes expressions related to the topic of the lesson, as in "Time and age" in Lesson 1, or expressions suitable at certain times or places, as in "At the station" in Lesson 10. Words introduced in the Supplement section are found in the Index of each volume.

B▶Reading and Writing

The Reading and Writing section aims to foster comprehension and writing ability by learning Japanese characters and by providing opportunities to practice both reading and writing. *Hiragana* is introduced in Lesson 1, followed by *katakana* in Lesson 2, and kanji in Lesson 3 and following. From Lesson 3, each lesson contains the following components:

●Kanji list

Each new kanji introduced in a lesson is contained in a list, each with about 15 kanji. This makes it easy to memorize a few each day, rather than be overwhelmed with so many at once.

Among the readings shown in (4) and (5), *hiragana* indicates the *kun'yomi*, or Japanese readings for a kanji, while *katakana* indicates the *on'yomi*, or Chinese reading. Both *kun'yomi* and *on'yomi* are sometimes altered in compounds of two or more kanji. For example, the ordinary pronunciation of 学 is "*gaku*," which becomes "*ga(k)*" when the kanji is used in the word 学校. Such derivative readings are also included in (4) and (5).

Although some kanji have many readings, only those readings that are useful at an elementary level are included.

Shaded readings and words in each lesson should be memorized. The others are for reference, so students don't need to memorize them. A practice sheet for each kanji is provided in the Reading and Writing section of the Workbook. Students should practice writing the kanji repeatedly, according to the stroke order shown on the kanji list in the textbook.

●Practice

GENKI I consists of kanji practice, readings for comprehension, questions about the content of the readings, and writing practice. Kanji practice includes various types of questions, such as having students reconstruct a kanji from its various parts or make new words by combining kanji. By tackling these problems, students will realize the goal of practice—to become more proficient in their use of kanji. Basically, the readings are short and deal with subjects familiar to the students. They are easy to understand if the student has learned the vocabulary and grammar taught previously in the Dialogue and Grammar section. When readings include new words, a corresponding word list is provided. Finally, composition topics are given for writing practice.

GENKI II contains readings for comprehension, questions about the content of the readings, and writing practice. The readings employ various styles of Japanese, ranging from letters and fables to essays and advertisements. With a knowledge of the previously learned vocabulary, grammar, and kanji, the readings are easy to understand but grow longer and more difficult in later lessons. Word lists are provided for newly introduced vocabulary. Finally, composition topics are introduced.

C▶ Appendix

Volumes 1 and 2 both contain an Index. The Japanese-English Index, in *hiragana* order, lists words found in the Vocabulary and Supplement section of each lesson. The number next to a word indicates the lesson in which the word was introduced. In the English-Japanese Index, English equivalents to Japanese words are arranged in alphabetical order.

Also included in the Appendix are tables of verb conjugations as well as sound inflections of the expressions related to numbers.

Ⅲ Orthography and font

The basic text is written in kanji and *hiragana*. Kanji is used for the most commonly used characters, those that appear in the official list of Joyo Kanji. *Hiragana* is used instead, however, when the Joyo Kanji equivalent would not be necessary for beginning students of Japanese.

So that students can easily study the Dialogue and Grammar section, the pronunciation of every kanji is indicated in *hiragana*. However, to lessen the burden on the students and allow them to study on their own, Greetings and Lessons 1 and 2 are represented in *hiragana* and *katakana*, as well as by romanized forms. It is best not to rely too much on the romanizations, but use them only as a learning aid. Students study *hiragana* and *katakana* in Lessons 1 and 2, respectively, of the Reading and Writing section.

Students study kanji from Lesson 3 in the Reading and Writing section, where pronunciations of the kanji already presented are not indicated in *hiragana*, in order to promote the students' increasing acquisition of kanji.

The Japanese in the basic text is set mainly in the Textbook font, which resembles handwriting and serves as a good model for students. Students will encounter a variety of fonts used for Japanese materials, however, and should be aware that the shape of some characters differ considerably, depending on the font used. Note especially that with some characters, we find two separate strokes in one style are merged into a single stroke.

Example:	Textbook font	Mincho font	Gothic font	Handwriting
	さ	さ	さ	さ
	き	き	き	き
	り	り	り	り
	ら	ら	ら	ら
	こ	こ	こ	こ
	や	や	や	や

Japanese Writing System

There are three kinds of characters in Japanese: *hiragana*, *katakana*, and kanji.[1] All three characters can be seen in a single sentence.

テレビを見ます。

katakana kanji *hiragana*

I watch television.

Hiragana and *katakana*, like the alphabet, represent sounds. As you can see in the above example, *hiragana* has a roundish shape and is used for conjugation endings, function words, and native Japanese words not covered by kanji. *Katakana*, which has rather straight lines, is normally used for writing loanwords and foreign names. For example, the Japanese word for "television" is written in *katakana* as テレビ (*terebi*). Kanji, or Chinese characters, represent not just sounds but also meanings. Mostly, kanji are used for nouns and the stems of verbs and adjectives.

① H i r a g a n a

1. Basic Hiragana Syllables

There are forty-six basic *hiragana* syllables, which are listed below. Once you memorize this chart, you will have the skill to transcribe all of the Japanese sounds.

あ *a*	い *i*	う *u*	え *e*	お *o*
か *ka*	き *ki*	く *ku*	け *ke*	こ *ko*
さ *sa*	し **shi*	す *su*	せ *se*	そ *so*
た *ta*	ち **chi*	つ **tsu*	て *te*	と *to*
な *na*	に *ni*	ぬ *nu*	ね *ne*	の *no*
は *ha*	ひ *hi*	ふ *fu*	へ *he*	ほ *ho*

---

[1] There is another writing system called *rōmaji* (Roman letters) which is used for station names, signs, and so on.

ま *ma*	み *mi*	む *mu*	め *me*	も *mo*
や *ya*		ゆ *yu*		よ *yo*
ら *ra*	り *ri*	る *ru*	れ *re*	ろ *ro*
わ *wa*				を ****o*
ん *n*				

*The syllables し, ち, and つ are romanized as *shi*, *chi*, and *tsu*, respectively, which is closer to the English pronunciation.

**を is also pronounced as "*wo*."

The romanization is given for general pronunciation reference.

2. Hiragana with Diacritical Marks

You can transcribe 23 additional sounds by adding diacritical marks. With a pair of short diagonal strokes (ˋ), the unvoiced consonants *k*, *s*, *t*, and *h* become voiced consonants *g*, *z*, *d*, and *b*, respectively. The consonant *h* changes to *p* with the addition of a small circle (˚).

が *ga*	ぎ *gi*	ぐ *gu*	げ *ge*	ご *go*
ざ *za*	じ *ji*	ず *zu*	ぜ *ze*	ぞ *zo*
だ *da*	*ぢ *ji*	*づ *zu*	で *de*	ど *do*
ば *ba*	び *bi*	ぶ *bu*	べ *be*	ぼ *bo*
ぱ *pa*	ぴ *pi*	ぷ *pu*	ぺ *pe*	ぽ *po*

*ぢ (*ji*) and づ (*zu*) are pronounced the same as じ (*ji*) and ず (*zu*), respectively, and have limited use.

3. Transcribing Contracted Sounds

Small や, ゆ, and よ follow after letters in the second column (*i*-vowel *hiragana*, except い) and are used to transcribe contracted sounds. The contracted sound represents a single syllable.

きゃ *kya*	きゅ *kyu*	きょ *kyo*		ぎゃ *gya*	ぎゅ *gyu*	ぎょ *gyo*
しゃ *sha*	しゅ *shu*	しょ *sho*		じゃ *ja*	じゅ *ju*	じょ *jo*
ちゃ *cha*	ちゅ *chu*	ちょ *cho*				
にゃ *nya*	にゅ *nyu*	にょ *nyo*				
ひゃ *hya*	ひゅ *hyu*	ひょ *hyo*		びゃ *bya*	びゅ *byu*	びょ *byo*
みゃ *mya*	みゅ *myu*	みょ *myo*		ぴゃ *pya*	ぴゅ *pyu*	ぴょ *pyo*
りゃ *rya*	りゅ *ryu*	りょ *ryo*				

4. Transcribing Double Consonants

There is another small letter つ, which is used when transcribing double consonants such as *tt* and *pp*.

Examples: かった   *ka__tt__a*   (won)   cf. かた   *kata*   (shoulder)

          さっか   *sa__kk__a*   (writer)

          はっぱ   *ha__pp__a*   (leaf)

          ざっし   *za__ss__hi*   (magazine)

Note that double consonant *n*'s, as in *sannen* (3 years), are written with ん + a *hiragana* with an initial *n* sound (な, に, ぬ, ね, or の).

Examples: さんねん   *sa__nn__en*   (3 years)

          あんない   *a__nn__ai*   (guide)

5. Other Issues Relating to Transcription and Pronunciation

A. Long Vowels

When the same vowel is placed one right after the other, the pronunciation of the vowel becomes about twice as long as the single vowel. Be sure to hold the sound long enough, because the length of the vowel can change one word to another.

aa	おばあさん	*obaasan*	(grandmother)	cf. おばさん	*obasan*	(aunt)
ii	おじいさん	*ojiisan*	(grandfather)	cf. おじさん	*ojisan*	(uncle)
uu	すうじ	*suuji*	(number)			

ee   The long *ee* sound is usually transcribed by adding an い to an *e*-vowel *hiragana*. There are a few words, however, in which え is used instead of い.

えいが	*eega*	(movie)
おねえさん	*oneesan*	(big sister)

oo   The long *oo* sound is in most cases transcribed by adding an う to an *o*-vowel *hiragana*. There are, however, words in which the long vowel is transcribed with an お, for historical reasons.

ほうりつ	*hooritsu*	(law)
とお	*too*	(ten)

B. Pronunciation of ん

ん "*n*" is treated like a full syllable, in terms of length. Its pronunciation varies, however, depending on the sound that follows it. Japanese speakers are normally not aware of the different sound values of ん. Therefore, you do not need to worry too much about its pronunciation.[2]

C. Vowels to Be Dropped

The vowels *i* and *u* are sometimes dropped when placed between voiceless consonants (*k*, *s*, *t*, *p*, and *h*), or at the end of an utterance preceded by voiceless consonants.

Example: すきです *s(u)kides(u)* (I like it.)

---

[2]One variety of the ん pronunciation merits discussing here. When it is followed by a vowel or at the end of an utterance, ん indicates that the preceding vowel is long and nasalized. (Nasalized vowels are shown here with a tilde above vowel letters. You hear nasalized vowels in French words such as "bon," or the English interjection "uh-uh," as in "no.")

れんあい	*rẽai*	(romance)
ほん	*hõ*	(book)

Followed by *n*, *t*, *d*, *s*, and *z* sounds, ん is pronounced as "n."

おんな	*onna*	(woman)

Followed by *m*, *p*, and *b* sounds, ん is pronounced as "m."

さんぽ	*sampo*	(stroll)

Followed by *k* and *g* sounds, ん is pronounced as "ng" as in "song."

まんが	*maŋga*	(comics)

D. Accent in the Japanese Language

Japanese has a pitch accent: all syllables are pronounced basically either in high or low pitch. Unlike the English stress accent in which stressed syllables tend to be pronounced longer and louder, in Japanese each syllable is pronounced approximately in equal length and stress. The pitch patterns in Japanese vary greatly, depending on the region of the country.

Examples: あさ $a_{\overline{sa}}$ (morning)

なまえ $_{\overline{na}}{}^{ma\ e}$ (name)

たかい $_{\overline{ta}}{}^{ka}{}_{i}$ (high)

Ⅱ **K a t a k a n a**

ア *a*	イ *i*	ウ *u*	エ *e*	オ *o*
カ *ka*	キ *ki*	ク *ku*	ケ *ke*	コ *ko*
サ *sa*	シ **shi*	ス *su*	セ *se*	ソ *so*
タ *ta*	チ **chi*	ツ **tsu*	テ *te*	ト *to*
ナ *na*	ニ *ni*	ヌ *nu*	ネ *ne*	ノ *no*
ハ *ha*	ヒ *hi*	フ *fu*	ヘ *he*	ホ *ho*
マ *ma*	ミ *mi*	ム *mu*	メ *me*	モ *mo*
ヤ *ya*		ユ *yu*		ヨ *yo*
ラ *ra*	リ *ri*	ル *ru*	レ *re*	ロ *ro*
ワ *wa*				ヲ *o*
ン *n*				

*The syllables シ, チ, and ツ are romanized as *shi*, *chi*, and *tsu*, respectively, to give a closer English pronunciation.

ガ *ga*	ギ *gi*	グ *gu*	ゲ *ge*	ゴ *go*
ザ *za*	ジ *ji*	ズ *zu*	ゼ *ze*	ゾ *zo*
ダ *da*	*ヂ *ji*	*ヅ *zu*	デ *de*	ド *do*
バ *ba*	ビ *bi*	ブ *bu*	ベ *be*	ボ *bo*

パ *pa*	ピ *pi*	プ *pu*	ペ *pe*	ポ *po*

*ヂ (*ji*) and ヅ (*zu*) are pronounced the same as ジ (*ji*) and ズ (*zu*), respectively, and have limited use.

キャ *kya*	キュ *kyu*	キョ *kyo*
シャ *sha*	シュ *shu*	ショ *sho*
チャ *cha*	チュ *chu*	チョ *cho*
ニャ *nya*	ニュ *nyu*	ニョ *nyo*
ヒャ *hya*	ヒュ *hyu*	ヒョ *hyo*
ミャ *mya*	ミュ *myu*	ミョ *myo*
リャ *rya*	リュ *ryu*	リョ *ryo*

ギャ *gya*	ギュ *gyu*	ギョ *gyo*
ジャ *ja*	ジュ *ju*	ジョ *jo*

ビャ *bya*	ビュ *byu*	ビョ *byo*
ピャ *pya*	ピュ *pyu*	ピョ *pyo*

The pronunciation of *katakana* and its combinations are the same as those of *hiragana,* except for the following points.

(1) The long vowels are written with ー.

Examples:	カー	*kaa*	(car)
	スキー	*sukii*	(ski)
	スーツ	*suutsu*	(suit)
	ケーキ	*keeki*	(cake)
	ボール	*booru*	(ball)

When you write vertically, the ー mark needs to be written vertically also.

Example:

ボール→　ボ
　　　　　｜
　　　　　ル

(2) Additional combinations with small vowel letters are used to transcribe foreign sounds that originally did not exist in Japanese.

Examples:	ウィ	ハロウィーン	*harowiin*	(Halloween)
	ウェ	ハイウェイ	*haiwee*	(highway)
	ウォ	ミネラルウォーター	*mineraruwootaa*	(mineral water)
	シェ	シェリー	*sherii*	(sherry)
	ジェ	ジェームス	*jeemusu*	(James)
	チェ	チェック	*chekku*	(check)
	ファ	ファッション	*fasshon*	(fashion)
	フィ	フィリピン	*firipin*	(Philippine)
	フェ	カフェ	*kafe*	(cafe)
	フォ	カリフォルニア	*kariforunia*	(California)
	ティ	パーティー	*paatii*	(party)
	ディ	ディスコ	*disuko*	(disco)
	デュ	デューク	*dyuuku*	(Duke)

(3) The sound "v" is sometimes written with ヴ. For example, the word "Venus" is sometimes written as ビーナス or ヴィーナス.

会話・文法編
かいわ　ぶんぽう　へん

会話・文法編 ● もくじ
かい わ ぶん ぽう へん

あいさつ
Greetings

おはよう。	Ohayoo.	Good morning.
おはよう ございます。	Ohayoo gozaimasu.	Good morning. (polite)
こんにちは。	Konnichiwa.	Good afternoon.
こんばんは。	Konbanwa.	Good evening.
さようなら。	Sayoonara.	Good-bye.
おやすみなさい。	Oyasuminasai.	Good night.
ありがとう。	Arigatoo.	Thank you.
ありがとう ございます。	Arigatoo gozaimasu.	Thank you. (polite)
すみません。	Sumimasen.	Excuse me.; I'm sorry.
いいえ。	Iie.	No.; Not at all.
・いってきます。	Ittekimasu.	I'll go and come back.
・いってらっしゃい。	Itterasshai.	Please go and come back.
・ただいま。	Tadaima.	I'm home.
・おかえりなさい。	Okaerinasai.	Welcome home.
いただきます。	Itadakimasu.	Thank you for the meal. (before eating)
ごちそうさま。	Gochisoosama.	Thank you for the meal. (after eating)
はじめまして。	Hajimemashite.	How do you do?
どうぞ よろしく。	Doozo yoroshiku.	Nice to meet you.

表現ノート
ひょうげん

おはよう/ありがとう▶ *Ohayoo* is used between friends and family members, while *ohayoo gozaimasu* is used between less intimate acquaintances, similarly with *arigatoo* and *arigatoo gozaimasu*. The rule of thumb is: if you are on a first-name basis with someone, go for the shorter versions. If you would address someone as Mr. or Ms., use the longer versions. To give a concrete example, the social expectation is such that students are to use the longer variants when they speak with a professor.

さようなら▶ There are several good-bye expressions in Japanese, the choice among which depends on the degree of separation. *Sayoonara* indicates that the speaker does not expect to see the person spoken to before she "turns a page in her life"; not until a new day arrives, or until fate brings the two together again, or until they meet again in the other world.

> じゃあ、また。　Jaa, mata.
> (between friends, expecting to see each other again fairly soon)
> しつれいします。　Shitsureeshimasu.
> (taking leave from a professor's office, for example)
> いってきます。　Ittekimasu.
> (leaving home)

すみません▶ *Sumimasen* means (1) "Excuse me," to get another person's attention, (2) "I'm sorry," to apologize for the trouble you have caused, or (3) "Thank you," to show appreciation for what someone has done for you.

いいえ▶ *Iie* is primarily "No," a negative reply to a question. In the dialogue, it is used to express the English phrase "Don't mention it," or "You're welcome," with which you point out that one is not required to feel obliged for what you have done for them.

いってらっしゃい/いってきます/ただいま/おかえりなさい▶ *Ittekimasu* and *itterasshai* is a common exchange used at home when a family member leaves. The person who leaves says *ittekimasu*, which literally means "I will go and come back." And the family members respond with *itterasshai*, which means "Please go and come back."

　Tadaima and *okaeri* are used when a person comes home. The person who arrives home says *tadaima* (I am home right now) to the family members, and they respond with *okaerinasai* (Welcome home).

れんしゅう Practice

Act out the following situations with your classmates.

1. You meet your host family for the first time. Greet them.
2. It is one o'clock in the afternoon. You see your neighbor Mr. Yamada.
3. You come to class in the morning. Greet your teacher. Greet your friends.
4. On a crowded train, you stepped on someone's foot.
5. You dropped your book. Someone picked it up for you.
6. It is eight o'clock at night. You happen to meet your teacher at the convenience store.
7. You are watching TV with your host family. It is time to go to sleep.
8. You are leaving home.
9. You have come back home.
10. You are going to start eating.
11. You have finished eating.

第1課 だい いっ か | L E S S O N ······· 1

あたらしいともだち New Friends

かいわ Ｄｉａｌｏｇｕｅ

Mary, an international student who just arrived in Japan, talks to a Japanese student.

Ⅰ

1 メアリー： すみません。いま なんじ ですか。
  めありい
  Mearii   Sumimasen.　Ima　nanji desu ka.

(handwritten annotations: now, what, time)

2 たけし： じゅうにじ はん です。
  Takeshi   Juuniji han desu.

3 メアリー： ありがとう ございます。
  めありい
  Mearii   Arigatoo   gozaimasu.

4 たけし： いいえ。
  Takeshi   Iie.

Ⅱ

1 たけし： あの、りゅうがくせいですか。
Takeshi Ano, ryuugakusee desu ka.

2 メアリー： ええ。アリゾナだいがくの がくせいです。
Mearii Ee. Arizona daigaku no gakusee desu.

3 たけし： そうですか。せんもんは なんですか。
Takeshi Soo desu ka. Senmon wa nan desu ka.

4 メアリー： にほんごです。いま にねんせいです。
Mearii Nihongo desu. Ima ninensee desu.

Ⅰ

Mary: Excuse me. What time is it now?

Takeshi: It's half past twelve.

Mary: Thank you.

Takeshi: You're welcome.

Ⅱ

Takeshi: Um . . . are you an international student?

Mary: Yes. I am a student at the University of Arizona.

Takeshi: I see. What is your major?

Mary: Japanese. I am a sophomore now.

たんご
Vocabulary

*	あの	ano	um . . .
*	いま	ima	now
	えいご	eego	English (language)
*	ええ	ee	yes
*	がくせい	gakusee	student
*	〜ご	. . . go	language ex. にほんご (*nihon-go*) Japanese language
	こうこう	kookoo	high school
◐	ごご	gogo	P.M.
◑	ごぜん	gozen	A.M.
	〜さい	. . . sai	. . . years old
	〜さん	. . . san	Mr./Ms. . . .
*	〜じ	. . . ji	o'clock ex. いちじ (*ichiji*) one o'clock
	〜じん	. . . jin	people ex. にほんじん (*nihon-jin*) Japanese people
	せんせい	sensee	teacher; Professor . . .
*	せんもん	senmon	major
*	そうです	soo desu	That's right.
*	だいがく	daigaku	college; university
	でんわ	denwa	telephone
	ともだち	tomodachi	friend
	なまえ	namae	name
◉	なん/なに	nan/nani	what
*	にほん	Nihon	Japan
*	〜ねんせい	. . . nensee	. . . year student ex. いちねんせい (*ichinensee*) first-year student
	はい	hai	yes
*	はん	han	half ex. にじはん (*nijihan*) half past two
	ばんごう	bangoo	number
*	りゅうがくせい	ryuugakusee	international student
	わたし	watashi	I

* Words that appear in the dialogue

ADDITIONAL VOCABULARY

Countries

アメリカ	Amerika	U.S.A.
イギリス	Igirisu	Britain
オーストラリア	Oosutoraria	Australia
かんこく	Kankoku	Korea
スウェーデン	Sueeden	Sweden
ちゅうごく	Chuugoku	China

Majors

かがく	kagaku	science
アジアけんきゅう	ajiakenkyuu	Asian studies
けいざい	keezai	economics
こくさいかんけい	kokusaikankee	international relations
コンピューター	konpyuutaa	computer
じんるいがく	jinruigaku	anthropology
せいじ	seeji	politics
ビジネス	bijinesu	business
ぶんがく	bungaku	literature
れきし	rekishi	history

Occupations

しごと	shigoto	job; work; occupation
いしゃ	isha	doctor
かいしゃいん	kaishain	office worker
こうこうせい	kookoosee	high school student
しゅふ	shufu	housewife
だいがくいんせい	daigakuinsee	graduate student
だいがくせい	daigakusee	college student
べんごし	bengoshi	lawyer

Family

おかあさん	okaasan	mother
おとうさん	otoosan	father
おねえさん	oneesan	older sister
おにいさん	oniisan	older brother
いもうと	imooto	younger sister
おとうと	otooto	younger brother

ぶんぽう　Ｇ ｒ ａ ｍ ｍ ａ ｒ

1 ｜ X は Y です

"It is 12:30." "I am a student." "My major is the Japanese language." These sentences will all be translated into Japanese using an appropriate noun and the word *desu*.

～です。　　*It is . . .*

じゅうにじはんです。　　*(It) is half past twelve.*
Juuniji han desu.

がくせいです。　　*(I) am a student.*
Gakusee desu.

にほんごです。　　*(My major) is the Japanese language.*
Nihongo desu.

Note that none of these sentences has a "subject," like the "it," "I," and "my major" found in their English counterparts. Sentences without subjects are very common in Japanese; Japanese speakers actually tend to omit subjects whenever they think it is clear to the listener what or who they are referring to.

What are we to do, then, when it is not clear what is being talked about? To make explicit what we are talking about, we can say:

_____は　にほんごです。　　_____ *is the Japanese language.*
　　　　wa　nihongo desu.

Where _____ stands for the thing that is talked about, or the "topic," which is later in the sentence identified as *nihongo*. For example,

せんもんは　にほんごです。　　*(My) major is the Japanese language.*
Senmon wa　　nihongo desu.

Similarly, one can use the pattern *X wa Y desu* to identify a person or a thing X as item Y.

X は Y です。　　*X is Y. As for X, it is Y.*

わたしは　スー・キムです。　　*I am Sue Kim.*
Watashi wa　Suu Kimu desu.

やましたさんは せんせいです。
Yamashita san wa   sensee desu.

Mr. Yamashita is a teacher.

メアリーさんは アメリカじんです。
Mearii san wa   amerikajin desu.

Mary is an American.

Wa is a member of the class of words called "particles." So is the word *no*, which we will turn to later in this lesson. Particles attach themselves to phrases and indicate how the phrases relate to the rest of the sentence.

Note also that nouns like *gakusee* and *sensee* in the above examples stand alone, unlike their English translations "student" and "teacher," which are preceded by "a." In Japanese, there is no item that corresponds to "a," nor is there any item that corresponds to the plural "-s" at the end of a noun. Without background situations, a sentence like *gakusee desu* is therefore ambiguous between the singular and the plural interpretations; it may mean "We are/you are/they are students," as well as "I am/you are/she is a student."

2   Question Sentences

It is very easy to form questions in Japanese. Basically, all you need to do is add *ka* at the end of a statement.

りゅうがくせいです。
Ryuugakusee desu.
(I am) an international student.

りゅうがくせいですか。[1]
Ryuugakusee desu ka.
(Are you) an international student?

The above sentence, *Ryuugakusee desu ka*, is a "yes/no" question. Question sentences may also contain a "question word" like *nan*[2] (what). In this lesson, we learn how to ask, and answer, questions using the following question words: *nanji* (what time), *nansai* (how old), *nannensee* (what year in school). Note carefully that the order of words in a sentence may be quite different from what you find in your language.

せんもんは なんですか。
Senmon wa   nan desu ka.
What is your major?

（せんもんは）えいごです。
(Senmon wa)   eego desu.
(My major) is English.

---

[1] It is not customary to write a question mark at the end of a question sentence in Japanese.

[2] The Japanese question word for "what" has two pronunciations: *nan* and *nani*. *Nan* is used immediately before *desu* or before a "counter" like *ji* (o'clock). The other form, *nani*, is used before a particle. *Nani* is also used in the combination *nanijin* (person of what nationality).

いま なんじですか。
Ima　nanji desu ka.
What time is it now?

（いま）くじです。
(Ima)　kuji desu.
It is nine o'clock.

メアリーさんは なんさいですか。
Mearii san wa　　　nansai desu ka.
How old are you, Mary?

じゅうきゅうさいです。
Juukyuusai desu.
I'm nineteen years old.

なんねんせいですか。
Nannensee desu ka.
What year are you in college?

にねんせいです。
Ninensee desu.
I'm a sophomore.

でんわばんごうは なんですか。
Denwa bangoo wa　　　nan desu ka.
What is your telephone number?

186の7343です。
Ichi hachi roku no nana san yon san desu.
It is 186-7343.

3 　noun₁の noun₂

No is a particle that connects two nouns. The phrase *Toozai daigaku no gakusee* means "(a) student at Tozai University." The second noun *gakusee* provides the main idea[3] (being a student) and the first one *Toozai daigaku* makes it more specific (not a high school, but a college student). *No* is very versatile. In the first example below, it acts like the possessive ("x's") in English, but that is not the only role *no* can play. See how it connects two nouns in the following examples.

たけしさんの でんわばんごう
Takeshi san no　　denwa bangoo
Takeshi's phone number

だいがくの せんせい
daigaku no　　　sensee
a college professor

にほんごの がくせい
nihongo no　　　gakusee
a student of the Japanese language

にほんの だいがく
nihon no　　　daigaku
a college in Japan

Observe that in the first two examples, the English and Japanese words are arranged in the same order, while in the last two, they are in the opposite order. Japanese seems to be more consistent in arranging ideas here; the main idea always comes at the end, with any further description placed before it.

---

[3]Here is what we mean by the "main idea." In the phrase *Takeshi san no denwa bangoo* (Takeshi's phone number), the noun *denwa bangoo* (phone number) is the main idea, in the sense that if something is Takeshi's phone number, it is a phone number. The other noun *Takeshi san* is not the main idea, because Takeshi's phone number is not Takeshi.

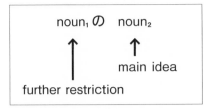

A phrase of the form "noun₁ *no* noun₂" acts more or less like one big noun. You can put it wherever you can put a noun, as in the following example:

Takeshi san no   okaasan wa   kookoo no   sensee desu.

Takeshi's *mother* is a *high school* *teacher.*

表現ノート
ひょうげん

Expression Notes ②

あの▶ *Ano* indicates that you have some reservations about saying what you are going to say next. You may be worried about interrupting something someone is currently doing, or sounding rude and impolite for asking personal questions, for example.

はい/ええ▶ Both *hai* and *ee* mean "yes" in response to yes-no questions. Compared to *hai*, *ee* is more conversational and relaxed. In more informal situations, *un* is used.

    Hai is also used to respond to a knock at the door or to the calling of one's name, meaning "Here," as follows. (*Ee* cannot be replaced in this case.)

Teacher:	スミスさん？ すみ す Sumisu san?	*Mr. Smith?*
Student:	はい。 Hai	*Here.*

そうですか▶ *Soo desu ka* acknowledges that you have understood what was just said. "Is that so?" or "I see."

Pronunciation of は▶ The particle は is pronounced "*wa*," not "*ha*." It should be written with は. All other instances of "*wa*" are written with わ.

わたしの でんわばんごうは 37-8667です。
Watashi no denwa bangoo wa san nana no hachi roku roku nana desu.
My telephone number is 37-8667.

There are a few exceptions, such as *konnichiwa* (good afternoon) and
konbanwa (good evening). They are usually written with こんにちは and こ
んばんは.

Numbers ▶ Many number words have more than one pronunciation. Refer
to the table at the end of this book for a general picture.

- 0 ゼロ and れい are both commonly used.
- 1 いち, but pronounced as いっ in いっぷん (one minute) and いっさ
  い (one-year old).
- 2 に all the time. When you are reading out each digit separately,
  as when you give your phone number, it may be pronounced with
  a long vowel, as にい.
- 3 さん all the time. The part that follows it may change shape, as
  in さんぷん, instead of さんふん.
- 4 よん is the most basic, but fourth-year student is よねんせい and
  four o'clock is よじ. In some combinations that we will later
  learn, it is read as し (as in しがつ, April). The part that follows
  this number may change shape too, as in よんぷん.
- 5 ご all the time. When read out separately, it may be pronounced
  with a long vowel, as ごう.
- 6 ろく, but pronounced as ろっ in ろっぷん.
- 7 なな is the most basic, but seven o'clock is しちじ.
- 8 はち, but usually pronounced as はっ in はっぷん and はっさい.
- 9 きゅう is the most basic, but nine o'clock is くじ.
- 10 じゅう, but pronounced as じゅっ in じゅっぷん and じゅっさい.

Giving one's telephone number ▶ The particle *no* is usually placed in
between the local exchange code and the last four digits. Therefore, the
number 012-345-6789 is *zero ichi ni, san yon go no, roku nana hachi kyuu.*

せんせい▶ The word *sensee* is usually reserved for describing somebody
else's occupation. *Watashi wa sensee desu* makes sense, but may sound
slightly arrogant, because the word *sensee* actually means an "honorable
master." If you (or a member of your family) are a teacher, and if you want
to be really modest, you can use the word *kyooshi* instead.

さん▶ *San* is placed after a name as a generic title. It goes both with a given
name and a family name. Children are referred to as *chan* (and boys in

particular as *kun*), rather than as *san*. Professors and doctors are usually referred to with the title *sensee*. *San* and other title words are never used in reference to oneself.

Referring to the person you are talking to ▶ The word for "you," *anata*, is not very commonly used in Japanese. Instead, we use the name and a title like *san* and *sensee* to refer to the person you are talking to. Therefore, a sentence like "Ms. Hart, are you Swedish?" should be:

ハートさんは スウェーデンじんですか。
Haato san wa sueedenjin desu ka.

instead of ハートさん、あなたは スウェーデンじんですか。
Haato san,   anata wa sueedenjin desu ka.

Japanese names ▶ When Japanese give their name, they say their family name first and given name last. Usually, they don't have middle names. When they introduce themselves, they often say only their family name. Here are some typical Japanese names.

Family name	Given name	
	Men	Women
さとう Satoo	ひろし Hiroshi	ゆうこ Yuuko
すずき Suzuki	いちろう Ichiroo	めぐみ Megumi
たかはし Takahashi	けんじ Kenji	くみこ Kumiko
たなか Tanaka	ゆうき Yuuki	なおみ Naomi
いとう Itoo	まさひろ Masahiro	きょうこ Kyooko

れんしゅう Ｐｒａｃｔｉｃｅ

Ⅰ すうじ (Numbers) 🔊

0	ゼロ／れい zero ree				
1	いち ichi	11	じゅういち juuichi	30	さんじゅう sanjuu
2	に ni	12	じゅうに juuni	40	よんじゅう yonjuu
3	さん san	13	じゅうさん juusan	50	ごじゅう gojuu
4	よん／し／（よ） yon shi (yo)	14	じゅうよん／じゅうし juuyon juushi	60	ろくじゅう rokujuu
5	ご go	15	じゅうご juugo	70	ななじゅう nanajuu
6	ろく roku	16	じゅうろく juuroku	80	はちじゅう hachijuu
7	なな／しち nana shichi	17	じゅうなな／じゅうしち juunana juushichi	90	きゅうじゅう kyuujuu
8	はち hachi	18	じゅうはち juuhachi	100	ひゃく hyaku
9	きゅう／く kyuu ku	19	じゅうきゅう／じゅうく juukyuu juuku		
10	じゅう juu	20	にじゅう nijuu		

A. Read the following numbers. 🔊

   (a) 5   (b) 9   (c) 7   (d) 1   (e) 10

   (f) 8   (g) 2   (h) 6   (i) 4   (j) 3

B. Read the following numbers. 🔊

   (a) 45   (b) 83   (c) 19   (d) 76   (e) 52

   (f) 100   (g) 38   (h) 61   (i) 24   (j) 97

C. What are the answers? 🔊

   (a) 5+3 (b) 9+1 (c) 3+4 (d) 6−6 (e) 10+9 (f) 8−7 (g) 40−25

Ⅱ じかん (Time)

いちじ ichiji	にじ niji	さんじ sanji	<u>よじ</u> yoji	ごじ goji
ろくじ rokuji	しちじ shichiji	はちじ hachiji	くじ kuji	じゅうじ juuji
じゅういちじ juuichiji	じゅうにじ juuniji	いちじはん ichiji han		

A. Look at the following pictures and answer the questions.

Example: Q：いま なんじですか。
Ima nanji desu ka.

A：いちじはんです。
Ichiji han desu.

Ex.

(1)

(2)

(3)

(4)

(5)

(6)

B. Answer the questions.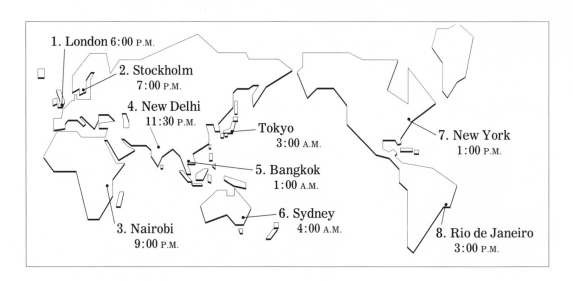

Example: Q：とうきょうは　いま　なんじですか。
Tookyoo wa　　ima　　nanji desu ka.

A：ごぜん　さんじです。
Gozen　　sanji desu.

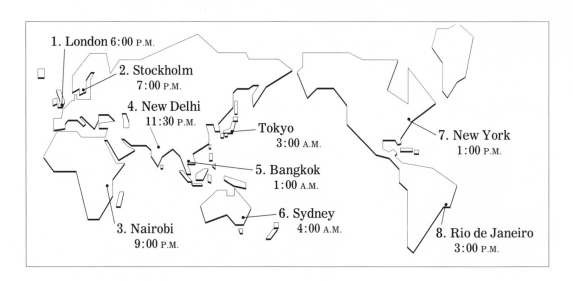

1. London 6:00 P.M.
2. Stockholm 7:00 P.M.
4. New Delhi 11:30 P.M.
Tokyo 3:00 A.M.
7. New York 1:00 P.M.
5. Bangkok 1:00 A.M.
3. Nairobi 9:00 P.M.
6. Sydney 4:00 A.M.
8. Rio de Janeiro 3:00 P.M.

Ⅲ でんわばんごう (Telephone Numbers)

A. Read the following people's telephone numbers.

Example: やました　283-9547　→　にはちさんの　きゅうごよんなな
Yamashita　　　　　　　　ni hachi san no　kyuu go yon nana

1. メアリー　　951-0326
   Mearii
2. たけし　　　362-4519
   Takeshi
3. スー　　　　691-4236
   Suu
4. ロバート　　852-1032
   Robaato

B. Pair Work—Read the dialogue below with your partner.

A：でんわばんごうは　なんですか。
Denwa bangoo wa　　nan desu ka.

B：283-9547です。
Ni hachi san no kyuu go yon nana desu.

A：283-9547ですね。
　　　Ni hachi san no kyuu go yon nana desu ne.

B：はい、そうです。
　　　Hai,　　soo desu.

C. Group Work—Use the dialogue above and ask three classmates their telephone numbers.

name	telephone number
(　　　　　　　　　)	(　　　　　　　　　　　　)
(　　　　　　　　　)	(　　　　　　　　　　　　)
(　　　　　　　　　)	(　　　　　　　　　　　　)

Ⅳ にほんごの がくせい

Translate the following phrases into Japanese using の (no). 🔊

Example:　student of the Japanese language　→　にほんごの がくせい
　　　　　　　　　　　　　　　　　　　　　　　　　　　nihongo no　　gakusee

1. my teacher
2. my telephone number
3. my name
4. Takeshi's major
5. Mary's friend
6. student of the University of London
7. teacher of the Japanese language
8. high school teacher

Ⅴ メアリーさんは アメリカじんです

A. Look at the chart on the next page and describe each person using the cues in (a) through (e). 🔊

1. たけしさん　　2. スーさん　　3. ロバートさん　　4. やましたせんせい
　　Takeshi san　　　　Suu san　　　　　Robaato san　　　　　Yamashita sensee

(a) nationality
　　Example:　メアリーさん　→　メアリーさんは アメリカじんです。
　　　　　　　　Mearii san　　　　　　Mearii san wa　　　　amerikajin desu.

(b) year in school
　　Example:　メアリーさん　→　メアリーさんは にねんせいです。
　　　　　　　　Mearii san　　　　　　Mearii san wa　　　　ninensee desu.

(c) age

Example: メアリーさん → メアリーさんは じゅうきゅうさいです。
Mearii san   Mearii san wa   juukyuu sai desu.

(d) school

Example: メアリーさん → メアリーさんは アリゾナだいがくの
Mearii san   Mearii san wa   Arizona daigaku no

がくせいです。
gakusee desu.

(e) major

Example: メアリーさん → メアリーさんの せんもんは にほんごです。
Mearii san   Mearii san no   senmon wa   nihongo desu.

	Hart, Mary	きむらたけし Kimura Takeshi	Kim, Sue	Smith, Robert	やましたせんせい Yamashita sensee
Nationality	American	Japanese	Korean (かんこくじん) kankokujin	British (イギリスじん) igirisujin	Japanese
Year	2nd year	4th year	3rd year	4th year	
Age	19	22	20	22	47
School	U. of Arizona	Tozai Univ.	Seoul Univ.	U. of London	Tozai Univ.
Major	Japanese	history (れきし) rekishi	computer (コンピューター) konpyuutaa	business (ビジネス) bijinesu	(Japanese teacher)

B. Pair Work—Ask and answer questions using the given cues.

Example 1: メアリーさん／アメリカじん
Mearii san   amerikajin

Q：メアリーさんは アメリカじんですか。
Mearii san wa   amerikajin desu ka.

A：ええ、そうです。
Ee,   soo desu.

Example 2: メアリーさん／さんねんせい
めありい
Mearii san　　　　　sannensee

　　Q：メアリーさんは　さんねんせいですか。
めありい
Mearii san wa　　　　　sannensee desu ka.

　　A：いいえ、にねんせいです。
Iie,　　　　ninensee desu.

1. メアリーさん／アリゾナだいがくの　がくせい
めありい　　　　ありぞな
Mearii san　　　Arizona daigaku no　　　gakusee

2. メアリーさん／いちねんせい
めありい
Mearii san　　　ichinensee

3. たけしさん／にほんじん
Takeshi san　　　nihonjin

4. たけしさん／にほんだいがくの　がくせい
Takeshi san　　　Nihon daigaku no　　　gakusee

5. たけしさん／じゅうきゅうさい
Takeshi san　　　juukyuusai

6. スーさん／スウェーデンじん
すう　　　　すうぇえでん
Suu san　　　sueedenjin

7. スーさんの　せんもん／けいざい (economics)
すう
Suu san no　　　senmon　　　keezai

8. ロバートさんの　せんもん／ビジネス
ろばあと　　　　　　　　　　びじねす
Robaato san no　　　senmon　　　bijinesu

9. ロバートさん／よねんせい
ろばあと
Robaato san　　　yonensee

10. ロバートさん／にじゅういっさい
ろばあと
Robaato san　　　nijuuissai

11. やましたせんせい／にほんじん
Yamashita sensee　　　nihonjin

12. やましたせんせい／ハワイだいがくの　せんせい
はわい
Yamashita sensee　　　Hawai daigaku no　　　sensee

Ⅵ おとうさんは　かいしゃいんです

A. Look at the chart below and describe each person with regard to (a) and (b). 🔊

1. おかあさん　　　2. おにいさん　　　3. いもうと
okaasan　　　　　　oniisan　　　　　　imooto

(a) occupation/school

Example:　おとうさん　→　メアリーさんの　おとうさんは　かいしゃいんです。
otoosan　　　　　　めありい
　　　　　　　　　　　Mearii san no　　　otoosan wa　　　kaishain desu.

(b) age

Example:　おとうさん　→　メアリーさんの　おとうさんはよんじゅうはっさいです。
　　　　　　otoosan　　　　　 Mearii san no　　　 otoosan wa　　　 yonjuuhassai desu.

Mary's host family

	おとうさん otoosan (father)	おかあさん okaasan (mother)	おにいさん oniisan (elder brother)	いもうと imooto (younger sister)
Occupation/ School	かいしゃいん kaishain (works for a company)	しゅふ shufu (housewife)	だいがくいんせい daigakuinsee (graduate student)	こうこうせい kookoosee (high school student)
Age	48	45	23	16

B.　Answer the questions using the chart above.

1.　おとうさんは　かいしゃいんですか。
　　Otoosan wa　　　kaishain desu ka.

2.　おとうさんは　なんさいですか。
　　Otoosan wa　　　nansai desu ka.

3.　おかあさんは　せんせいですか。
　　Okaasan wa　　　sensee desu ka.

4.　おかあさんは　なんさいですか。
　　Okaasan wa　　　nansai desu ka.

5.　おにいさんは　かいしゃいんですか。
　　Oniisan wa　　　kaishain desu ka.

6.　おにいさんは　なんさいですか。
　　Oniisan wa　　　nansai desu ka.

7.　いもうとは　だいがくせいですか。
　　Imooto wa　　　daigakusee desu ka.

8.　いもうとは　なんさいですか。
　　Imooto wa　　　nansai desu ka.

Ⅶ まとめの れんしゅう (Review Exercises)

A. Class Activity—Ask five classmates questions and fill in the chart below.

Example questions:

- おなまえは？ (What is your name?)
  Onamae wa?
- どこから きましたか。 (Where do you come from?)
  Doko kara　kimashita ka.
- しごと (occupation) は なんですか。
  Shigoto wa　nan desu ka.
- なんねんせいですか。
  Nannensee desu ka.
- なんさいですか。
  Nansai desu ka.
- せんもんは なんですか。
  Senmon wa　nan desu ka.

Name	Nationality	Occupation/School	Age	Major, etc.

B. Self-introduction—Introduce yourself to the class.

Example:

はじめまして。メアリー・ハートです。
Hajimemashite.　Mearii Haato desu.
アリゾナだいがくの がくせいです。いま
Arizona daigaku no　gakusee desu.　Ima
にねんせいです。せんもんは にほんごです。
ninensee desu.　Senmon wa　nihongo desu.
じゅうきゅうさいです。どうぞ よろしく。
Juukyuusai desu.　Doozo　yoroshiku.

C. Class Activity—Ask your classmates what their majors are, and find someone who has the following major.

Example:　Q：せんもんは　なんですか。
　　　　　　　　Senmon wa　　　nan desu ka.

　　　　　　　A：にほんごです。
　　　　　　　　Nihongo desu.

name

1. Japanese　　　＿＿＿＿＿＿＿＿＿＿＿＿＿

2. economics　　＿＿＿＿＿＿＿＿＿＿＿＿＿

3. English　　　　＿＿＿＿＿＿＿＿＿＿＿＿＿

4. history　　　　＿＿＿＿＿＿＿＿＿＿＿＿＿

5. business　　　＿＿＿＿＿＿＿＿＿＿＿＿＿

じかん・とし
Time / Age

Time

hours

1	いちじ ichiji
2	にじ niji
3	さんじ sanji
4	よじ yoji
5	ごじ goji
6	ろくじ rokuji
7	しちじ shichiji
8	はちじ hachiji
9	くじ kuji
10	じゅうじ juuji
11	じゅういちじ juuichiji
12	じゅうにじ juuniji

minutes

1	いっぷん ippun	11	じゅういっぷん juuippun
2	にふん nifun	12	じゅうにふん juunifun
3	さんぷん sanpun	13	じゅうさんぷん juusanpun
4	よんぷん yonpun	14	じゅうよんぷん juuyonpun
5	ごふん gofun	15	じゅうごふん juugofun
6	ろっぷん roppun	16	じゅうろっぷん juuroppun
7	ななふん nanafun	17	じゅうななふん juunanafun
8	はっぷん／はちふん happun　　hachifun	18	じゅうはっぷん／ juuhappun
9	きゅうふん kyuufun		じゅうはちふん juuhachifun
10	じゅっぷん juppun	19	じゅうきゅうふん juukyuufun
		20	にじゅっぷん nijuppun
		30	さんじゅっぷん sanjuppun

Age　　なんさいですか。／おいくつですか。　(How old are you?)
Nansai desu ka.　　　Oikutsu desu ka.

The counter suffix 〜さい is used to indicate "-years old."

1	いっさい issai	5	ごさい gosai	9	きゅうさい kyuusai
2	にさい nisai	6	ろくさい rokusai	10	じゅっさい jussai
3	さんさい sansai	7	ななさい nanasai	11	じゅういっさい juuissai
4	よんさい yonsai	8	はっさい hassai	20	はたち* hatachi

*For 20 years old, はたち (*hatachi*) is usually used, although にじゅっさい (*nijussai*) can be used.

第2課 だいにか | L E S S O N ⋯⋯⋯⋯⋯2

かいもの Shopping

かいわ D i a l o g u e

Ⓘ Mary goes to a flea market.

1 メアリー：　　　すみません。これは　いくらですか。
　めありい
　Mearii　　　　　Sumimasen.　Kore wa　ikura desu ka.

2 みせのひと：　　それは　さんぜんえんです。
　Mise no hito　　Sore wa　sanzen en desu.

3 メアリー：　　　たかいですね。じゃあ、あのとけいは　いくらですか。
　めありい
　Mearii　　　　　Takai desu ne.　Jaa,　ano tokee wa　ikura desu ka.

4 みせのひと：　　あれは　さんぜんごひゃくえんです。
　Mise no hito　　Are wa　sanzengohyaku en desu.

5 メアリー：　　　そうですか。あれも　たかいですね。
　めありい
　Mearii　　　　　Soo desu ka.　Are mo　takai desu ne.

6 みせのひと：　　これは　せんはっぴゃくえんですよ。
　Mise no hito　　Kore wa　senhappyaku en desu yo.

7 メアリー：　　　じゃあ、そのとけいを　ください。
　めありい
　Mearii　　　　　Jaa,　sono tokee o　kudasai.

*　　　　　　　　*　　　　　　　　*

A man finds a wallet on the ground.

8 しらないひと：これは　だれの　さいふですか。
　Shiranai hito　　Kore wa　dare no　saifu desu ka.

9 メアリー：　　　わたしの　さいふです。
　めありい
　Mearii　　　　　Watashi no　saifu desu.

　　　　　　　　　ありがとうございます。
　　　　　　　　　Arigatoo gozaimasu.

Ⅱ After shopping, Mary goes to a restaurant.

1 ウエートレス：いらっしゃいませ。メニューを　どうぞ。
　うええとれす　　　　　　　　　　　めにゅう
　Ueetoresu　　　Irasshaimase.　Menyuu o　doozo.

2 メアリー：　　　　どうも。　これは　なんですか。
　Mearii　　　　　　Doomo.　　Kore wa　nan desu ka.

3 ウエートレス：どれですか。　ああ、　とんかつです。
　Ueetoresu　　　　Dore desu ka.　Aa,　　tonkatsu desu.

4 メアリー：　　　　とんかつ？　さかなですか。
　Mearii　　　　　　Tonkatsu?　Sakana desu ka.

5 ウエートレス：いいえ、　さかなじゃありません。　にくです。おいしいですよ。
　Ueetoresu　　　　Iie,　　sakana ja arimasen.　　Niku desu.　Oishii desu yo.

6 メアリー：　　　　じゃあ、　これを　おねがいします。
　Mearii　　　　　　Jaa,　　kore o　onegaishimasu.

　　　　　　　　　　　　＊　　　　　　　＊　　　　　　　＊

7 メアリー：　　　　すみません、おてあらいは　どこですか。
　Mearii　　　　　　Sumimasen,　otearai wa　doko desu ka.

8 ウエートレス：あそこです。
　Ueetoresu　　　　Asoko desu.

Ⅰ

Mary: Excuse me. How much is this?

Vendor: It is 3,000 yen.

Mary: It's expensive. Well then, how much is that watch?

Vendor: That is 3,500 yen.

Mary: I see. That is expensive, too.

Vendor: This is 1,800 yen.

Mary: Then, I'll take that watch.

　　　　　＊　　　　　＊　　　　　＊

Stranger: Whose wallet is this?

Mary: It's my wallet. Thank you very much.

Ⅱ

Waitress: Welcome. Here's the menu.

Mary: Thank you. What is this?

Waitress: Which one? Oh, it is *tonkatsu* (pork cutlet).

Mary: *Tonkatsu*? Is it fish?

Waitress: No, it is not fish. It is meat. It is delicious.

Mary: Then, I'll have this.

　　　　　＊　　　　　＊　　　　　＊

Mary: Excuse me. Where is the restroom?

Waitress: It is over there.

たんご

V o c a b u l a r y

W o r d s   T h a t   P o i n t

* これ	kore	this one
* それ	sore	that one
* あれ	are	that one (over there)
* どれ	dore	which one
この	kono	this . . .
* その	sono	that . . .
* あの	ano	that . . . (over there)
どの	dono	which . . .
* あそこ	asoko	over there
* どこ	doko	where
* だれ	dare	who

F o o d

* おいしい	oishii	delicious
* さかな	sakana	fish
* とんかつ	tonkatsu	pork cutlet
* にく	niku	meat
* メニュー めにゅう	menyuu	menu
やさい	yasai	vegetable

T h i n g s

えんぴつ	enpitsu	pencil
かさ	kasa	umbrella
かばん	kaban	bag
くつ	kutsu	shoes
* さいふ	saifu	wallet
ジーンズ じいんず	jiinzu	jeans
じしょ	jisho	dictionary
じてんしゃ	jitensha	bicycle
しんぶん	shinbun	newspaper
テープ てえぷ	teepu	tape
* とけい	tokee	watch; clock
トレーナー とれえなあ	toreenaa	sweat shirt

* Words that appear in the dialogue

ノート	nooto	notebook
ペン	pen	pen
ぼうし	booshi	hat; cap
ほん	hon	book

Places

* おてあらい	otearai	restroom
きっさてん	kissaten	cafe
ぎんこう	ginkoo	bank
としょかん	toshokan	library
ゆうびんきょく	yuubinkyoku	post office

Countries

アメリカ	Amerika	U.S.A.
イギリス	Igirisu	Britain
かんこく	Kankoku	Korea
ちゅうごく	Chuugoku	China

Majors

けいざい	keezai	economics
コンピューター	konpyuutaa	computer
ビジネス	bijinesu	business
れきし	rekishi	history

Family

| おかあさん | okaasan | mother |
| おとうさん | otoosan | father |

Money Matters

* いくら	ikura	how much
* ～えん	. . . en	. . . yen
* たかい	takai	expensive

Expressions

* いらっしゃいませ	irasshaimase	Welcome (to our store)
* (～を)おねがいします	(. . . o) onegaishimasu	. . . , please.
* (～を)ください	(. . . o) kudasai	Please give me . . .
* じゃあ	jaa	then . . . ; if that is the case, . . .
* (～を)どうぞ	(. . . o) doozo	Here it is.
* どうも	doomo	Thank you.

ぶんぽう Grammar

1 これ それ あれ どれ

What do we do when we want to talk about things that we do not know the names of? We say "this thing," "that one," and so forth. In Japanese, we use *kore*, *sore*, and *are*.

これは いくらですか。   *How much is this?*
Kore wa   ikura desu ka.

それは さんぜんえんです。   *That is 3,000 yen.*
Sore wa   sanzen en desu.

Kore refers to a thing that is close to you, the speaker ("this thing here"). *Sore* is something that is close to the person you are talking to ("that thing in front of you"), and *are* refers to a thing that is neither close to the speaker nor the listener ("that one over there").

あれは わたしの ペンです。
Are wa   watashi no   pen desu.

これは わたしの ペンです。   それは わたしの ペンです。
Kore wa   watashi no   pen desu.   Sore wa   watashi no   pen desu.

There is also an expression *dore* for "which." Here we will learn to use *dore* in sentences like:

どれですか。   *Which one is it (that you are talking about)?*
Dore desu ka.

In this lesson, we will not explore the full extent to which the word *dore* can be put to use, because there is a slight complication with question words like *dore*. Question words like *dore* and *nani* cannot be followed by the particle *wa*. Instead, you must use the particle *ga* and say:

どれが あなたの ペンですか。
Dore ga anata no pen desu ka.　　　*Which one is your pen?*

2　この/その/あの/どの ＋ noun

If you want to be slightly more specific than *kore*, *sore*, and *are*, you can use *kono*, *sono*, and *ano* together with a noun. (Note here that the *re* series must always stand alone, while the *no* series must always be followed by a noun.) Thus, if you know that the item in your hand is a watch (*tokee*), instead of:

これは いくらですか。
Kore wa ikura desu ka.　　　*How much is this?*

you can say:

このとけいは いくらですか。
Kono tokee wa ikura desu ka.　　　*How much is this watch?*

Similarly, if you are talking about a watch that is held by the person you are talking to, you can say:

そのとけいは さんぜんえんです。
Sono tokee wa sanzen en desu.　　　*That watch is 3,000 yen.*

And if the watch is far from both the speaker and the listener, you can say:

あのとけいは さんぜんごひゃくえんです。
Ano tokee wa sanzengohyaku en desu.　　　*That watch over there is 3,500 yen.*

If you already know that one of several watches is 3,500 yen but do not know which, you can say:

どのとけいが さんぜんごひゃくえんですか。
Dono tokee ga sanzengohyaku en desu ka.　　　*Which watch is 3,500 yen?*

Since *dono* is a question word, just like *dore* discussed above, we cannot use the particle *wa* with it; we must use *ga*.

To summarize:

これ（は〜）	この noun（は〜）	close to the person speaking
それ（は〜）	その noun（は〜）	close to the person listening
あれ（は〜）	あの noun（は〜）	far from both people
どれ（が〜）	どの noun（が〜）	unknown

3   だれの noun

In Lesson 1, we learned how to say things like *Mearii san no denwa bangoo* (Mary's phone number) and *Takeshi san no okaasan* (Takeshi's mother). We now learn how to ask who something belongs to. The question word for "who" is *dare*, and for "whose," we simply add the particle *no*.

これは だれの かばんですか。
Kore wa dare no   kaban desu ka.
Whose bag is this?

それは スーさんの かばんです。
Sore wa   Suu san no   kaban desu.
That is Sue's bag.

4   ここ そこ あそこ どこ

We will learn just one more *ko-so-a-do* set in this lesson: *koko*, *soko*, *asoko*, and *doko* are words for places.

ここ	*here, near me*
そこ	*there, near you*
あそこ	*over there*
どこ	*where*

You can ask for directions by saying:

すみません、ゆうびんきょくは どこですか。   *Excuse me, where is the post office?*
Sumimasen,   yuubinkyoku wa   doko desu ka.

If you are close by, you can point toword the post office and say:

（ゆうびんきょくは） あそこです。   *(The post office is) right over there.*
(Yuubinkyoku wa)   asoko desu.

We will learn how to give more specific directions in Lesson 4.

5 noun も

In Lesson 1, we learned how to say "Item A is this, item B is that." We now learn how to say "Item A is this, and item B is this, too."

たけしさんは　にほんじんです。
Takeshi san wa　nihonjin desu.

Takeshi is a Japanese person.

みちこさん<u>も</u>　にほんじんです。
Michiko san mo　nihonjin desu.

Michiko is Japanese, <u>too</u>.

Note that these two sentences are almost identical in shape. This is natural, as they both claim that a certain person is Japanese. The second sentence, however, is different from the first in that we do not find the particle *wa* in it. We have *mo* instead. *Mo* is a particle that indicates that that item, *too*, has the given property. One thing that you should watch out for is exactly where the particle is placed. In English, the word "too" can be placed after the sentence as a whole, as in the example above. Not so in Japanese. In the above example, *mo* must directly follow *Michiko san*.

6 noun じゃありません

To negate a statement of the form *X wa Y desu*, where Y is a noun, you replace *desu* with *ja arimasen*.[2]

やまださんは　がくせいじゃありません。
Yamada san wa　gakusee ja arimasen.

Mr. Yamada is not a student.

---

[1] We cannot use *mo* to describe a situation like the following: Our friend, Pat, has dual citizenship; Pat is a Japanese, but at the same time, she is an American. To describe the second half of this situation, we cannot say, *Patto mo amerikajin desu*, because the sentence would mean that Pat, in addition to somebody that has been mentioned, is an American. Neither can we say, *Patto wa amerikajin mo desu*. (Japanese speakers would say, *Patto wa amerikajin demo arimasu*.)

[2] In the dialogues, there are two sentences that end with *desu*, which call for special attention: *Are mo takai desu ne* (That one too is expensive), and *Oishii desu yo* (It is delicious). These sentences cannot be negated by replacing *desu* with *ja arimasen*, because *takai* and *oishii* are not nouns. *Are mo takai ja arimasen* and *oishii ja arimasen* are therefore not grammatical. Instead, one would have to say *takaku arimasen* and *oishiku arimasen*. We will learn about the conjugation pattern of adjectives in Lesson 5.

Ja in *ja arimasen* is a contraction of *dewa*. In written Japanese, the uncontracted form is more common; thus, the above sentence more likely appears in writing as *Yamada san wa gakusee dewa arimasen*.

affirmative:	（Ｘ は）Ｙ です。	*X is Y.*
negative:	（Ｘ は）Ｙ <u>じゃありません</u>。	*X is not Y.*

7　～ね/～よ

Statements often end with the tags *ne* or *yo*, depending on the way the speaker views the interaction with the listener. If the speaker is seeking the listener's confirmation or agreement to what has been said, then *ne* ("right?") could be added.

リーさんの　せんもんは　ぶんがくですね。　　*Ms. Lee, your major is literature, right?*
Rii san no　　　senmon wa　　bungaku desu ne.

これは　にくじゃありませんね。　　*This is not meat, is it?*
Kore wa　niku ja arimasen ne.

Another particle, *yo* ("I tell you"), is added to a statement if the speaker wants to assure the listener of what has been said. With *yo* added, a statement becomes an authoritative decree.

とんかつは　さかなじゃありませんよ。
Tonkatsu wa　　　sakana ja arimasen yo.
Let me assure you. "Tonkatsu" is not fish.

スミスさんは　イギリスじんですよ。
Sumisu san wa　　　igirisujin desu yo.
(In case you're wondering,) Mr. Smith is British.

表現ノート
ひょうげん

(〜を)ください▶ *(. . . o) kudasai* is "Please give me X." You can use it to request (concrete) items in general.

(〜を)おねがいします▶ *(. . . o) onegaishimasu* too is a request for item X. When used to ask for a concrete object, *(. . . o) onegaishimasu* sounds slightly more upscale than *(. . . o) kudasai*. It is heard often when ordering food at a restaurant ("I will have . . ."). *(. . . o) onegaishimasu* can also be used to ask for "abstract objects," such as repairs, explanations, and understanding.

(〜を)どうぞ▶ *(. . . o) doozo* is used when an offer is made with respect to item X. In the dialogue, the restaurant attendant uses it when she is about to hand the menu to the customer. It may also be used when a person is waiting for you to come forth with item X; a telephone operator, asking for your name, would probably say *Onamae o doozo*. (*O* is a politeness marker. Therefore *onamae* is "your honorable name.")

On the pronunciation of number words ▶ Note that the words for 300, 600, 800, 3,000 and 8,000 involve sound changes. "Counters" whose first sound is *h*, like *hyaku* (hundred), generally change shape after 3, 6, and 8. Some counters that begin with *s*, like *sen* (thousand), change shape after 3 and 8. Refer to the table at the end of the volume.

Big numbers ▶ In addition to the digit markers for tens (*juu*), hundreds (*hyaku*), and thousands (*sen*), which are found in Western languages as well, Japanese uses the marker for tens of thousands (*man*). Thus 20,000, for example, is *niman* ($=2 \times 10,000$), rather than *nijuusen* ($=20 \times 1,000$). While the next unit marker in Western languages is one million, Japanese describes that number as $100 \times 10,000$, that is, *hyakuman*.

More complicated numbers can be considered the sums of smaller numbers, as in the following examples.

234,567	=	$23 \times 10,000$	にじゅうさんまん	(nijuusanman)
		$4 \times 1,000$	よんせん	(yonsen)
		5×100	ごひゃく	(gohyaku)
		6×10	ろくじゅう	(rokujuu)
		7	なな	(nana)

れんしゅう Ｐｒａｃｔｉｃｅ

Ⅰ すうじ (Numbers) 🔊

100	ひゃく hyaku		1,000	せん sen		10,000	いちまん ichiman
200	にひゃく nihyaku		2,000	にせん nisen		20,000	にまん niman
300	さんびゃく sanbyaku		3,000	さんぜん sanzen		30,000	さんまん sanman
400	よんひゃく yonhyaku		4,000	よんせん yonsen		40,000	よんまん yonman
500	ごひゃく gohyaku		5,000	ごせん gosen		50,000	ごまん goman
600	ろっぴゃく roppyaku		6,000	ろくせん rokusen		60,000	ろくまん rokuman
700	ななひゃく nanahyaku		7,000	ななせん nanasen		70,000	ななまん nanaman
800	はっぴゃく happyaku		8,000	はっせん hassen		80,000	はちまん hachiman
900	きゅうひゃく kyuuhyaku		9,000	きゅうせん kyuusen		90,000	きゅうまん kyuuman

A. Read the following numbers. 🔊

(a) 34   (b) 67   (c) 83   (d) 99   (e) 125

(f) 515   (g) 603   (h) 850   (i) 1,300   (j) 3,400

(k) 8,900   (l) 35,000   (m) 64,500   (n) 92,340

B. Look at the pictures and answer how much the things are. 🔊

Example: Q：ペンは いくらですか。
ぺ ん
Pen wa　ikura desu ka.

A：はちじゅうえんです。
Hachijuu en desu.

Ex. ペン
¥80

(1) えんぴつ
¥50

(2) かさ
¥1,000

(3) しんぶん
¥110

(4) ほん
¥1,500

(5) テープ
¥600

(6) くつ
¥3,500

(7) とけい
¥10,000

(8) かばん
¥20,000

(9) じしょ
¥8,000

(10) ジーンズ
¥9,000

(11) じてんしゃ
¥25,000

(12) ノート
¥450

(13) ぼうし
¥2,800

C. Pair Work—One of you looks at picture A and the other looks at picture B (p. 50). (Don't look at the other picture.) Find out the price of all items.

Example:　A：えんぴつは いくらですか。
　　　　　　　 Enpitsu wa　　ikura desu ka.

　　　　　　B：ひゃくえんです。
　　　　　　　 Hyaku en desu.

¥

Picture A

Ⅱ これは なんですか

A. Items (1) through (6) are near you, and items (7) through (12) are near your friend. Your friend asks what these things are. Answer the questions. Pay attention to これ (*kore*) and それ (*sore*).

Example 1:　Your friend：それは なんですか。
　　　　　　　　　　　Sore wa 　nan desu ka.
　　　　　　　　　You：これは ペンです。
　　　　　　　　　　　　　Kore wa 　pen desu.

Example 2:　Your friend：これは なんですか。
　　　　　　　　　　　Kore wa 　nan desu ka.
　　　　　　　　　You：それは トレーナーです。
　　　　　　　　　　　　　Sore wa 　toreenaa desu.

B. Look at the picture and tell what each building is. 🔊

Example:　Q：あれは　なんですか。
　　　　　　　Are wa　　nan desu ka.

　　　　　　A：あれは　としょかんです。
　　　　　　　Are wa　　toshokan desu.

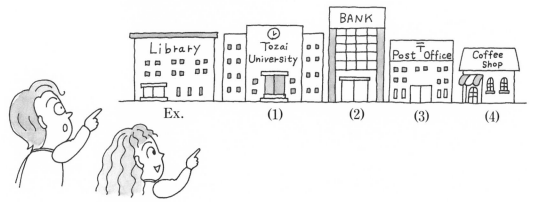

C. Pair Work—Point out five things in the classroom and ask your partner what they are using これ (kore), それ (sore), or あれ (are). Refer to the picture on p. 53 for the vocabulary.

Example 1:

A：あれは　なんですか。
　　Are wa　　nan desu ka.

B：あれは　とけいです。
　　Are wa　　tokee desu.

Example 2:

A：それは　なんですか。
　　Sore wa　　nan desu ka.

B：これは　ペンです。
　　Kore wa　　pen desu.

D. Pair Work—One of you looks at card A and the other looks at card B (p. 51). Ask and answer questions to find out the price of each item. Use この (kono), その (sono), or あの (ano) appropriately.

Example:　Customer：このほんは　いくらですか。
　　　　　　　　　　　　　Kono hon wa　　ikura desu ka.

　　　　　　Store attendant：にせんひゃくえんです。
　　　　　　　　　　　　　　　　Nisen hyaku en desu.

Card A

¥2,100

¥12,600

(2)

¥4,200

(3)

(4)
wallet

ABC

¥7,350

Ex.　¥315

Book

(5)

(1)

¥2,100

Part I. You are a store attendant. Tell the customer how much each item is.

Part II. You are a customer. Ask for the prices of items (1)-(5).

Ⅲ これは だれの かさですか

Pair Work—Point at each item below (picture A) and ask whose it is. Your partner will refer to the picture B (p. 52) and tell you who it belongs to.

Example: A：これは だれの かさですか。
Kore wa　dare no　kasa desu ka.

B：メアリーさんの かさです。
Mearii san no　　　kasa desu.

Picture A

(1)　　　　(2)　　　　(3)　　　　(4)　　　　(5)

Switch roles with your partner.

(6)　　　　(7)　　　　(8)　　　　(9)　　　　(10)

Ⅳ やまださんも にほんじんです

Look at the pictures below and describe each picture.

Example:

おとうさんは にほんじんです。
Otoosan wa　　　nihonjin desu.

おかあさんも にほんじんです。
Okaasan mo　　　nihonjin desu.

Ex.　Japanese
Father　　　　　　Mother

(1) second year

Mary   Tanaka

(2) ¥5,800

(3) 22-years old

Takeshi   Robert

(4) とけい
tokee

(5) vegetable

(6) U. of London students

Robert   Nancy

Ⓥ メアリーさんは にほんじんじゃありません
　　め　あ　り　い

A. Look at the chart on the next page and answer the questions. 🕪

Example:　Q：メアリーさんは にほんじんですか。
　　　　　　　　　　め あ り い
　　　　　　　　Mearii san wa　　　　　nihonjin desu ka.

　　　　　　A：いいえ、にほんじんじゃありません。アメリカじんです。
　　　　　　　　　　　　　　　　　　　　　　　　　あ め り か
　　　　　　　　lie,　　　　nihonjin ja arimasen.　　　　　Amerikajin desu.

1. たけしさんは ちゅうごくじんですか。
   Takeshi san wa　　　chuugokujin desu ka.

2. ロバートさんは アメリカじんですか。
   　ろ ば あ と　　　　あ め り か
   Robaato san wa　　　amerikajin desu ka.

3. やましたせんせいは かんこくじんですか。
   Yamashita sensee wa　　　kankokujin desu ka.

4. ロバートさんの せんもんは にほんごですか。
   　ろ ば あ と
   Robaato san no　　　senmon wa　　　nihongo desu ka.

5. スーさんの せんもんは けいざいですか。
   　す う
   Suu san no　　　senmon wa　　　keezai desu ka.

6. たけしさんは とうざいだいがくの がくせいですか。
   　　　　　　　　　　た う
   Takeshi san wa　　　Toozai daigaku no　　　gakusee desu ka.

7. メアリーさんは ロンドンだいがくの がくせいですか。
   Mearii san wa　　　Rondon daigaku no　　　gakusee desu ka.

8. たけしさんは にねんせいですか。
   Takeshi san wa　　　ninensee desu ka.

9. スーさんは いちねんせいですか。
   Suu san wa　　　ichinensee desu ka.

10. ロバートさんは よねんせいですか。
   Robaato san wa　　　yonensee desu ka.

	Hart, Mary	きむらたけし Kimura Takeshi	Kim, Sue	Smith, Robert	やましたせんせい Yamashita sensee
Nationality	American	Japanese	Korean	British	Japanese
School	U. of Arizona	Tozai Univ.	Seoul Univ.	U. of London	Tozai Univ.
Major	Japanese	history	computer	business	(Japanese teacher)
Year	2nd year	4th year	3rd year	4th year	

B. Pair Work—Ask your partner whose belongings items (1) through (7) are. Your partner will refer to the picture on the next page and answer the questions.

Example:　A：これは メアリーさんの さいふですか。
　　　　　　　Kore wa　Mearii san no　　　saifu desu ka.
　　　　　　B：いいえ、メアリーさんの さいふじゃありません。
　　　　　　　Iie,　　Mearii san no　　　saifu ja arimasen.
　　　　　　A：これは リーさんの さいふですか。
　　　　　　　Kore wa　Rii san no　　saifu desu ka.
　　　　　　B：ええ、リーさんの さいふです。
　　　　　　　Ee,　　Rii san no　　saifu desu.

Ex.

(1) 　(2) 　(3) 　(4) 　(5) 　(6) 　(7)

メアリー
Mearii

リー
Rii

ようこ
Yooko

Ⅵ まとめの れんしゅう (Review Exercises)

A. Role Play—One student is a store attendant. The other is a customer. Use Dialogue Ⅰ as a model.

B. Role Play—One student is a waiter/waitress. The other student goes to a restaurant. Look at the menu below and order some food or drink, using Dialogue Ⅱ as a model.

Pair Work (I) C.

Example:　A：えんぴつは　いくらですか。
　　　　　　　　Enpitsu wa　　ikura desu ka.
　　　　　　B：ひゃくえんです。
　　　　　　　　Hyaku en desu.

 ¥100

Picture B

 ¥　　　　　¥　　　　　¥　　　　　¥3,700

¥4,500　　　¥9,000　　　¥　　　　　¥7,000

Pair Work Ⅱ D.

Example:　Customer：このほんは　いくらですか。
　　　　　　　　Kono hon wa　ikura desu ka.

　　　　Store attendant：にせんひゃくえんです。
　　　　　　　　Nisen hyaku en desu.

Card B

(1)
¥1,050

(2)　　wallet
¥7,350

Ex.　(3)
Book
¥2,100　¥53

(5)
¥3,780

ABC

(4)
¥9,450

Part I. You are a customer. Ask for the price of items (1)-(5).

Part II. You are a store attendant. Tell the customer how much each item is.

Pair Work Ⅲ

Example:　A：これは だれの かさですか。
　　　　　　　Kore wa　dare no　kasa desu ka.
　　　　　　B：メアリーさんの かさです。
　　　　　　　Mearii san no　　　kasa desu.

Picture B

スー
Suu

たけし
Takeshi

メアリー
Mearii

ロバート
Robaato

やましたせんせい
Yamashita sensee

きょうしつ
In the Classroom

でんき
denki

こくばん
kokuban

テレビ
terebi

カーテン
kaaten

ドア
doa

ビデオ
bideo

まど
mado

じしょ
jisho

ほん
hon

えんぴつ
enpitsu

けしゴム
keshigomu

つくえ
tsukue

ペン
pen

いす
isu

かばん
kaban

Useful Expressions

わかりました。 Wakarimashita.	I understand./I understood.
わかりません。 Wakarimasen.	I don't understand./I don't know.
ゆっくり いってください。 Yukkuri　　　itte kudasai.	Please speak slowly.
もういちど いってください。 Moo ichido　　　itte kudasai.	Please say it again.
ちょっと まってください。 Chotto　　　matte kudasai.	Please wait.

第3課 LESSON 3
デートの約束 Making a Date

会話 Dialogue 🔊

Ⅰ Mary and Takeshi are talking.

1 たけし： メアリーさん、週末はたいてい何をしますか。

2 メアリー： そうですね。たいていうちで勉強します。でも、ときどき映画を見ま

3 　　　　　 す。

4 たけし： そうですか……じゃあ、土曜日に映画を見ませんか。

5 メアリー： 土曜日はちょっと……

6 たけし： じゃあ、日曜日はどうですか。

7 メアリー： いいですね。

Ⅱ On Sunday morning, at Mary's host family's.

1 メアリー： おはようございます。

2 お母さん： おはよう。早いですね。

3 メアリー： ええ、今日は京都に行きます。京都で映画を見ます。

4 お母さん： いいですね。何時ごろ帰りますか。

5 メアリー： 九時ごろです。

6 お母さん： 晩ごはんは？

7 メアリー： 食べません。

8 お母さん： そうですか。じゃあ、いってらっしゃい。

9 メアリー： いってきます。

Takeshi: Mary, what do you usually do on the weekend?

Mary: Let's see. I usually study at home. But I sometimes see movies.

Takeshi: I see . . . then, would you like to see a movie on Saturday?

Mary: Saturday is not a good day. (lit., Saturday is a little bit [inconvenient] . . .)

Takeshi: Then, how about Sunday?

Mary: That's fine.

Mary: Good morning.

Host mother: Good morning. You are early, aren't you?

Mary: Yes, I'm going to Kyoto today. I will see a movie in Kyoto.

Host mother: Good. Around what time will you come back?

Mary: Around nine.

Host mother: How about dinner?

Mary: I will not eat.

Host mother: I see. Well, have a nice day.

Mary: Good-bye.

単語
たん ご

V o c a b u l a r y

N o u n s

Entertainment and Sports

*	えいが	映画	movie
	おんがく	音楽	music
	ざっし	雑誌	magazine
	スポーツ		sports
	デート		date (romantic, not calendar)
	テニス		tennis
	テレビ		TV
	ビデオ		video tape; VCR

Foods and Drinks

	あさごはん	朝御飯	breakfast
	おさけ	お酒	sake; alcohol
	おちゃ	お茶	green tea
	コーヒー		coffee
*	ばんごはん	晩御飯	dinner
	ハンバーガー		hamburger
	ひるごはん	昼御飯	lunch
	みず	水	water

Places

	いえ	家	home; house
*	うち		home; house; my place
	LL エルエル		language lab
	がっこう	学校	school

Time

	あさ	朝	morning
	あした		tomorrow
	いつ		when
*	きょう	今日	today
*	〜ごろ		at about
	こんばん	今晩	tonight
*	しゅうまつ	週末	weekend
*	どようび	土曜日	Saturday
*	にちようび	日曜日	Sunday

* Words that appear in the dialogue

| まいにち | 毎日 | every day |
| まいばん | 毎晩 | every night |

U - v e r b s

* いく	行く	to go (*destination* に/へ)
* かえる	帰る	to go back; to return (*destination* に/へ)
きく	聞く	to listen; to hear (〜を)
のむ	飲む	to drink (〜を)
はなす	話す	to speak; to talk (*language* を/で)
よむ	読む	to read (〜を)

R u - v e r b s

おきる	起きる	to get up
* たべる	食べる	to eat (〜を)
ねる	寝る	to sleep; to go to sleep
* みる	見る	to see; to look at; to watch (〜を)

I r r e g u l a r   V e r b s

くる	来る	to come (*destination* に/へ)
* する		to do (〜を)
* べんきょうする	勉強する	to study (〜を)

A d j e c t i v e s

| * いい | | good |
| * はやい | 早い | early |

A d v e r b s

あまり＋ negative		not much
ぜんぜん＋ negative	全然	not at all
* たいてい	大抵	usually
* ちょっと		a little
* ときどき	時々	sometimes
よく		often; much

E x p r e s s i o n s

* そうですね		That's right.; Let me see.
* でも		but
* どうですか		How about . . . ?; How is . . . ?

文法 G r a m m a r
ぶん ぽう

1 Verb Conjugation

Verbs in Japanese conjugate, or take various shapes. In this lesson, we learn three forms: (1) the "dictionary forms," (2) the present tense affirmative forms, and (3) the present tense negative forms.[1] There are two kinds of verbs that follow regular conjugation patterns, and an example of each is below.

	ru-verb	u-verb
verb bases	tabe	ik
dictionary forms	食べる (to eat) た	行く (to go) い
present, affirmative	食べます た	行きます い
present, negative	食べません た	行きません い
stems	食べ た	行き い

食べる belongs to the group of verbs called the "ru-verbs." Ru-verbs are so called, because た you add the suffix ru to the verb base (tabe, in the above example) to form the dictionary form. For the two long forms we learn in this lesson, you simply add the suffixes masu and masen, instead of ru, to the bases. We learn four ru-verbs in this lesson:

食べる	寝る	起きる	見る
た	ね	お	み
食べます	寝ます	起きます	見ます
た	ね	お	み

Another major group of verbs is called the "u-verbs." The dictionary form of an u-verb like 行く can be broken down into the base (ik in the above example) and the suffix u. The い long forms like 行きます and 行きません, then, are formed with the base plus suffixes い   い imasu and imasen. You may find the u-verb conjugations slightly more difficult than the ru-verb conjugations, because of the extra vowel i. We learn six u-verbs in this lesson:

飲む	読む	話す	聞く	行く	帰る
の	よ	はな	き	い	かえ
飲みます	読みます	話します	聞きます	行きます	帰ります
の	よ	はな	き	い	かえ

---

[1]The use of the term "dictionary forms" is by no means restricted to listings in a dictionary. They also appear in various constructions in actual sentences. We will learn their uses in later chapters. Don't be misled by the names given to the long forms too; the "present tense" in Japanese can indicate both the "present" and the "future." We will return to this issue in Section 2 below. For the moment, we will concentrate on the forms, not the meaning of these verbs.

In later lessons, we will have many opportunities to refer to the parts like 食べ and 行き, which come before ます and ません in the long forms. For the sake of ease of reference, we will call these parts (same as bases with *ru*-verbs, and bases plus *i* with *u*-verbs) "stems."

In addition to *ru*-verbs and *u*-verbs, there are two "irregular verbs." Note that the vowels in their bases are different in the short (dictionary) forms and the long forms.

	irregular verbs	
dictionary forms	する (to do)	くる (to come)
present, affirmative	します	きます
present, negative	しません	きません
stems	し	き

These two verbs are also used to form compound verbs. In this lesson, we learn the verb 勉強する, which conjugates just like the verb する.

It is important to remember which verb belongs to which conjugation class. It is a good idea, therefore, to memorize each verb as a set: instead of memorizing just the dictionary form, try to memorize the dictionary form *and* the present tense affirmative, like 行く ー 行きます. This is especially important with verbs that end with the *hiragana* る, because they may be irregular verbs like する and くる, or *ru*-verbs, or *u*-verbs whose bases just happen to end with the consonant *r*. If you know the verb classes and the rules that apply to them, you know why it is wrong to say ×見ります and ×帰ます.[2]

	見る (= a *ru*-verb)	帰る (= an *u*-verb that ends with る)
verb bases	*mi*	*kaer*
long forms	見ます／見ません	帰ります／帰りません
stems	見	帰り

---

[2]Things are not as bad as you might expect after reading the above paragraph. The key lies in the second from the last syllable in a dictionary form. The irregular verbs set aside, if you see the vowels *a*, *o*, or *u* right before the final る, you can be absolutely sure that they are *u*-verbs. (We have not learned any such verbs yet.) Unfortunately for us, the logic does not follow in the other direction; there are *ru*-verbs and *u*-verbs that have the vowels *i* and *e* before the final る. 寝る has the vowel *e* before る and is a *ru*-verb. 帰る, on the other hand, has the same sound sequence, but is an *u*-verb.

2　Verb Types and the "Present Tense"

In this lesson we learn about a dozen verbs that describe basic human actions. These are often called "action verbs," and the "present tense" of these verbs either means (1) that a person habitually or regularly engages in these activities, or (2) that a person will, or is planning to, perform these activities in the future.

Habitual actions:

私 (わたし) はよくテレビを見 (み) ます。　　　　*I often watch TV.*

メアリーさんはときどき朝 (あさ) ごはんを食 (た) べません。　*Mary sometimes doesn't eat breakfast.*

Future actions:

私 (わたし) はあした京都 (きょうと) に行 (い) きます。　　*I will go to Kyoto tomorrow.*

スーさんは今日 (きょう) うちに帰 (かえ) りません。　　*Sue will not return home today.*

3　Particles

Nouns used in sentences generally must be followed by particles, which indicate the relations that the nouns bear to the verbs.[3] In this lesson, we learn four particles: で, に, へ, and を.

で　The particle で indicates where the event described by the verb takes place.[4]

図書館 (としょかん) で本 (ほん) を読 (よ) みます。　　*I will read books in the library.*

うちでテレビを見 (み) ます。　　*I will watch TV at home.*

に　The particle に has many meanings, but here we will learn two: (1) the goal toward which things move, and (2) the time at which an event takes place.

(1) goal of movement

私 (わたし) は今日学校 (きょうがっこう) に行 (い) きません。　*I will not go to school today.*

私 (わたし) はうちに帰 (かえ) ります。　　*I will return home.*

---

[3] In spoken language, particles are often "dropped." We will learn more about such cases in Lesson 15.

[4] In later lessons, we will be introduced to verbs that require particles other than で to express location.

(2) time

日曜日に京都に行きます。 *I will go to Kyoto on Sunday.*

十一時に寝ます。 *I will go to bed at eleven.*

(Some time words stand alone, without the particle に tagging along, which will be discussed in Section 4 below.)

Approximate time references can be made by substituting ごろ or ごろに for に. Thus,

十一時ごろ(に)寝ます。 *I will go to bed at about eleven.*

へ The particle へ, too, indicates the goal of movement. The sentences in (1) above therefore can be rewritten using へ instead of に. Note that this particle is pronounced "*e.*"

私は今日学校へ行きません。 *I will not go to school today.*

私はうちへ帰ります。 *I will return home.*

Note that へ may replace the particle に only in the goal-of-movement sense. The particle に for time references and other uses, which we will learn about in later lessons, cannot be so replaced.

を The particle を indicates "direct objects," the kind of things that are directly involved in, or affected by, the event. Note that this particle is pronounced "*o.*"

コーヒーを飲みます。 *I drink coffee.*

テープを聞きます。 *I listen to tapes.*

テレビを見ます。 *I watch TV.*

4 Time Reference

You need the particle に with (1) the days of the week like "on Sunday," and (2) numerical time expressions, like "at 10:42," and "in September."

日曜日に行きます。 *I will go on Sunday.*

十時四十二分に起きます。 *I get up at 10:42.*

九月に帰ります。 　　　　　　　*I will go back in September.*

You do not use the particle に with (1) time expressions defined relative to the present moment, such as "today" and "tomorrow," (2) expressions describing regular intervals, such as "every day," and (3) the word for "when."

あした来ます。 　　　　　　　　*I will come tomorrow.*

毎晩テレビを見ます。 　　　　　*I watch TV every evening.*

いつ行きますか。 　　　　　　　*When will you go?*

You normally do not use に with (1) the parts of a day, like "in the morning" and "at night," and (2) the word for "weekend." Unlike words like あした and ~~毎晩~~ above, however, these words are sometimes followed by に, depending on styles, emphases, and personal preferences.

朝(に)新聞を読みます。 　　　　*I read the newspaper in the morning.*

週末(に)何をしますか。 　　　　*What will you do on weekends?*

5　～ませんか

You can use ませんか (= the present tense negative verb, plus the question particle) to extend an invitation. It should be noted that its affirmative counterpart, ますか, *cannot* be so used. Thus a sentence like 昼ごはんを食べますか can only be construed as a question, not as an invitation.

昼ごはんを食べませんか。　　*What do you say to having lunch with me?*
いいですね。　　　　　　　　*Sounds great.*

テニスをしませんか。　　　　*Will you play tennis with me?*
うーん、ちょっと。　　　　　*Um, it's slightly (inconvenient for me at this moment).*

6　Word Order

Japanese sentences are fairly flexible in the arrangement of elements that appear in them. Generally, sentences are made up of several noun-particle sequences followed by a verb or an adjective, which in turn is often followed by a sentence-final particle such as か, ね, or よ. Among the noun-particle sequences, their relative orders are to a large extent free.

A typical sentence, therefore, looks like the following, but several other arrangements of noun-particle sequences are also possible.

私は 今日 図書館で 日本語を 勉強します。
わたし きょう としょかん にほんご べんきょう
topic   time   place   object   verb

I will study Japanese in the library today.

私は よく 七時ごろ うちへ 帰ります。
わたし しちじ かえ
topic frequency   time   goal   verb

I often go back home at around seven.

7 Frequency Adverbs

You can add a frequency adverb such as 毎日 (everyday), よく (often), and ときどき
まいにち
(sometimes) to a sentence to describe how often you do something.

私はときどき喫茶店に行きます。   *I sometimes go to a coffee shop.*
きっさてん い

In this lesson, we also learn two adverbs which describe how *infrequent* an activity or an event is; ぜんぜん (never; not at all) and あまり (not often; not very much). These adverbs anticipate the negative at the end of the sentence. If you use ぜんぜん or あまり, in other words, you need to conclude the sentence with ません.

私はぜんぜんテレビを見ません。   *I do not watch TV at all.*
わたし み

たけしさんはあまり勉強しません。   *Takeshi does not study much.*
べんきょう

8 The Topic Particle は

As we saw in Lesson 1, the particle は presents the topic of one's utterance ("As for item X, it is such that . . ."). It puts forward the item that you want to talk about and comment on. You may have noted that the topic phrases in sentences such as メアリーさんは三年生
さんねんせい
です (Mary is a third-year student), and 私の専門は日本語です (My major is Japanese
わたし せんもん にほんご
language), are the subjects of those sentences. A topic phrase, however, need not be the subject of a sentence. We see three sentences in the dialogue of this lesson where nonsubject phrases are made topics with the help of the particle は.

メアリーさん、週末はたいてい何をしますか。
しゅうまつ なに
Mary, what do you usually do on the weekend?

今日は京都に行きます。
I'm going to Kyoto today.

In the above two examples, は promotes time expressions as the topic of each sentence. Its effects can be paraphrased like these: "Let's talk about weekends; what do you do on weekends?" "Let me say what I will do today; I will go to Kyoto."

晩ごはんは？
How about dinner?

食べません。
I will not eat.

In this example, は is used in directing the listener's attention and thereby inviting a comment or completion of a sentence. You may also note that the broached topic, 晩ごはん, does not stand in subject relation to the verb, but is rather its direct object.

表現ノート
ひょうげん

Expression Notes ④

行く/来る▶ When you move to a place where the hearer is, you say "I'm coming." in English. However in the same situation, 私は行きます is used in Japanese. 来る is a movement toward the place where the speaker is. 行く is a movement in a direction away from the speaker.

ちょっと▶ ちょっと literally means "a little," "a bit," "a small amount," as in ちょっとください (Please give me a little) and ちょっと待ってください (Please wait for a moment). It is commonly used for a polite refusal. In this case, it means "inconvenient," "impossible," and so on. Japanese people don't normally reject requests, suggestions, or invitations with いいえ (No), because it sounds too direct.

A：土曜日に映画を見ませんか。   *Will you see a movie on Saturday?*
B：土曜日は、ちょっと。   *Saturday is not convenient.*
    (lit., Saturday is a little bit.)

練習 Practice
れん しゅう

�Ⅰ 図書館で本を読みます
と しょ かん ほん よ

A. Change the following verbs into ～ます and ～ません. 🔊

Example: たべる → たべます

たべる → たべません

1. のむ   2. きく   3. みる   4. する   5. はなす

6. いく   7. くる   8. かえる   9. ねる   10. よむ

11. おきる   12. べんきょうする

B. Look at the pictures below and make sentences using the cues. 🔊

(a) Add the appropriate verbs to the following direct objects.

Example: 雑誌 → 雑誌を読みます。
ざっ し   ざっ し よ

Ex. 雑誌   (1) テープ   (2) テニス   (3) ハンバーガー
ざっ し

library/2:00   L.L./4:30   school/Saturday   McDonald's/5:00

(4) コーヒー   (5) テレビ   (6) 日本語
に ほん ご

coffee shop/3:00   home/tonight   college/every day

(b) Add the place to the above sentences.

Example:　library　→　図書館で雑誌を読みます。
　　　　　　　　　　　と しょかん　ざっ し　　よ

C.　Look at the pictures below and make sentences using the cues.

Example:　go to the post office　→　郵便局に行きます。
　　　　　　　　　　　　　　　　　　ゆうびんきょく　い

Ex.　go to the post office　(1) go to the library　(2) come to school

1:00

3:00

8:30

(3) come to the coffee shop　(4) return home　(5) return to the U. S.

5:30

tomorrow

D.　Pair Work—Make questions, using verbs we have learned in this lesson.

Example:　A：図書館で雑誌を読みますか。
　　　　　　　　　と しょかん　ざっ し　　よ
　　　　　　　B：ええ、読みます。／いいえ、読みません。
　　　　　　　　　　　　よ　　　　　　　　　　よ

E. Pair Work—Guessing game

Ask questions and find out the items your partner has chosen.

---

1. Before you start, both of you will choose one item in each row of the table and mark it.
2. In each row, using the verb and one of the four items, make a yes-or-no-question sentence and find out which item your partner has chosen.
3. You can ask at most two questions with one verb. If you have guessed correctly the item your partner has chosen, you score a point. Your partner will not give away the right answer when you ask a wrong question.
4. When you have asked questions about all the verbs in the table, switch roles with your partner and answer their questions.
5. Tabulate the score. You win the game if you have scored higher than your partner.

Example:　A：学校に行きますか。
　　　　　B：いいえ、行きません。
　　　　　A：喫茶店へ行きますか。
　　　　　B：はい、行きます。(A guessed what B marked, therefore A won.)

～に行きます	post office	school	coffee shop	library
～を見ます	TV	movie	video	cartoon（まんが）
～を飲みます	sake	green tea	water	coffee
～を読みます	book	newspaper	magazine	Japanese book
～をします	date	study	telephone	tennis

Ⅱ 何時に起きますか
なん じ お

A. Look at Mary's schedule and answer the following questions. 🔊

Mary's Schedule

7:30 A.M.	get up
8:00	eat breakfast
8:30	go to school
12:00	eat lunch
3:00 P.M.	drink coffee
4:00	play tennis
5:00	go home
6:30	eat dinner
7:00	watch TV
8:00	study
11:30	go to bed

1. メアリーさんは何時に起きますか。
   なん じ お
2. メアリーさんは何時に学校に行きますか。
   なん じ がっこう い
3. メアリーさんは何時に昼ごはんを食べますか。
   なん じ ひる た
4. メアリーさんは何時にコーヒーを飲みますか。
   なん じ の
5. メアリーさんは何時にうちに帰りますか。
   なん じ かえ
6. メアリーさんは何時に勉強しますか。
   なん じ べんきょう
7. メアリーさんは何時に寝ますか。
   なん じ ね

B. Pair Work—Ask your partner what time they do the following things.

Example: A：何時に起きますか。
            なん じ お
         B：八時に起きます。
            はち じ お

Your partner's schedule

time	
( )	get up
( )	eat breakfast
( )	go to school
( )	eat lunch
( )	go home
( )	go to bed

C. Look at the pictures in Ⅰ-B (p. 65) and Ⅰ-C (p. 66), and add the time expressions to the sentences. 🔊

Example: 2:00 → 二時に図書館で本を読みます。
                 に じ としょかん ほん よ

Ⅲ コーヒーを飲みませんか

A. Make suggestions using the cues below. 🔊

Example: drink coffee → コーヒーを飲みませんか。

1. see a movie　　2. come to my house　　3. play tennis
4. eat dinner　　5. study in the library　　6. talk at a coffee shop
7. drink tea at home　　8. listen to the music

B. Pair Work—Ask your friend out for the activities in the pictures.

Example: A：映画を見ませんか。
B：いいですね。／ううん、ちょっと……。

Ex.　　　　　(1)　　　　　(2)　　　　　(3)

(4)　　　　　(5)　　　　　(6)

Ⅳ 毎日本を読みます
まいにちほん　　　　よ

How often do you do the following activities? Answer the questions using the expressions below.

Example: Q：本を読みますか。
ほん　よ

A：ええ、よく読みます。／いいえ、あまり読みません。
よ　　　　　　　　　　　　　　　　　よ

1. スポーツをしますか。
2. 雑誌を読みますか。
ざっし　よ
3. 図書館に行きますか。
としょかん　い
4. 映画を見ますか。
えいが　み
5. コーヒーを飲みますか。
の
6. 日本の音楽を聞きますか。
にほん　おんがく　き
7. 朝ごはんを食べますか。
あさ　　　　た

毎日
まいにち
よく ⎫
ときどき ⎭ 〜ます
あまり ⎫
ぜんぜん ⎭ 〜ません

Ⅴ まとめの練習 (Review Exercises)
れんしゅう

A. Answer the following questions.

1. 何時に起きますか。
なんじ　お
2. どこで勉強しますか。
べんきょう
3. いつテレビを見ますか。
み
4. スポーツをしますか。
5. 週末はどこに行きますか。
しゅうまつ　　　　い
6. 朝、何を食べますか。
あさ　なに　た
7. 今晩、何をしますか。
こんばん　なに
8. 毎晩、何時ごろ寝ますか。
まいばん　なんじ　　　ね

B. Tell your classmates what your plans are today/tomorrow/on the weekend.

Example: 今日は二時にLLに行きます。三時に図書館で日本語を勉強します。
きょう　にじ　エルエル　い　　　さんじ　としょかん　にほんご　べんきょう
六時ごろうちに帰ります。
ろくじ　　　　　かえ

C. Class Activity—Find someone who . . .

name

1. gets up at 7 o'clock.   _____

2. eats breakfast every day.   _____

3. speaks French.   _____

4. watches TV at home.   _____

5. listens to Japanese music.   _____

6. plays tennis.   _____

D. Suggest to a classmate that you do something together over the weekend. Use Dialogue Ⅰ as a model.

Example:　A：Bさんはテニスをしますか。

　　　　　B：はい。

　　　　　A：じゃあ、日曜日_{にちようび}にテニスをしませんか。

　　　　　B：日曜日_{にちようび}はちょっと……。

　　　　　A：そうですか。じゃあ、土曜日_{どようび}はどうですか。

　　　　　B：ええ、いいですね。

第4課 ┃ L E S S O N ⋯⋯⋯⋯4
初めてのデート The First Date
はじ

会話 Dialogue
かい わ

(I) Mary goes downtown.

1 メアリー： すみません。マクドナルドはどこですか。

2 知らない人： あのデパートの前ですよ。
　 し　　ひと 　　　　　　　　　　　まえ

3 メアリー： ありがとうございます。

(II) In the evening, at Mary's host family's house.

1 メアリー： ただいま。

2 お父さん： おかえりなさい。映画はどうでしたか。
　 とう 　　　　　　　　　　　えいが

3 メアリー： 見ませんでした。たけしさんは来ませんでした。
　　　　　　み 　　　　　　　　　　　　　　　　き

4 お父さん： えっ、どうしてですか。
　 とう

5 メアリー： わかりません。だから、一人で本屋とお寺に行きました。
　　　　　　　　　　　　　　　　 ひとり　ほんや　　てら　い

6 お父さん： 人がたくさんいましたか。
　 とう 　　ひと

7 メアリー： はい。お寺で写真をたくさん撮りました。
　　　　　　　　てら　しゃしん　　　　　　と

8 　　　　　 デパートにも行きました。はい、おみやげです。
　　　　　　　　　　　　　い

9 お父さん： ありがとう。
　 とう

10 お母さん： あっ、メアリーさん、
　 かあ

11 　　　　　 さっき電話がありましたよ。
　　　　　　　　てんわ

Ⅲ On the phone.

1 たけし： はい、木村です。

2 メアリー： もしもし、たけしさんですか。メアリーです。

3 たけしさん、今日来ませんでしたね。

4 たけし： 行きましたよ。ハーゲンダッツの前で一時間待ちました。

5 メアリー： えっ。ハーゲンダッツじゃありませんよ。マクドナルドですよ。

6 たけし： マクドナルド……ごめんなさい！

Ⅰ

Mary: Excuse me. Where is McDonald's?

Stranger: It is in front of that department store.

Mary: Thank you.

Ⅱ

Mary: I'm home.

Host father: Welcome home. How was the movie?

Mary: I didn't see it. Takeshi didn't come.

Host father: Oh, why?

Mary: I don't know. So, I went to a bookstore and a temple alone.

Host father: Were there a lot of people?

Mary: Yes. I took many pictures at the temple. I also went to a department store.
Here's a souvenir for you.

Host father: Thank you.

Host mother: Oh, Mary, you had a phone call a little while ago.

Ⅲ

Takeshi: This is Kimura.

Mary: Hello, is this Takeshi? This is Mary. Takeshi, you didn't come today, did you?

Takeshi: I went there. I waited for one hour in front of the Häagen-Dazs place.

Mary: Not Häagen-Dazs. McDonald's!

Takeshi: McDonald's . . . I'm sorry!

単語 _{たんご}

Ｖｏｃａｂｕｌａｒｙ

Nouns

Activities

アルバイト		part-time job
かいもの	買い物	shopping
クラス		class

People and Things

あなた		you
いぬ	犬	dog
* おみやげ	お土産	souvenir
こども	子供	child
ごはん	御飯	rice; meal
* しゃしん	写真	picture; photograph
つくえ	机	desk
てがみ	手紙	letter
ねこ	猫	cat
パン		bread
* ひと	人	person

Places

* おてら	お寺	temple
こうえん	公園	park
スーパー		supermarket
* デパート		department store
バスてい	バス停	bus stop
びょういん	病院	hospital
ホテル		hotel
* ほんや	本屋	bookstore
まち	町	town; city
レストラン		restaurant

Time

きのう	昨日	yesterday
* さっき		a little while ago
* ～じかん	～時間	hour
cf. いちじかん	一時間	one hour

* Words that appear in the dialogue

せんしゅう	先週	last week
とき	時	when . . . ; at the time of . . .
		(〜の)
げつようび	月曜日	Monday
かようび	火曜日	Tuesday
すいようび	水曜日	Wednesday
もくようび	木曜日	Thursday
きんようび	金曜日	Friday

U-verbs

	あう	会う	to meet; to see (a person)
			(*person* に)
*	ある		there is . . . (〜が)
	かう	買う	to buy (〜を)
	かく	書く	to write (*person* に *thing* を)
*	とる	撮る	to take (pictures) (〜を)
*	まつ	待つ	to wait (〜を)
*	わかる		to understand (〜が)

Ru-verb

| * | いる | | (a person) is in . . . ; stays at . . . |
| | | | (*place* に) |

Adverbs and Other Expressions

	〜ぐらい		about (approximate measurement)
*	ごめんなさい		I'm sorry.
*	だから		so; therefore
*	たくさん		many; a lot
	〜と		together with (a person)
*	どうして		why
*	ひとりで	一人で	alone
*	もしもし		Hello? (used on the phone)

Location Words

	みぎ	右	right (〜の)
	ひだり	左	left (〜の)
*	まえ	前	front (〜の)
	うしろ	後ろ	back (〜の)
	なか	中	inside (〜の)
	うえ	上	on (〜の)

した	下	under	（〜の）
そば		near	（〜の）
となり	隣	next	（〜の）
あいだ	間	between	（ A と B の）
そこ		there	
ここ		here	

文法 Grammar
ぶん ぽう

1 Xがあります/います

X があります means "there is/are X (nonliving thing)." The particle が introduces, or presents, the item X. You can use あります when you want to say that there is something at a certain location.

あそこにマクドナルドがあります。　　　*There's a McDonald's over there.*

Note that あります is different from other verbs we have seen so far on the following three counts. One, it calls for the particle に, rather than で, for the place description. Two, the place description usually comes at the beginning of the sentence. Three, the thing description is usually followed by the particle が, rather than は.

You can also use あります to say that you *have* or *own* something.[1]

テレビがありません。　　　　　　　　*I don't have a TV.*

時間がありますか。　　　　　　　　　*Do you have time?*
じ かん

We also use あります when we want to say that *an event will take place.*[2]

火曜日にテストがあります。　　　　　*There will be an exam on Tuesday.*
か ようび

あしたは日本語のクラスがありません。　*There will be no Japanese class tomorrow.*
に ほん ご

When you want to present a *person* or some other sentient being, rather than a thing, you need to use the verb います.[3] Thus,

---

[1] Note the difference between:
　テレビがありません (I don't have a TV), the negative version of テレビがあります, and
　テレビじゃありません (It isn't a TV), the negative version of テレビです.

[2] In a minor detail which we will not discuss any further here, when あります is used in the sense of an event taking place, the place description is followed by the particle で, like normal verbs and unlike the other uses of あります. Note also that some time expressions (such as 日曜日に) come with the particle に, and some others (such as あした) do not (see Lesson 3). The rule applies to the あります sentences as well.

[3] Note that the same verb "is" in English comes out differently in Japanese:
　あそこに留学生がいます。　　*There is an international student over there.*
　　　りゅう がく せい
　メアリーさんは留学生です。　*Mary is an international student.*
　　　　　　　りゅう がく せい
　います and あります are strictly for descriptions of existence and location, while です is for description of an attribute of a person or a thing.

あそこに留学生がいます。　　　　　*There's an international student over there.*

(place に)	thing が	あります	*There is/are . . .*
	person が	います	

2　Describing Where Things Are

We learned in Lesson 2 that to ask for the location of item X, you can use the word どこ (where) and say X はどこですか.

マクドナルドはどこですか。　　　　*Where's McDonald's?*

In response, one can, of course, point and say:

マクドナルドは { あそこ / そこ / ここ } です。　　*McDonald's is* { *over there.* / *right there near you.* / *right here.* }

In this lesson, we will learn to describe locations in more detail. More specifically, we learn to describe the location of an item relative to another item, as in "X is in front of Y." The Japanese version looks like X は Y の前です.

（マクドナルドは）あのデパートの前です。
It's in front of that department store.

Other useful words describing locations are as follows:

location words

X は Y の { みぎ / ひだり / まえ / うしろ / なか / うえ / した / そば[4] / となり[5] } です。	*X is* { *to the right of* / *to the left of* / *in front of* / *behind* / *inside* / *on/above* / *under/beneath* / *near* / *next to* } *Y.*
X は Y と Z のあいだです。	*X is between Y and Z.*

銀行は図書館の<u>となり</u>です。
ぎんこう　　としょかん
The bank is next to the library.

かさはテーブルの<u>下</u>です。
　　　　　　　　　した
The umbrella is under the table.

レストランはデパートと病院の<u>間</u>です。
　　　　　　　　　　　びょういん　あいだ
The restaurant is between the department store and the hospital.

One can use any of the above location words together with a verb to describe an event that occurs in the place. To use these phrases with verbs such as 食べる and 待つ, one will need
　　　　　　　　　　　　　　　　　　　　　　　　　た　　　　　　　　ま
the particle で.

私はハーゲンダッツの<u>前</u>でメアリーさんを待ちました。
わたし　　　　　　　　　　まえ　　　　　　　　　　　ま
I waited for Mary in front of the Häagen-Dazs place.

3　Past Tense

The past tense forms of verbs look like the following, where ～ stands for the stem of a verb.

	affirmative	negative
present tense	～<u>ます</u>	～<u>ません</u>
past tense	～<u>ました</u>	～<u>ませんでした</u>

メアリーさんは九時ごろうちに帰りました。　　*Mary returned home at about nine.*
　　　　　　　くじ　　　　　　　かえ

私はきのう日本語を勉強しませんでした。　　*I did not study Japanese yesterday.*
わたし　　　にほんご　べんきょう

The various details of formation of the long forms that we learned in Lesson 3, like the *ru*-verb/*u*-verb/irregular verb distinctions, all apply to the past tense forms as well.

---

[4]Another word for "near" that is also commonly used is ちかく.

[5]Both XはYのとなりです and XはYのよこです describe situations where two items (X and Y) are found side by side. For a となり sentence to be considered appropriate, items X and Y need to belong to the same category; two people, two buildings, and so forth. In contrast, an item can be よこ in relation to another item even if they are quite distinct.

　　◯電話はトイレの<u>よこ</u>です。　　　*The telephone is by the restroom.*
　　　でんわ
　　✕電話はトイレの<u>となり</u>です。　　(odd)
　　　でんわ

The past tense versions of "X は Y です" sentences look like the following.

	affirmative	negative
present tense	〜です	〜じゃありません
past tense	〜<u>でした</u>	〜じゃありません<u>でした</u>[6]

山下先生は東西大学の学生でした。
やましたせんせい　とうざいだいがく　がくせい
Mr. Yamashita was a student at Tozai University.

あれは日本の映画じゃありませんでした。
にほん　えいが
That was not a Japanese movie.

4　たくさん

Expressions of quantity in Japanese are rather different from those in English. In Japanese, if you want to add a quantity word like たくさん to the direct object of a sentence, you can either place it before the noun, or after the particle を.

私は京都で
わたし　きょうと
{ 写真をたくさん
　しゃしん
　たくさん写真を
　　　　しゃしん }
撮りました。
と
I took many pictures in Kyoto.

{ 野菜をたくさん
　やさい
　たくさん野菜を
　　　　やさい }
食べました。
た
I ate a lot of vegetables.

5　一時間
いちじかん

The duration of an activity is expressed with a bare noun, like 一時間. Such a noun stands
いちじかん
alone (that is, not followed by any particle) and usually appears immediately before the verb.

メアリーさんはそこでたけしさんを一時間待ちました。
いちじかん　ま
Mary waited for Takeshi there for an hour.

For an approximate measurement, you can add ぐらい[7] after 〜時間.
じかん

---

[6]As was the case with the present tense じゃありません, written language would more likely have ではあ
りませんでした, instead of the contracted form じゃありませんでした.

[7]As we learned in Lesson 3, for "at about a certain time" we have another word ごろ.

私はきのう日本語を三時間ぐらい勉強しました。
I studied Japanese for about three hours yesterday.

6　と

The particle と has two functions. One is to connect two nouns A *and* B.[8]

日本語と英語を話します。　　　*I speak Japanese <u>and</u> English.*

京都と大阪に行きました。　　　*I went to Kyoto <u>and</u> Osaka.*

The other meaning of と is "together with"; it describes *with whom* you do something.[9]

メアリーさんはスーさんと韓国に行きます。
Mary will go to Korea <u>with</u> Sue.

7　も

We learned in Lesson 2 that we use the particle も in reference to the second item which shares a common attribute with the first. You can also use も when two or more people perform the same activity.

私はきのう京都に行きました。　　*I went to Kyoto yesterday.*

山下先生もきのう京都に行きました。　*Professor Yamashita went to Kyoto yesterday, too.*

Or when someone buys, sees, or eats two or more things.

メアリーさんはくつを買いました。　*Mary bought shoes.*

メアリーさんはかばんも買いました。　*Mary bought a bag, too.*

In both cases, も directly marks an item on the list of things or people that have something in common. Observe that も *replaces* the particles は, が, or を in these sentences.

You can also use も when you go to two places, do something on two different occasions, and so forth.

---

[8]You can use と to connect nouns only. We will learn about connecting verbs and sentences in Lesson 6.

[9]"With" as in "with chopsticks" requires another particle. See Lesson 10.

私は先週京都に行きました。　　　*I went to Kyoto last week.*

大阪にも行きました。　　　*I went to Osaka, too.*

ロバートさんは土曜日にパーティーに行きました。
Robert went to a party on Saturday.

日曜日にもパーティーに行きました。
He went to a party on Sunday, too.

We put も *after* the particle に in these sentences. More generally, particles other than は, が, and を are used together with も, rather than being replaced by it.

表現ノート　　　Expression Notes ⑤

X の前▶ X の前 is often used in the sense of "across (the street) from X" or "opposite X." You may also hear another word that is used in the sense of across, namely, X のむかい.

　If something is behind X, or farther away from a street and cannot be directly seen because of the intervening X, in addition to calling it X の後ろ, you can also describe it as being X のうら.

えっ/あっ▶ In the dialogues, we observe Mary's host father saying えっ, and her host mother saying あっ. えっ is like the incredulous "what?" that you use when you have heard something that is hard to believe. あっ is used when you have suddenly noticed or remembered something. The small っ at the end of these little words indicates that these words, when pronounced, are very short.

二時間半▶ 半 (half) appears after the unit word like 時間. Thus, "two hours and a half" is 二時間半, rather than 二半時間.

もしもし▶ もしもし is "hello," which is used only in telephone conversations. Some people use もしもし when they place a call. Some other people use it when they receive a call.

練習 Practice
れん しゅう

① 大学があります
だいがく

A. Look at the picture and tell what you see, using あります or います.

B. Answer the following questions.

1. あなたの町に日本のレストランがありますか。
   まち　にほん

2. あなたの家に猫がいますか。
   いえ　ねこ

3. あなたの学校に何がありますか。
   がっこう　なに

4. あなたの学校に日本人の学生がいますか。
   がっこう　にほんじん　がくせい

5. デパートに何がありますか。
   なに

6. この教室 (classroom) にだれがいますか。
   きょうしつ

7. 動物園 (zoo) に何がいますか。
   どうぶつえん　なに

8. あなたの国 (country) に何がありますか。
   くに　なに

9. あなたの家に何がありますか。
   いえ　なに

C. Look at Takeshi's schedule for the week and answer the following questions. 🔊

	School	After School
Monday	French English Computer	
Tuesday	History	club activity
Wednesday	French English Computer	
Thursday	History	club activity
Friday	English (TEST)	party
Saturday	NO SCHOOL	date
Sunday	NO SCHOOL	part-time job

club activity	クラブ
party	パーティー
test	テスト

Example:　Q：月曜日にフランス語のクラスがありますか。
　　　　　　A：はい、あります。

1. 月曜日に英語のクラスがありますか。
2. 火曜日にコンピューターのクラスがありますか。
3. 木曜日にフランス語のクラスがありますか。
4. 土曜日にクラスがありますか。
5. 水曜日に何がありますか。
6. 金曜日に何がありますか。
7. 日曜日に何がありますか。

D. Pair Work—Write down your next week's schedule and ask each other what plans you have on each day of the week.

Example:　A：月曜日に何がありますか。
　　　　　　B：日本語のクラスがあります。

	Your Schedule	Your Partner's Schedule
月曜日 げつようび		
火曜日 かようび		
水曜日 すいようび		
木曜日 もくようび		
金曜日 きんようび		
土曜日 どようび		
日曜日 にちようび		

Ⅱ 図書館はどこですか
   としょかん

A. Look at the picture and tell where the following things are. 🔊

Example: 図書館
        としょかん
    → 図書館は大学の後ろです。
      としょかん　だいがく　うし
      図書館はスーパーのとなりです。
      としょかん

1. 郵便局   2. 喫茶店   3. バス停
   ゆうびんきょく   きっさてん   てい
4. 公園   5. スーパー   6. 病院
   こうえん   びょういん

B. Look at the picture and tell where the following things are. 🔊

Example: 本 → 本はつくえの上です。
        ほん   ほん   うえ

1. えんぴつ

2. ラケット (racket)

3. 時計
   とけい
4. 電話
   でんわ
5. かばん

6. ぼうし

C. Pair Work—Ask and answer questions to find where the buildings are.
One student looks at map A. The other student looks at map B (p. 93). Don't
look at the other's map.

Example:　A：公園はどこですか。
　　　　　　　こうえん
　　　　　　B：公園はホテルのとなりです。
　　　　　　　こうえん

Map A

喫茶店
きっさてん

ホテル　公園　スーパー
　　　　こうえん

病院
びょういん

デパート

レストラン

図書館　銀行
としょかん　ぎんこう

Ask where the following
places are.

1.　大学　　　　2.　バス停
　　だいがく　　　　　　　てい
3.　高校　　　　4.　本屋
　　こうこう　　　　　　　ほんや
5.　郵便局
　　ゆうびんきょく

Ⅲ 先生は二十二歳でした
せんせい　にじゅうにさい

A. Look at the information about Prof. Yamashita 25 years ago and answer the
questions. 🔊

Twenty-five years ago, Prof. Yamashita was
　　twenty-two years old
　　senior at a college
　　good student
　　his major—Japanese history

Example:

　Q：山下先生は大学生 (college student) でしたか。
　　やましたせんせい　だいがくせい
　A：はい、山下先生は大学生でした。
　　　　やましたせんせい　だいがくせい

　Q：山下先生は十九歳でしたか。
　　やましたせんせい　じゅうきゅうさい
　A：いいえ、山下先生は十九歳じゃありませんでした。
　　　　やましたせんせい　じゅうきゅうさい

1. 山下先生は子供でしたか。
　やましたせんせい　こども
2. 山下先生は一年生でしたか。
　やましたせんせい　いちねんせい
3. 山下先生はいい学生でしたか。
　やましたせんせい　　がくせい
4. 山下先生の専門は英語でしたか。
　やましたせんせい　せんもん　えいご
5. 山下先生の専門は歴史でしたか。
　やましたせんせい　せんもん　れきし

B. Pair Work—Guessing game

Ask questions and find out the prices your partner has chosen.

---

1. Before you start, both of you will choose one price in each row of the table and mark it.

2. In each row, use the item and one of the four prices, make a yes-or-no-question sentence and find out which price your partner has chosen.

3. You can ask at most two questions with one item. If you have guessed correctly the price your partner has chosen, you score a point. Your partner will not give away the right answer when you ask a wrong question.

4. When you have asked questions about all the items in the table, switch roles with your partner and answer their questions.

5. Tabulate the score. You win the game if you have scored higher than your partner.

Example:　A：そのかばんは二万円でしたか。
　　　　　　　　　　にまんえん
　　　　　　B：いいえ、二万円じゃありませんでした。
　　　　　　　　　　　にまんえん
　　　　　　A：一万五千円でしたか。
　　　　　　　　いちまんごせんえん
　　　　　　B：はい、そうです。

かばん	￥5,000	￥10,000	￥15,000	￥20,000
かさ	￥600	￥1,000	￥1,300	￥2,000
ぼうし	￥1,600	￥2,000	￥2,400	￥3,000
トレーナー	￥3,500	￥4,000	￥6,500	￥8,000
時計 とけい	￥3,000	￥10,000	￥17,000	￥25,000

C. Pair Work—Suppose you got one thing as a birthday present and choose it from the items on the next page. Your partner guesses what you got. Answer your partner's questions.

Example:　B：プレゼントはかばんでしたか。
　　　　　　A：ええ、かばんでした。
　　　　　　　　いいえ、かばんじゃありませんでした。

Ⅳ 月曜日に何をしましたか
<small>げつようび　なに</small>

A. Change the following verbs into 〜ました and 〜ませんでした. 🔊

Example:　たべる　→　たべました

　　　　　　たべる　→　たべませんでした

1. はなす　2. かう　3. よむ　4. かく　5. くる　6. まつ　7. おきる　8. わかる

9. する　10. とる　11. ある　12. ねる　13. きく　14. かえる　15. のむ

B. The pictures below show what Mary did last week. Tell what she did. 🔊

Example:　メアリーさんは月曜日に図書館で勉強しました。
<small>　　　　　　　　げつようび　としょかん　べんきょう</small>

Ex. Monday　　　(1) Tuesday　　　(2) Wednesday　　　(3) Thursday

in the library　　　at home　　　at school　　　at a coffee shop

(4) Friday　　　(5) Saturday　　　(6) Sunday

at a friend's house　　　in Kyoto　　　at a department store

C. Look at the pictures in B and answer the questions. 🔊

Example: Q：メアリーさんは月曜日に図書館で勉強しましたか。
        A：はい、勉強しました。
        Q：メアリーさんは月曜日に映画を見ましたか。
        A：いいえ、見ませんでした。

1. メアリーさんは火曜日に手紙を書きましたか。
2. メアリーさんは水曜日に喫茶店に行きましたか。
3. メアリーさんは木曜日に日本人の友だちに会いましたか。
4. メアリーさんは金曜日にお寺に行きましたか。
5. メアリーさんは土曜日にテニスをしましたか。
6. メアリーさんは日曜日に買い物をしましたか。

D. Look at the pictures above and answer the questions. 🔊

Example: Q：メアリーさんは月曜日に何をしましたか。
        A：図書館で勉強しました。

1. メアリーさんは水曜日に何をしましたか。
2. メアリーさんは火曜日に何をしましたか。
3. メアリーさんはいつ映画を見ましたか。
4. メアリーさんはいつ買い物をしましたか。
5. メアリーさんは金曜日にどこで晩ごはんを食べましたか。
6. メアリーさんは木曜日にどこで友だちに会いましたか。

E. Pair Work—Ask what your partner did on Monday, Tuesday, etc.

Example: A：月曜日に何をしましたか。
        B：テニスをしました。

Ⓥ 子供の時よく本を読みましたか

Pair Work—Using the expressions below, ask your partners how often they did the following activities when they were a child or in high school.

Example:　A：子供の時／高校の時 よく本を読みましたか。
　　　　　　B：はい、よく読みました。
　　　　　　　　いいえ、あまり読みませんでした。

1. 勉強する
2. スポーツをする
3. 映画を見る
4. 公園に行く
5. 手紙を書く
6. デートをする

毎日	
よく	
ときどき	〜ました
あまり	
ぜんぜん	〜ませんでした

Ⅵ コーヒーも飲みます

A. Compare sentences (a) and (b), and change sentence (b) using も.

Example:　(a) ハンバーガーは二百円です。
　　　　　　(b) コーヒーは二百円です。　→　コーヒーも二百円です。

1. (a) たけしさんは時計を買いました。
   (b) たけしさんはかばんを買いました。
2. (a) ロバートさんは日本語を勉強します。
   (b) メアリーさんは日本語を勉強します。
3. (a) たけしさんは土曜日にアルバイトをします。
   (b) たけしさんは日曜日にアルバイトをします。
4. (a) メアリーさんはうちで日本語を話します。
   (b) メアリーさんは学校で日本語を話します。
5. (a) あした、メアリーさんはたけしさんに会います。
   (b) あした、メアリーさんはスーさんに会います。
6. (a) 先週、LL に行きませんでした。
   (b) きのう、LL に行きませんでした。

B. Describe the pictures using も.

Example: 山本さんは学生です。
やまもと　　　　　　がくせい

田中さんも学生です。
た　なか　　　　　　がくせい

Ex.　やまもと　たなか

student

(1)

きむら　やまぐち

go to a party

(2)

ごはん　　パン

(3)

コーヒー　おちゃ

(4)

I speak English　Hablo español

(5)

こうえん　　　　おてら

(6)

うち　　としょかん

(7)

どようび　　にちようび

(8)

かようび　もくようび

テスト　テスト

(9)

とうきょう

ひろしま

Ⅶ まとめの練習 (Review Exercises)

A. Answer the following questions.

1. 毎日、何時に起きますか。
2. たいてい何時間ぐらい寝ますか。
3. 毎日、何時間勉強しますか。
4. よくだれと昼ごはんを食べますか。
5. よく友だちに手紙を書きますか。
6. 先週、スポーツをしましたか。
7. きのう、どこで晩ごはんを食べましたか。
8. 先週、写真をたくさん撮りましたか。

B. Pair Work—A and B want to play basketball together. The following is A's schedule for this week. (B's schedule is on p. 93.) Play the roles of A and B with your partner. Ask each other what the other is doing and decide on what day you will play basketball.

Example:

A：バスケット(basketball)をしま

せんか。

B：いいですね。

A：月曜日はどうですか。

B：月曜日は図書館で勉強します。

火曜日は？

A's Schedule

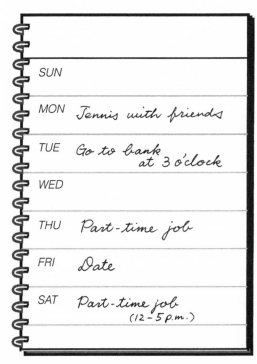

SUN	
MON	Tennis with friends
TUE	Go to bank at 3 o'clock
WED	
THU	Part-time job
FRI	Date
SAT	Part-time job (12 – 5 p.m.)

Pair Work Ⅱ C.

Example:　A：公園はどこですか。
　　　　　　　　こうえん

　　　　　　　B：公園はホテルのとなりです。
　　　　　　　　こうえん

Map B

大学
だいがく

ホテル　公園
　　　　こうえん

高校
こうこう

郵便局　デパート
ゆうびんきょく

図書館
としょかん

本屋
ほんや

バス停
てい

Ask where the following places are.

1. 病院　　　2. 喫茶店
　 びょういん　　 きっさてん

3. スーパー　　4. 銀行
　　　　　　　　 ぎんこう

5. レストラン

Pair Work Ⅶ B.

Example:

A：バスケット(basketball)をしま
　せんか。

B：いいですね。

A：月曜日はどうですか。
　 げつようび

B：月曜日は図書館で勉強します。
　 げつようび　　としょかん　べんきょう

　火曜日は？
　かようび

B's Schedule

SUN	6 p.m. Jogging
MON	Study in the library
TUE	
WED	Shopping in Osaka
THU	Dinner at friend's house
FRI	
SAT	

位置
いち

Locations

つくえの上
うえ

つくえのそば

つくえの下
した

かばんの中
なか

左　右
ひだり　みぎ

←　→
よこはま　とうきょう

やまださんの
となり

やまださんの
後ろ
うし

やまださんと
さとうさんの間
あいだ

やまださん

さとうさん

やまださんの前
まえ

日・週・月・年
ひ・しゅう・つき

Days / Weeks / Months / Years

Days

日曜日 にちようび	月曜日 げつようび	火曜日 かようび	水曜日 すいようび	木曜日 もくようび	金曜日 きんようび	土曜日 どようび
1 ついたち	**2** ふつか	**3** みっか	**4** よっか	**5** いつか	**6** むいか	
7 なのか	**8** ようか	**9** ここのか	**10** とおか	**11** じゅういちにち	**12** じゅうににち	**13** じゅうさんにち
14 じゅうよっか	**15** じゅうごにち	**16** じゅうろくにち	**17** じゅうしちにち	**18** じゅうはちにち	**19** じゅうくにち	**20** はつか
21 にじゅういちにち	**22** にじゅうににち	**23** にじゅうさんにち	**24** にじゅうよっか	**25** にじゅうごにち	**26** にじゅうろくにち	**27** にじゅうしちにち
28 にじゅうはちにち	**29** にじゅうくにち	**30** さんじゅうにち	**31** さんじゅういちにち			

Months

いちがつ（一月）————————January

にがつ（二月）————————February

さんがつ（三月）————————March

しがつ（四月）————————April

ごがつ（五月）————————May

ろくがつ（六月）————————June

しちがつ（七月）————————July

はちがつ（八月）————————August

くがつ（九月）————————September

じゅうがつ（十月）————————October

じゅういちがつ（十一月）—November

じゅうにがつ（十二月）——December

Time Words

Day	Week	Month	Year
おととい the day before yesterday	せんせんしゅう （先々週） the week before last	にかげつまえ （二か月前） the month before last	おととし the year before last
きのう（昨日） yesterday	せんしゅう（先週） last week	せんげつ（先月） last month	きょねん（去年） last year
きょう（今日） today	こんしゅう（今週） this week	こんげつ（今月） this month	ことし（今年） this year
あした tomorrow	らいしゅう（来週） next week	らいげつ（来月） next month	らいねん（来年） next year
あさって the day after tomorrow	さらいしゅう （再来週） the week after next	さらいげつ （再来月） the month after next	さらいねん （再来年） the year after next

第5課 LESSON 5

沖縄旅行 A Trip to Okinawa
おき なわ りょ こう

会 話 Dialogue
かい わ

Ⓘ Robert and Ken are vacationing in Okinawa.

1 ロバート： いい天気ですね。
てん き

2 けん： そうですね。でも、ちょっと暑いですね。
あつ

3 ロバート： わあ、きれいな海！
うみ

4 けん： 泳ぎましょう。
およ

            *   *   *

5 けん： ロバートさんはどんなスポーツが好きですか。
す

6 ロバート： サーフィンが好きです。
す

7 あした一緒にやりましょうか。
いっしょ

8 けん： でも、難しくありませんか。
むずか

9 ロバート： 大丈夫ですよ。
だいじょう ぶ

Ⅱ At the post office.

1 ロバート： すみません。はがきは、イギリスまでいくらですか。

2 郵便局員： 七十円です。
ゆうびんきょくいん　　　なな じゅうえん

3 ロバート： じゃあ、七十円切手を二枚お願いします。それから、五十円切手を一枚
なな じゅうえんきって　　にまい　ねが　　　　　　　　　　　　　ご じゅうえんきって　　いちまい

4 ください。

Ⅲ On Monday at school.

1 たけし： 　　ロバートさん、はがき、ありがとう。旅行は楽しかったですか。

2 ロバート： 　　ええ。沖縄の海はとてもきれいでしたよ。

3 たけし： 　　よかったですね。ぼくも海が大好きです。飛行機の切符は高かったで

4 　　　　　　　すか。

5 ロバート： 　　いいえ、あまり高くありませんでした。たけしさんのデートはどうで

6 　　　　　　　したか。

7 たけし： 　　……

Ⅰ

Robert: Nice weather.

Ken: Yes. But it is a little hot.

Robert: Wow, beautiful sea!

Ken: Let's swim.

*　　　　　*　　　　　*

Ken: What kind of sports do you like, Robert?

Robert: I like surfing. Shall we do it together tomorrow?

Ken: But isn't it difficult?

Robert: No.

Ⅱ

Robert: Excuse me. How much is a postcard to Britain?

Person at the post office: 70 yen.

Robert: Then, two 70-yen stamps, please. And one 50-yen stamp, please.

Ⅲ

Takeshi: Robert, thank you for the postcard. Did you enjoy the trip?

Robert: Yes. The sea was very beautiful in Okinawa.

Takeshi: Good. I like the sea very much, too. Was the airline ticket expensive?

Robert: No, it wasn't so expensive. How was your date, Takeshi?

Takeshi: . . .

単語
Vocabulary

Nouns

* うみ	海	sea
* きって	切手	postal stamps
* きっぷ	切符	ticket
* サーフィン		surfing
しゅくだい	宿題	homework
たべもの	食べ物	food
たんじょうび	誕生日	birthday
テスト		test
* てんき	天気	weather
のみもの	飲み物	drink
* はがき	葉書	postcard
バス		bus
* ひこうき	飛行機	airplane
へや	部屋	room
* ぼく	僕	I (used by men)
やすみ	休み	holiday; day off; absence
* りょこう	旅行	travel

い-adjectives

あたらしい	新しい	new
* あつい	暑い	hot (weather)
あつい	熱い	hot (objects)
いそがしい	忙しい	busy (people/days)
おおきい	大きい	large
おもしろい	面白い	interesting
こわい	怖い	frightening
さむい	寒い	cold (weather—not used for objects)
* たのしい	楽しい	fun
ちいさい	小さい	small
つまらない		boring
ふるい	古い	old (thing—not used for people)
* むずかしい	難しい	difficult

* Words that appear in the dialogue

| やさしい | | easy (problem); kind (person) |
| やすい | 安い | inexpensive; cheap (thing) |

な-adjectives

きらい(な)	嫌い	disgusted with; to dislike (〜が)
* きれい(な)		beautiful; clean
げんき(な)	元気	healthy; energetic
しずか(な)	静か	quiet
* すき(な)	好き	fond of; to like (〜が)
だいきらい(な)	大嫌い	to hate
* だいすき(な)	大好き	very fond of; to love
にぎやか(な)		lively
ハンサム(な)		handsome
ひま(な)	暇	not busy; to have a lot of free time

U-verbs

* およぐ	泳ぐ	to swim
きく	聞く	to ask (person に)
のる	乗る	to ride; to board (〜に)
* やる		to do; to perform (〜を)

Ru-verb

| でかける | 出かける | to go out |

Adverbs and Other Expressions

* いっしょに	一緒に	together
* それから		and then
* だいじょうぶ	大丈夫	It's okay.; Not to worry.; Everything is under control.
とても		very
どんな		what kind of . . .
* 〜まい	〜枚	[counter for flat objects]
* 〜まで		to (a place); as far as (a place); till (a time)

文法 Grammar
ぶん ぽう

1 Adjectives

There are two types of adjectives in Japanese. One type is called "い-adjectives," and the other type "な-adjectives." い and な are their last syllables when they modify nouns.

い-adjectives:

おもしろい映画   *an interesting movie*
えいが

きのう、おもしろい映画を見ました。   *I saw an interesting movie yesterday.*
えいが み

こわい先生   *a scary teacher*
せんせい

山下先生はこわい先生です。   *Professor Yamashita is a scary teacher.*
やましたせんせい せんせい

な-adjectives:

きれいな写真   *a beautiful picture*
しゃしん

京都できれいな写真を撮りました。   *I took a beautiful picture in Kyoto.*
きょうと しゃしん と

元気な先生   *an energetic teacher*
げんき せんせい

山下先生は元気な先生です。   *Professor Yamashita is an energetic teacher.*
やましたせんせい げんき せんせい

Japanese adjectives conjugate for tense (present and past), polarity (affirmative and negative), and so forth, just as verbs do. The two types of adjectives follow different conjugation patterns.

い-adjectives い-adjectives change shape as follows. You will want to be very careful here, because the pattern is rather complicated.

おもしろい		affirmative	negative
	present	おもしろいです	おもしろくありません
		It is interesting.	*It is not interesting.*
	past	おもしろかったです	おもしろくありませんでした
		It was interesting.	*It was not interesting.*

It is interesting (and confusing) that the idea of past tense is encoded differently in the affirmative and the negative polarities: (おもしろ)かった です is "past+affirmative," while (おもしろ)くありません でした is "negative+past.[1]"

Unlike verbs, adjectives conjugate fairly regularly. The only irregularity worth noticing at this stage is the behavior of the adjective いい (good). The first syllable of いい is changed to よ in all forms except the dictionary form and the long present tense affirmative form.[2]

いい (irregular)		affirmative	negative
	present	いいです	よくありません
	past	よかったです	よくありませんでした

な-adjectives　The conjugation pattern of な-adjectives is much more straightforward. It actually is exactly the same as the conjugation table of です which follows a noun, as discussed in Lesson 4.[3]

元気(な)		affirmative	negative
	present	元気です *She is healthy.*	元気じゃありません *She is not healthy.*
	past	元気でした *She was healthy.*	元気じゃありませんでした *She was not healthy.*

The final syllable な is dropped in these long forms of な-adjectives.

---

[1]Some speakers follow a more regular conjugation, where です is inert in both polarities. For these speakers, the chart looks like the following:

	affimative	negative
present	〜いです	〜くないです
past	〜かったです	〜くなかったです

[2]There actually are alternate forms, よい and よいです, but they are much less frequently used than いい and いいです.

[3]As with い-adjectives, some speakers prefer an alternative paradigm, such as the following:

	affimative	negative
present	〜です	〜じゃないです
past	〜でした	〜じゃなかったです

2 好き(な)/きらい(な)

In this lesson, we learn two な-adjectives that are very important from the grammatical point of view. They are 好き(な) (to be fond of; to like), and きらい(な) (to be disgusted with; to dislike). The meaning of these adjectives is relational, and you need two terms: a person to like or dislike something on the one hand, and a person or a thing on the other hand that is liked or disliked. In sentences, these two terms usually appear with the particles は and が, respectively.[4]

$$
\boxed{\text{X は Y が } \left\{ \begin{array}{c} \text{好き} \\ \text{きらい} \end{array} \right\} \text{です。} \qquad X \left\{ \begin{array}{c} \textit{likes} \\ \textit{dislikes} \end{array} \right\} Y.}
$$

ロバートさんは日本語のクラスが好きです。   *Robert likes his Japanese classes.*

山下先生は魚がきらいです。   *Professor Yamashita dislikes fish.*

The item that is liked or disliked can also be a person. You may want to be cautious using these words in reference to your preference for a specific person, however, because 好きです is usually taken to be an admission of one's *romantic* interest.[5]

Let us note three more things about 好き(な) and きらい(な) before we go on. One, if you like or dislike something (or somebody) very much, you can use the intensified forms of 好きです and きらいです, namely, 大好きです and 大きらいです. These forms are more common than the combinations of 好き(な) and きらい(な) and the degree modifier とても, to which we will turn shortly.

Two, when Japanese people want to say that they neither like nor dislike something, they usually say:

好きでもきらいでもありません。   *I neither like nor dislike (it).*

Three, you can use 好きな and きらいな as modifiers of nouns. For example, you can say things like:

---

[4]In contexts where you are contrasting two or more items, the particle は is used instead of が. Thus,
私は野菜は好きですが、肉はきらいです。   *I like* vegetables, *but I don't like* meat.
[5]In the expression of romantic or familial affection, the complex particle のことが can replace が. Thus,
たけしさんはメアリーさんのことが好きです。   ＝メアリーさんが好きです。
Takeshi is in love with Mary.

これは私の好きなテレビです。　　　*This is <u>my favorite</u> TV program.*
わたし　す

3　Degree Expressions

If you want to say things like "very hot," and "a little hot," you can add "degree adverbs" like とても (very) and ちょっと (a little; slightly) before adjectives.

沖縄の海はとてもきれいでした。　　*The sea was very beautiful in Okinawa.*
おきなわ　うみ

この部屋はちょっと暑いです。　　　*This room is a little hot.*
へや　　　　　あつ

Instead of having とても added to them, 好き(な) and きらい(な) have their own intensified forms, 大好き(な) (like very much) and 大きらい(な) (hate).
だいす　　　　　　　　　　　　　　だい

たけしさんはコーヒーが大好きです。
だいす
Takeshi likes coffee a lot.

キムさんはなっとうが大きらいです。
だい
Ms. Kim hates natto (a Japanese fermented soybean delicacy).

4　〜ましょう/〜ましょうか

Take a long form of a verb and replace the ending with ましょう or ましょうか and you will get the Japanese expression for "let's . . . ," which you can use to suggest a plan of action.

一緒に図書館で勉強しましょう。
いっしょ　としょかん　べんきょう
Let's study in the library together.

喫茶店でコーヒーを飲みましょうか。
きっさてん　　　　　　の
Shall we drink coffee at a coffee shop?

5　Counting

There are two important things you should know about counting items in Japanese. One, we use different number words for different kinds of items; the words used for counting people are different from the words used for counting books, for example. Two, number words often come *after*, rather than *before*, the items counted in a sentence.

リーさんは　切手を　三枚　買いました。　　　*Lee bought three stamps.*
きって　さんまい　か
　　　　　　item　number

The number word, 三枚, is made up of the numeral 三 and the "counter" 枚. This counter is used for sheets of paper and other flat objects. There will be other counters in later lessons—for people, for books, for sticklike objects, and so forth.

表現ノート
ひょうげん

Expression Notes ⑥

忙しい/にぎやか(な) ▶忙しい is used when we describe people and is not used for places. When you want to say that Tokyo is busy, you should use にぎやか(な).

たけしさんは忙しいです。	*Takeshi is busy.*
東京はにぎやかです。	*Tokyo is busy/lively.*

Note that the sentence below is also acceptable, since the subject "I" is omitted in the sentence.

日曜日は忙しいです。　＝日曜日は(私は)忙しいです。
I am busy on Sunday.

練習 Practice
れん しゅう

① 高いです
たか

A. Change the following adjectives into the affirmatives. 〔🔊〕

Example: たかい　→　たかいです

　　　　　げんきな　→　げんきです

1. やすい　　　2. あつい　3. さむい　　4. おもしろい　5. つまらない

6. いそがしい　7. いい　　8. しずかな　9. にぎやかな　10. きれいな

11. ひまな

B. Change the following adjectives into the negatives. 〔🔊〕

Example: やすい　→　やすくありません

　　　　　ひまな　→　ひまじゃありません

1. さむい　　　2. ふるい　3. こわい　　4. あたらしい　5. むずかしい

6. ちいさい　7. いい　　8. げんきな　9. しずかな　　10. きれいな

11. ハンサムな

C. Look at the pictures below and make sentences.

Example: この時計は高いです。
　　　　　とけい　たか
　　　　　この時計は安くありません。
　　　　　とけい　やす

Ex.　　　　　　(1)　　　　　　(2)　　　　　　(3)

(4)　　　　　(5)　　　　　(6)　　　　　(7)

(8)　　　　　(9)　　　　　(10)　　　　(11)

(12)　　　　(13)

D. Answer the following questions.

Example:　Q：日本語のクラスは難しいですか。
　　　　　　A：ええ、難しいです。／いいえ、難しくありません。

1. 今日はひまですか。　　　　　2. 先生はやさしいですか。
3. 学校は大きいですか。　　　　4. 部屋はきれいですか。
5. 日本の食べ物はおいしいですか。　6. 日本の食べ物は安いですか。

E. Pair Work—Make affirmative and negative sentences with your partner.

Example:　きれいな

　　　　→　友達の部屋はきれいです。でも、私の部屋はきれいじゃあり
　　　　　　ません。

1. おもしろい　　2. いい　　　3. こわい　　　4. おいしい
5. 高い　　　　　6. ハンサムな　7. 元気な　　　8. ひまな

F. Pair Work—Make your own sentences on the topics below using adjectives, and tell your partner.

Example: テストは難しくありません。やさしいです。
むずか

1. 私は
わたし
2. 私の町は
わたし まち
3. 私のとなりの人は
わたし ひと
4. 私の部屋は
わたし へ や
5. 東京は
とうきょう
6. ハワイは

Ⅱ 高かったです
たか

A. Change the following adjectives into the past affirmatives. 🔊

Example: たかい → たかかったです
げんきな → げんきでした

1. やすい   2. あつい 3. さむい   4. おもしろい   5. つまらない
6. いそがしい 7. いい   8. しずかな 9. にぎやかな   10. きれいな
11. ひまな

B. Change the following adjectives into the past negatives. 🔊

Example: やすい → やすくありませんでした
げんきな → げんきじゃありませんでした

1. たかい 2. たのしい   3. やさしい   4. つまらない 5. おおきい
6. いい   7. いそがしい 8. にぎやかな 9. しずかな   10. きれいな
11. ひまな

C. This is what Robert wrote down about the trip to Okinawa. Look at the memo and make sentences. 🔊

Ex. Okinawa—hot
1. food—not expensive
2. food—delicious
3. hotel—not big
4. hotel—new
5. restaurant—not quiet
6. sea—beautiful
7. surfing—interesting

Example:
沖縄は暑かったです。
おきなわ あつ

D. Pair Work—Use the chart below and practice a dialogue with your partner, substituting the underlined parts. A and B are talking about A's vacation.

Example: A is Robert.

→　A：<u>休みに沖縄に行きました</u>。
　　　　　　やす　　おきなわ　　い
　　B：そうですか。どうでしたか。
　　A：<u>とても暑かったです</u>。
　　　　　　　あつ

Ex. Robert	went to Okinawa	very hot
(1) Mary	saw a movie	scary
(2) Takeshi	stayed home（うちにいる）	very boring
(3) Sue	went to a party	not fun
(4) Mr. Yamashita	went to flea market（フリーマーケット）	not cheap
(5) 私 わたし		

Ⅲ 高い時計ですね
　　　たか　とけい

A. Look at the pictures and make comments on them.

Example:　時計　→　高い時計ですね。
　　　　　　とけい　　　たか　とけい

Ex.

(1) ホテル

(2) テレビ

(3) 宿題
　　しゅくだい

(4) 人
　　ひと

(5) 人
　　ひと

(6) 町
　　まち

(7) 部屋
　　へや

B. Answer the questions using the given cues. 🔊

Example:　Q：メアリーさんはどんな人ですか。
　　　　　　A：メアリーさんはやさしい人です。

Ex.　メアリー　　　　(1) スー　　　　(2) ロバート　　　　(3) たけし

　　kind　　　　　beautiful　　　　interesting　　　　energetic

Ⅳ 魚が好きですか

A. Pair Work—Choose the items from the following categories and ask your partners whether they like them.

Example:　A：メアリーさんは肉が好きですか。
　　　　　　B：はい、好きです／大好きです。
　　　　　　　　いいえ、きらいです／大きらいです。

1. Foods: meat／なっとう (fermented beans)／ice cream（アイスクリーム）
2. Sports: aerobics（エアロビクス）／skiing（スキー）／skating（スケート）
3. Music: hard rock（ハードロック）／jazz（ジャズ）／classical music（クラシック）
4. School Work: test／Japanese class／homework
5. Drinks: sake／green tea／coffee

＊ If you neither like it nor dislike it, you can use 好きでもきらいでもありません。

B. Answer the following questions.

1. どんなスポーツが好きですか。
2. どんな食べ物が好きですか。
3. どんな飲み物が好きですか。
4. どんな映画が好きですか。
5. どんな音楽が好きですか。

Ⓥ 映画を見ましょう
えい が　み

A. Change the following into ましょう sentences. 🕪

Example: 日本語を話す → 日本語を話しましょう。
に ほん ご　はな 　　　　　に ほん ご　はな

1. うちに帰る
かえ
2. 先生に聞く
せんせい　き
3. 映画を見る
えい が　み

4. はがきを買う
か
5. 出かける
で
6. 待つ
ま

7. 泳ぐ
およ
8. 写真を撮る
しゃしん　と
9. バスに乗る
の

B. Pair Work—Make follow-up suggestions using ましょうか.

Example: 寒いですね。
さむ
→ A：寒いですね。お茶を飲みましょうか。
さむ 　　　　ちゃ　の
B：そうしましょう。

1. 暑いですね。
あつ
2. 十二時ですね。
じゅうに じ
3. この宿題は難しいですね。
しゅくだい　むずか
4. あしたは先生の誕生日ですよ。
せんせい　たんじょう び
5. あのレストランはおいしいですよ。
6. あしたはテストがありますね。

Ⓥ まとめの練習 (Review Exercises)
れんしゅう

A. Pair Work—Ask your partner the following questions.

1. Were you busy last week?

2. Were you fine last week?

3. Was your high school big/old?

4. Was your watch expensive?

5. Is your bag new?

6. Is your room small/clean?

7. Is your teacher kind?

B. Class Activity—Show and tell

Bring pictures you took on a trip. Explain to your class where you went, what you did, how it was, etc. And later, other students will ask in detail about the trip.

Example questions:

どこに行きましたか。

天気はどうでしたか。

だれと行きましたか。

飛行機の切符はいくらでしたか。

C. Role Play—Using Dialogue Ⅱ as a model, buy some stamps and postcards.

郵便局で
ゆうびんきょく

At the Post Office

Useful Expressions

これ、お願いします。——————— *Can you take care of this, please?*
　　　 ねが

五十円切手を三枚ください。——— *Give me three 50-yen stamps, please.*
ごじゅうえんきって　さんまい

（航空便）でお願いします。——— *Make this (an airmail), please.*
こうくうびん　　 ねが

何日ぐらいかかりますか。——————— *How many days will it take?*
なんにち

百五十円になります。——————— *It will be 150 yen.*
ひゃくごじゅうえん

あと百円です。——————————— *Another 100 yen, please.*
　　ひゃくえん

Useful Vocabulary

窓口 ——————— counter
まどぐち

はがき ——————— postcard

小包 ——————— parcel
こづつみ

航空便 ——————— airmail
こうくうびん

保険 ——————— insurance
ほけん

書留 ——————— registered mail
かきとめ

切手 ——————— stamp
きって

エアログラム — aerogramme

封書 ——————— letter
ふうしょ

船便 ——————— surface mail
ふなびん

速達 ——————— special delivery
そくたつ

Postcard

Stamps

写真屋で
しゃしんや

At a Photo Shop

Customer:	すみません。焼き増しお願いします。
	Excuse me. I'd like a reprint, please.
Shop clerk:	はい。光沢ありでよろしいですか。
	Certainly. Would the glossy finish be all right?
Customer:	はい。
	Yes.
Shop clerk:	ここに名前と電話番号をお願いします。
	Please fill in your name and telephone number here.
Customer:	いつできますか。
	When will it be ready?
Shop clerk:	仕上がりは十五日の三時です。
	It will be ready at three o'clock on the 15th.
	この引き換え券を持ってきてください。
	Please bring this receipt.
Customer:	わかりました。じゃ、お願いします。
	All right. Thank you.
Shop clerk:	ありがとうございました。
	Thank you very much.

Useful Vocabulary

焼き増し —————— reprint
やま

現像 —————— development
げんぞう

光沢あり —————— glossy finish
こうたく

光沢なし —————— mat finish
こうたく

パノラマ —————— panoramic

スライド —————— slide

プリント —————— print

仕上がり —————— date/time something is ready
しあ

24枚撮り —————— 24-print roll
まいど

使い捨てカメラ —— disposable camera
つか　す

ネガ —————— negative

フィルム —————— film

電池 —————— battery
でんち

引き換え券 —————— receipt
ひ　か　けん

第6課 L E S S O N 6
ロバートさんの一日 A Day in Robert's Life
いち にち

会話 D i a l o g u e 🔊
かい わ

Ⓘ In the class.

1 山下先生： ロバートさん、次のページを読んでください。
やましたせんせい つぎ よ

2 ロバート： ……

3 山下先生： ロバートさん、起きてください。クラスで寝てはいけませんよ。
やましたせんせい お ね

4 ロバート： 先生、教科書を忘れました。
せんせい きょうかしょ わす

5 山下先生： 教科書を持ってきてくださいね。毎日使いますから。
やましたせんせい きょうかしょ も まいにちつか

6 ロバート： はい、すみません。

Ⅱ After class.

1 ス ー： ロバートさん、今日は大変でしたね。
きょう たいへん

2 ロバート： ええ。後でスーさんのノートを借りてもいいですか。
あと か

3 ス ー： ええ、いいですよ。

4 ロバート： ありがとう。すぐ返します。
かえ

5 ス ー： ロバートさん、あしたテストがありますよ。

6 ロバート： えっ。本当ですか。
ほんとう

7 ス ー： ええ。ロバートさん、金曜日に休みましたからね。
きんようび やす

8 ロバート： じゃあ、今日は家に帰って、勉強します。
きょう いえ かえ べんきょう

Ⅲ On the bus.

1 おばあさん： あの、すみません。このバスは市民病院へ行きますか。
しみんびょういん い

2 ロバート： ええ、行きますよ……あの、おばあさん、どうぞ座ってください。
い すわ

3 おばあさん： いいえ、けっこうです。すぐ降りますから。
お

4 ロバート： 　　そうですか。じゃあ、荷物を持ちましょうか。
5 おばあさん： 　　あ、どうもすみません。

Ⅰ

Prof. Yamashita: Robert, please read the next page.

Robert: . . .

Prof. Yamashita: Robert, please wake up. You cannot sleep in the class.

Robert: Mr. Yamashita, I forgot to bring the textbook.

Prof. Yamashita: Please bring your textbook with you. We use it everyday.

Robert: I understand. I'm sorry.

Ⅱ

Sue: Robert, you had a hard time today.

Robert: Yes. May I borrow your notebook later, Sue?

Sue: Yes.

Robert: Thank you. I'll return it soon.

Sue: Robert, we will have a test tomorrow.

Robert: Really?

Sue: Yes. You were absent from the class last Friday. (That's why you didn't know about it.)

Robert: Well then, I'll go home and study today.

Ⅲ

Old woman: Excuse me. Does this bus go to the city hospital?

Robert: Yes, it does. Take this seat, ma'am.

Old woman: No, thank you. I'll get off soon.

Robert: Is that so? Then, shall I carry your bag?

Old woman: Thank you.

単語
たんご

Vocabulary

Nouns

おかね	お金	money
* おばあさん		grandmother; old woman
おふろ	お風呂	bath
かんじ	漢字	kanji; Chinese character
* きょうかしょ	教科書	textbook
こんしゅう	今週	this week
* しみんびょういん	市民病院	Municipal Hospital
* つぎ	次	next
テレビゲーム		video game
でんき	電気	electricity
でんしゃ	電車	train
* にもつ	荷物	baggage
* ページ		page
まど	窓	window
よる	夜	night
らいしゅう	来週	next week
らいねん	来年	next year

な-adjective

* たいへん（な）	大変	tough (situation)

U-verbs

あそぶ	遊ぶ	to play; to spend time pleasantly
いそぐ	急ぐ	to hurry
おふろにはいる	お風呂に入る	to take a bath
* かえす	返す	to return (things) (*person* に *thing* を)
けす	消す	to turn off; to erase （〜を）
しぬ	死ぬ	to die
* すわる	座る	to sit down (*seat* に)
たつ	立つ	to stand up
たばこをすう	たばこを吸う	to smoke
* つかう	使う	to use （〜を）
てつだう	手伝う	to help (*person/task* を)

* Words that appear in the dialogue

はいる	入る	to enter　（〜に）
* もつ	持つ	to carry; to hold　（〜を）
* やすむ	休む	(1) to be absent (from . . .)　（〜を）
		(2) to rest

Ru-verbs

あける	開ける	to open (something)　（〜を）
おしえる	教える	to teach; to instruct　（*person* に *thing* を）
* おりる	降りる	to get off　（〜を）
* かりる	借りる	to borrow　（*person* に *thing* を）
しめる	閉める	to close (something)　（〜を）
つける		to turn on　（〜を）
でんわをかける	電話をかける	to make a phone call　（*person* に）
* わすれる	忘れる	to forget; to leave behind　（〜を）

Irregular Verbs

つれてくる	連れてくる	to bring (a person)　（〜を）
* もってくる	持ってくる	to bring (a thing)　（〜を）

Adverbs and Other Expressions

* あとで	後で	later on
おそく	遅く	(do something) late
* 〜から		because . . .
* けっこうです	結構です	That would be fine.; That wouldn't be necessary.
* すぐ		right away
* ほんとうですか	本当ですか	Really?
ゆっくり		slowly; leisurely; unhurriedly

文法 G r a m m a r
ぶん ぼう

1   *Te*-form

The main topic of this lesson is a new conjugation of verbs called the "*te*-form." *Te*-forms are a *very* important part of Japanese grammar. In this lesson, we will learn, among their various uses, to use them in:

- making requests (". . . , please.")
- giving and asking for permission ("You may . . ./May I . . .")
- stating that something is forbidden ("You must not . . .")
- forming a sentence that describes two events or activities. ("I did this and did that.")

The conjugation paradigm of *te*-forms is fairly complex, as we need to learn separate rules for *ru*-, *u*-, and irregular verbs. Furthermore, the rule for *u*-verbs is divided into five subrules.

First, with *ru*-verbs, the rule is very simple: Take る off and add て.

ru-verbs
食べる   →   食べて

U-verbs come in several groups, based on the final syllable of their dictionary forms.

u-verbs with final う, つ, and る[1]
会う   →   会って
待つ   →   待って

---

[1] As we discussed in Lesson 3, some verbs that end with the *hiragana* る are *ru*-verbs and some others are *u*-verbs. The rule of thumb for determining which verb is which is to examine the vowel before the final る syllable. If the vowel is *a*, *o*, or *u*, the verb, without any exceptions, is an *u*-verb. If the vowel is either *i* or *e*, the verb can be either an *u*-verb or a *ru*-verb. Statistically speaking, there are many more *ru*-verbs, than *u*-verbs in the *iru* and *eru* camp, but there are many important verbs in the minority, such as 入る (to enter), and 帰る (to return).

$$\left. \begin{array}{l} \textit{. . . aru} \\ \textit{. . . oru} \\ \textit{. . . uru} \end{array} \right\} = \text{always } \textit{u}\text{-verbs} \qquad \left. \begin{array}{l} \textit{. . . iru} \\ \textit{. . . eru} \end{array} \right\} = \text{often, but not always, } \textit{ru}\text{-verbs}$$

As far as *te*-forms are concerned, we observe that *u*-verbs that end with る will have a small つ, *ru*-verbs that end with る do not.

と<u>る</u>	➔	と<u>って</u>

u-verbs with final む, ぶ, and ぬ

読<u>む</u>	➔	読<u>んで</u>
遊<u>ぶ</u>	➔	遊<u>んで</u>
死<u>ぬ</u>	➔	死<u>んで</u>

u-verbs with final く

書<u>く</u>	➔	書<u>いて</u>

There is an important exception in this class:

行<u>く</u>	➔	行<u>って</u>

u-verbs with final ぐ

泳<u>ぐ</u>	➔	泳<u>いで</u>

u-verbs with final す

話<u>す</u>	➔	話<u>して</u>

The irregular verbs する and くる, and compound verbs built with them, conjugate as follows.

irregular verbs

する	➔	して
くる	➔	きて

Note that *te*-forms and stems (the forms you find before ます) are totally different constructs in the *u*-verb camp. A common mistake is to assume that the simple paradigm provided by the *ru*-verbs (食べて and 食べます) covers the *u*-verbs also, thus coming up with unwarranted forms such as ×会いて (see 会います) and ×読みて (see 読みます). It is probably easier, at this stage of learning, to memorize each verb as a set, as in 書く—書きます—書いて, than to apply the conjugation rules on the spot. Refer to the verb conjugation table at the end of this volume.

2 ～てください

Use a verbal *te*-form together with ください to make a polite request to another person "please do . . . for me.[2]"

教科書のテープを聞いてください。
Please listen to the tape that goes with the textbook.

すみません。ちょっと教えてください。
Excuse me. Please teach me a little. (= Tell me, I need your advice.)

3 ～てもいいです／～てはいけません

A verbal *te*-form plus もいいです means "you may do . . . ," which describes an activity that is permitted. To ask for permission, you can turn it into a question sentence, ～てもいいですか.

教科書を見てもいいですか。　　　　　*May I see the textbook?*

はい、見てもいいですよ。　　　　　　*Yes, you may.*

To deny somebody permission to do something, you can use the *te*-form plus はいけません.

いいえ、教科書を見てはいけません。　*No, you may not see the textbook.*

4 Describing Two Activities

You can use a *te*-form if you want to combine two or more verbs, as in describing a sequence of events or actions ("I did this and then I did that"). In other words, the *te*-form does the work of "and" with verbs. (Note that two verbs cannot be joined by と, which only connects nouns.)

ノートを借りて、コピーします。
I will borrow her notebook and xerox it.

---

[2] If you are talking to a very close friend or a member of your family, a *te*-form, by itself, can be used as a request.

　　　窓を開けて。　　　　*Open the window, will you?*

今日は、六時に起きて、勉強しました。
Today I got up at six and studied.

食堂に行って、昼ごはんを食べましょう。
Let's go to the cafeteria and have lunch.

The *te*-form of a verb can also be used to connect a verb more "loosely" with the rest of a sentence. In the first example below, the verb in the *te*-form describes the manner in which the action described by the second verb is performed. In the second example, the *te*-form describes the situation for which the apology is made.

バスに乗って、会社に行きます。
I go to work by bus. (I take a bus to work.)

教科書を忘れて、すみません。
I am sorry for not bringing in the textbook. (I left the book at home, and I am sorry.)

5 〜から

A sentence that ends with から (because) explains the reason or the cause of a situation, a proposal, and so forth.

(situation)。(explanation) **から**。[3]

私は今晩勉強します。あしたテストがありますから。
I will study this evening. (Because) we will have an exam tomorrow.

バスに乗りましょう。タクシーは高いですから。
Let's go by bus. (Because) taxis are expensive.

6 〜ましょうか

In Lesson 5 we learned ましょうか meaning "let's . . . ." ましょうか is also used in the sense of "let me do . . . ," in offering assistance. If you see somebody having a hard time opening the lid of a bottle, for example, you can offer help by saying:

（私が）やりましょうか。　　　　*I'll do it.*

---

[3]The explanation clause may also precede the situation clause. Thus the first example above can also be paraphrased as:

　あしたテストがありますから、私は今晩勉強します。

We will discuss this further in Lesson 9.

Or to a person who is carrying a heavy bag:

荷物を持ちましょうか。 *Shall I carry your bag?*

表現ノート
ひょうげん

遅く/遅い▶ Although both 遅い and 遅く mean "late," they have different usages, since 遅い is an adjective and 遅く is an adverb. 遅い modifies nouns or works as a predicate, and 遅く modifies verbs.

A：きのう一時に寝ました。 *I went to bed at one o'clock yesterday.*
B：遅いですね。 *It's late.*

週末には、十時ごろ起きて、遅い朝ごはんを食べます。
On weekends, I get up around 10:00 and eat late breakfast.

きのう、遅く寝ました。 *I went to bed late yesterday.*

You can also apply this rule to 早く／早い.

どうも▶ どうも is normally used with ありがとう, as in どうもありがとう (Thank you very much), or with すみません, as in どうもすみません (I am very sorry/Thank you very much). When used alone, it is an abbreviation of どうもありがとう or どうもすみません. Therefore, when you want to show your gratitude or regret, you can just say どうも instead of saying a long sentence. どうも functions in many ways, depending on the situation. Some people use どうも as "hello" or "good-bye."

お▶ Many words that begins with お can also be used without it. お in such words simply adds smoothness and nuance of social refinement, without changing the meaning of the words.

Example： お酒　お金　お風呂

練習 Practice
れん しゅう

① 窓を開けてください
まど あ

A. Change the following verbs into *te*-forms. 🔊

Example: おきる → おきて

1. たべる　2. かう　　3. よむ　　4. かく　　5. くる　　6. まつ

7. あそぶ　8. とる　　9. する　　10. いそぐ　11. いく　　12. ねる

13. しぬ　　14. はなす　15. かえる

B. Let's sing a *te*-form song!　(Battle Hymn of the Republic) 🔊

♪1.　あう　あって　まつ　まって　とる　とって
　　　よむ　よんで　あそぶ　あそんで　しぬ　しんで
　　　かく　かいて　けす　けして　いそぐ　いそいで
　　　みんな　*u*-verb　*te*-form
♪2.　うつる　って　むぶぬ　んで　く　いて　ぐ　いで
　　　(repeat twice)
　　　す　して　*u*-verb　*te*-form

C. What will you say when you want someone to do the following things? 🔊

Example:　to speak slowly　→　ゆっくり話してください。
　　　　　　　　　　　　　　　　　　はな

1. to call you tomorrow
2. to write a letter
3. to open the window
4. to drink tea
5. to teach you kanji
6. to bring a drink
7. to wait for you
8. to come with you
9. to go to a hospital
10. to return your book
11. to bring a friend
12. to stand up

D. What would you say in the following situations?

Example: 窓を開けてください。
まど あ

Ex.　　　　　　　　　　(1)　　　　　　　　　　(2)

(3)　　　　　　　　　　(4)　　　　　　　　　　(5)

E. Pair Work—Make your own request, such as "Please stand up" and "Please take a picture," and ask your partner to act it out.

Example:　A：コーヒーを飲んでください。　→　B pretends to drink coffee.
の

Ⅱ テレビを見てもいいですか/テレビを見てはいけません
　　　み　　　　　　　　　　　　　　　　　　み

A. You are staying with a host family. Ask your host family for permission to do the following things.

Example: テレビを見る　→　テレビを見てもいいですか。
み　　　　　　　　み

1. たばこを吸う　　　2. 電話をかける　　　3. 朝、お風呂に入る
す　　　　　　　　　でんわ　　　　　　　　　あさ　ふろ　はい

4. 遅く帰る　　　　　5. 友だちを連れてくる　6. 音楽を聞く
おそ かえ　　　　　とも　　つ　　　　　　おんがく き

7. 夜、出かける　　　8. テレビゲームをする
よる で

B. What would you say in the following situations? Make sentences with 〜てもいいですか.

1. You are in class. You realize you need to go to the bathroom as soon as possible.
2. You are in class. You feel sick and want to return home.
3. You have forgotten to do the homework. You are sure you can bring it in tomorrow.
4. You want to ask your teacher something, but you cannot phrase it in Japanese.
5. You want to smoke in a coffee shop, and there is someone sitting nearby.
6. You are at a friend's house，and suddenly remember that you need to make a phone call.
7. You have run into a celebrity. Conveniently, you have a camera with you.
8. You have arrived at a classroom. The air is stuffy.
9. You and your friend are in a dark room, and you feel somewhat uncomfortable.

C. You are a strict parent. Tell your child not to do the following things using the cues in A. 〔◦)〕

Example: テレビを見る　→　テレビを見てはいけません。

D. Tell the class what we can and can't do at school and at a host family's house.

Example: 学校でたばこを吸ってはいけません。
ホストファミリー (host family) のうちで朝お風呂に入ってもいいです。

Ⅲ 朝起きて、コーヒーを飲みます

A. Look at the pictures below and combine the pictures using *te*-forms. 〔◦)〕

Example: 朝起きて、コーヒーを飲みます。

(2)   (3)

(4)   (5)

B. Change the following into *te*-forms and make the rest of the sentences.

Example: 朝起きる   →   朝起きて、新聞を読みます。
　　　　　　あさお　　　　　　　あさお　　　しんぶん　よ

1. 友だちのうちに行く   2. うちに帰る   3. 電車を降りる
　とも　　　　　い　　　　　　　　かえ　　　　　　　てんしゃ　お
4. 友だちに会う   5. お風呂に入る   6. 大学に行く
　とも　　　あ　　　　　　　　　ふ　ろ　はい　　　　だいがく　い

Ⅳ バスに乗ります。時間がありませんから。
　　　　　　　の　　　　　じ かん

A. Add reasons to the following sentences.

Example: バスに乗ります。   →   バスに乗ります。時間がありませんから。
　　　　　　　　の　　　　　　　　　　　　の　　　　　じ かん

1. 先週は大変でした。   2. あの映画を見ません。
　せんしゅう　たいへん　　　　　　　　　えい が　み
3. あのレストランに行きました。   4. きのうクラスを休みました。
　　　　　　　　　　い　　　　　　　　　　　　　　　　やす
5. (name of a friend) が大好きです。
　　　　　　　　　　　だい す

B. Pair Work—Ask each other why you think the following.

Example: 朝ごはんを食べません。

→ Ａ：私は朝ごはんを食べません。

Ｂ：どうしてですか。

Ａ：あまりお金がありませんから。Ｂさんは？

Ｂ：私も朝ごはんを食べません。朝、忙しいですから。

1. 今週は大変です。
2. あしたはひまです。
3. 週末、(name of a movie) を見ます。
4. きのう、(name of a restaurant) に行きました。
5. お金がぜんぜんありません。
6. 来年は日本語を勉強しません。
7. 来週、(name of a place) に行きます。
8. 自転車を買います。

Ⓥ テレビを消しましょうか

Pair Work—Propose to do the following things, using ましょうか.

Example: テレビを消す

→ Ａ：テレビを消しましょうか。

Ｂ：すみません。お願いします。／いいえ、けっこうです。

1. 窓を開ける
2. テレビをつける
3. 手伝う
4. 先生に聞く
5. 電話をかける
6. 荷物を持つ
7. 飲み物を持ってくる
8. 電気を消す
9. 写真を撮る
10. 窓を閉める

Ⅵ まとめの練習 (Review Exercises)

A. Role Play—Play the roles of A and B with your partner.

Example:

<table>
<tr><td>

Example-A

You are short of money and want to borrow some money from your friend.

</td><td>

Example-B

You are going on a trip tomorrow. You don't have money to lend to your friend.

</td></tr>
</table>

A：すみませんが、お金を借りてもいいですか。

B：お金ですか。どうして。

A：あしたは友だちの誕生日ですから。

B：でも、私もお金がありません。あした、旅行に行きますから。

(1)

<table>
<tr><td>

1-A

You have a date tomorrow and want to borrow a car from your friend.

</td><td>

1-B

You just bought a brand-new car and don't want anyone to use it.

</td></tr>
</table>

(2)

<table>
<tr><td>

2-A

You lost your Japanese textbook, but you need to study for a test tomorrow.

</td><td>

2-B

You have a big test in Japanese and need your textbook to prepare for the test.

</td></tr>
</table>

(3)

<table>
<tr><td>

3-A

You are asked to return your friend's video today, but you forgot to bring it. You want to return it tomorrow.

</td><td>

3-B

You asked your friend to return your video today. You need it today because you want to watch it together with another friend.

</td></tr>
</table>

(4)

4-A	4-B
You are now in your friend's house. You see a cake that looks very delicious. You love cakes.	You just baked a cake for your mother's birthday. Your friend is in your house now.

B. Answer the following questions.

1. 今週の週末、何をしますか。　（Answer with "〜て、〜。"）
   こんしゅう　しゅうまつ　なに
2. 子供の時、よく何をしましたか。　（Answer with "〜て、〜。"）
   こども　とき　　　なに
3. 図書館で何をしてはいけませんか。
   としょかん　なに
4. 電車の中でたばこを吸ってもいいですか。
   でんしゃ　なか　　　　す
5. 大学に何を持ってきますか。
   だいがく　なに　も
6. よく電車に乗りますか。
   　　でんしゃ　の
7. 先週、宿題を忘れましたか。
   せんしゅう　しゅくだい　わす
8. 子供の時、どこで遊びましたか。
   こども　とき　　　　あそ
9. 子供の時、よくお母さんを手伝いましたか。
   こども　とき　　　かあ　　　てつだ
10. 図書館でよく本を借りますか。
    としょかん　　　ほん　か
11. よくクラスを休みますか。
    　　　　　やす

道を聞く／教える
みち　き　　　おし

Directions

Useful Expressions

まっすぐ行く
い

(go straight)

右に曲がる
みぎ　ま

(turn right)

左に曲がる
ひだり　ま

(turn left)

一つ目の信号を右に曲がる
ひと　め　しんごう　みぎ　ま

(turn right at the first signal)

二つ目の角を左に曲がる
ふた　め　かど　ひだり　ま

(turn left at the second corner)

道を渡る
みち　わた

(cross the street)

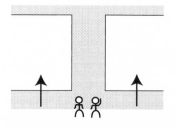

道の左側　　　　　道の右側
みち　ひだりがわ　　　　みち　みぎがわ

(left side of the street)　　(right side of the street)

Directions

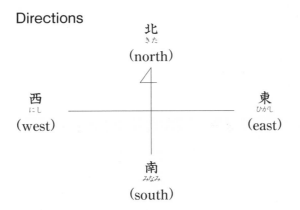

北
きた
(north)

西
にし
(west)

東
ひがし
(east)

南
みなみ
(south)

*　　　　　*　　　　　*

A：すみません。郵便局はどこですか。
ゆうびんきょく
Excuse me, where is a post office?

B：まっすぐ行って、三つ目の角を右に曲がって
い　　　みっ　め　かど　みぎ　ま
ください。郵便局は道の右側にありますよ。
ゆうびんきょく　みち　みぎがわ
*Go straight and turn right at the third
corner. The post office is on the right
side of the street.*

A：どうもありがとうございます。
Thank you very much.

第7課 | L E S S O N ·······················7

家族の写真 Family Picture
かぞく　しゃしん

会話 D i a l o g u e
かいわ

📶

Ⅰ Sue is showing a picture of her family to her roommate, Michiko.

1　みちこ：　これはスーさんの家族の写真ですか。
かぞく　しゃしん

2　スー：　ええ。

3　みちこ：　スーさんはどれですか。

4　スー：　これです。高校の時はめがねをかけていました。
こうこう　とき

5　みちこ：　かわいいですね。

6　スー：　これは父です。
ちち

7　　アメリカの会社に勤めています。
かいしゃ　つと

8　みちこ：　背が高くて、ハンサムですね。
せ　たか

9　　これはお姉さんですか。
ねえ

10　スー：　ええ。姉は結婚しています。
あね　けっこん

11　　今ソウルに住んでいます。
いま　す

12　　子供が一人います。三歳です。
こども　ひとり　さんさい

13　みちこ：　そうですか。あっ、猫がいますね。
ねこ

14　　でも、ちょっと太っていますね。
ふと

15　スー：　ええ、よく食べますから。
た

Ⅱ A phone rings in Sue and Michiko's room.

1　ロバート：　みちこさん、今何をしていますか。
いまなに

2　みちこ：　別に何もしていません。今、スーさんの写真を見ています。
べつ　なに　いま　しゃしん　み

3　ロバート：　そうですか。おもしろいビデオがありますから、よかったら見に来ま
み　き

4　　せんか。

5　みちこ：　いいですね。スーさんも一緒に行ってもいいですか。
いっしょ　い

₆ ロバート：　もちろん。

₇ みちこ：　　じゃあ、すぐ行きます。

Ⅰ

Michiko: Is this your family picture, Sue?

Sue: Yes.

Michiko: Which is you?

Sue: This. I was wearing glassses when I was in high school.

Michiko: You are cute.

Sue: This is my father. He works for an American company.

Michiko: He is tall and handsome. Is this your elder sister?

Sue: Yes. My sister is married. She lives in Seoul now. She has one child. He is three years old.

Michiko: I see. Oh, there is a cat. But he is a little fat.

Sue: Yes, because he eats a lot.

Ⅱ

Robert: Michiko, what are you doing now?

Michiko: I'm not doing anything especially. I am looking at Sue's pictures.

Robert: I see. I have an interesting video, so if you like, would you like to come to see it?

Michiko: That sounds good. Is it all right if Sue comes with me?

Robert: Of course.

Michiko: We'll come right now.

単語
たんご

▌ V o c a b u l a r y ▐ 🔊

N o u n s

* あね	姉	(my) older sister
アパート		apartment
いもうと	妹	younger sister
うた	歌	song
おとうと	弟	younger brother
おとこのひと	男の人	man
おにいさん	お兄さん	older brother
* おねえさん	お姉さん	older sister
おんなのひと	女の人	woman
* かいしゃ	会社	company
* かぞく	家族	family
かみ	髪	hair
きょうだい	兄弟	brothers and sisters
くに	国	country; place of origin
くるま	車	car
コンビニ		convenience store
しょくどう	食堂	cafeteria; dining commons
* ちち	父	(my) father
Tシャツ ティー		T-shirt
め	目	eye
* めがね	眼鏡	glasses

い - a d j e c t i v e s

あたまがいい	頭がいい	bright; smart; clever (conjugates like いい)
かっこいい		great-looking (conjugates like いい)
* かわいい		cute
* せがたかい	背が高い	tall
せがひくい	背が低い	short (stature)
ながい	長い	long
はやい	速い	fast
みじかい	短い	short (length)

* Words that appear in the dialogue

な-adjectives

| しんせつ（な） | 親切 | kind |
| べんり（な） | 便利 | convenient |

U-verbs

うたう	歌う	to sing
かぶる		to put on (a hat)
しる	知る	to get to know
しっています	知っています	I know
しりません	知りません	I do not know
* すむ	住む	to live （〜にすんでいます）
はく		to put on (items below your waist)
* ふとる	太る	to gain weight
ふとっています	太っています	to be on the heavy side

Ru-verbs

* （めがねを）かける		to put on (glasses)
きる	着る	to put on (clothes above your waist)
* つとめる	勤める	to work for （〜につとめています）
やせる		to lose weight
やせています		to be thin

Irregular Verb

| * けっこんする | 結婚する | to get married （〜と） |

Adverbs and Other Expressions

が		but
* なにも ＋ negative	何も	not . . . anything
〜にん	〜人	[counter for people]
* ひとり	一人	one person
ふたり	二人	two people
* べつに ＋ negative	別に	not . . . in particular
* もちろん		of course
* よかったら		if you like

文法 G r a m m a r
ぶん ぽう

1 ～ている

A verbal "*te*-form," when followed by the helping verb いる, means either of the following:[1]

   (a) *an action in progress,* or
   (b) *a past event that is connected with the present.*

Which of these two senses a given verb is used in is to a large extent determined by the semantic characteristics of the verb. The verbs we have learned so far can be roughly divided into three groups based on their semantics.

   (1) verbs that describe continuous *states*
   (2) verbs that describe *activities* that last for some time
   (3) verbs that describe *changes* that are more or less instantaneous

We have not seen many Group 1 verbs. So far we only have ある and いる. The *te*-forms of these verbs are never used together with the helping verb いる, so we will have nothing to say about them in this section.

Many verbs belong to Group 2. They include verbs such as 食べる, 読む, and 待つ. When the *te*-form of a verb in this group is followed by the helping verb いる, we have a sentence describing *an action in progress*.

スーさんは今勉強しています。 いまべんきょう	*Sue is studying right now.*
たけしさんは英語の本を読んでいます。 えいご ほん よ	*Takeshi is reading a book in English.*

You can also use a ～ています sentence to describe what a person does by occupation. The first example below therefore has two interpretations: one, you are teaching English right at this moment; and two, you are an English language teacher (but are not necessarily in class right now).

---

[1] The distinction between いる and ある that we learned in Lesson 4 does not apply to this helping verb ～ている: you can use ～ている both for living things and for inanimate objects.

私は英語を教えています。
I teach English. /I am teaching English (right now).

メアリーさんは日本語を勉強しています。
Mary studies Japanese. /Mary is studying Japanese (right now).

Verbs in Group 3 describe changes from one state to another. If you get married, or 結婚する, for example, your status changes from being single to being married. With these verbs,[2] ている indicates a past occurrence of a change which has retained its significance until the present moment. In other words, ている describes *the result of a change*.[3]

山下先生は結婚しています。   *Professor Yamashita is married.*[4]

みちこさんは窓のそばに座っています。   *Michiko is seated near the window.*

Here are some more examples of verbs that are commonly used in the ～ている framework.

持つ	→	持っている (has)	スーさんはお金をたくさん持っています。 *Sue has a lot of money.*
知る	→	知っている (knows)	山下先生は英語を知っています。 *Professor Yamashita knows English.*
太る	→	太っている (is overweight)	トムさんはちょっと太っています。 *Tom is a little overweight.*
やせる	→	やせている (is thin)	私の弟はとてもやせています。 *My younger brother is very thin.*

---

[2]Among the verbs we have learned so far, verbs such as 起きる, 行く, 帰る, 来る, わかる, 出かける, 乗る, 座る, 死ぬ, 消す, 忘れる, 借りる, 降りる, 持ってくる, 連れてくる, 結婚する, 太る, やせる, 着る belong to Group 3. In most cases you can determine whether a verb belongs to Group 2 or 3 by checking if the verb allows for a phrase describing duration, such as 一時間. Compare, for example,

   ◯ 私はきのう一時間本を読みました。   *I read a book for an hour yesterday.*
   ✕ 私は一時間死にました。(Ungrammatical, much as the English translation "I died for an hour" which
                is also odd.)

読む thus belongs to Group 2, and 死ぬ to Group 3.

[3]In Lesson 9, we will observe that this *result of a change* reading is actually not restricted to verbs in Group 3, but can be associated with those in Group 2 in certain contexts.

[4]Note that the sentence does *not* mean Professor Yamashita *is getting married*.

| 着る
_き | → | 着ている
_き
(wears) | メアリーさんはＴシャツを着ています。
Mary is wearing/wears a T-shirt. |

| 起きる
_お | → | 起きている
_お
(is awake) | お父さんは起きています。
Dad is up and awake. |

| 住む
_す | → | 住んでいる
_す
(lives in) | 父と母は東京に住んでいます。
My father and mother live in Tokyo. |

| 勤める
_{つと} | → | 勤めている
_{つと}
(works for) | 私の姉は日本の会社に勤めています。
My older sister works for a Japanese company. |

着る → 着ている (wears) メアリーさんはＴシャツを着ています。 *Mary is wearing/wears a T-shirt.*

起きる → 起きている (is awake) お父さんは起きています。 *Dad is up and awake.*

住む → 住んでいる (lives in) 父と母は東京に住んでいます。 *My father and mother live in Tokyo.*

勤める → 勤めている (works for) 私の姉は日本の会社に勤めています。 *My older sister works for a Japanese company.*

Note that verbs like 行く and 来る belong to this group. Thus 行っている and 来ている indicate the current states that result from prior movements, *not* movements that are currently in progress. You may want to be careful with what the following sentences mean.

中国に行っています。 　*Somebody has gone to/is in China.*
　　　　　　　　　　　 Not: *She is going to China.*

うちに来ています。 　*Somebody has come over to visit.*
　　　　　　　　　 Not: *Somebody is coming over.*

Finally, a note on conjugation. The helping verb いる conjugates as a *ru*-verb. Thus we have long forms as in the following example.

食べている _た		affirmative	negative
	present	食べています _た *He is eating.*	食べていません _た *He is not eating.*
	past	食べていました _た *He was eating.*	食べていませんでした _た *He was not eating.*

2　髪が長いです
　　_{かみ}　_{なが}

To describe somebody who has long hair, one could say:

トムさんの髪は長いです。　　*Tom's hair is long.*
　　　　_{かみ}　_{なが}

But in fact it would be far more natural in Japanese to say:

トムさんは髪が長いです。　　　*Tom has long hair.*
　　　　　　かみ　なが　　　　　　*(=As for Tom, he has long hair.)*

This applies not only to discussions of the length of one's hair, but to descriptions of a person's physical attributes in general.

$$
A さんは
\left\{
\begin{array}{c}
目_{め} \\
耳_{みみ} \\
手_{て} \\
足_{あし} \\
\vdots
\end{array}
\right\}
が
\left\{
\begin{array}{c}
大きい_{おお} \\
小さい_{ちい} \\
かわいい \\
\vdots
\end{array}
\right\}
\qquad
$$

Person A has a body part which is . . .

In idiomatic collocations, we also have:

背が高い　　　*is tall*
せ　たか

背が低い　　　*is short*
せ　ひく

頭がいい　　　*is bright/smart*
あたま

3　*Te*-forms for Joining Sentences

In the last lesson, we discussed the use of verbal *te*-forms to join sentences. い- and な-adjectives and です after nouns also have *te*-forms, which can be used to combine two elements to form longer sentences.

The *te*-form of an い-adjective is formed by substituting くて for the final い. The *te*-form of a な-adjective and a noun＋です sequence is formed by adding で to the base or the noun.

い-adjectives:	安い やす	→	安くて やす
irregular :	いい	→	よくて
な-adjectives:	元気(な) げんき	→	元気で げんき
noun ＋ です:	日本人です にほんじん	→	日本人で にほんじん

あの店の食べ物は安くて、おいしいです。
The food at that restaurant is <u>inexpensive</u> <u>and</u> delicious.

あの人はいつも元気で、おもしろいです。
That person is always <u>energetic</u> <u>and</u> fun to be with.

山下先生は日本人で、四十歳ぐらいです。
Professor Yamashita is <u>a Japanese</u> <u>and</u> he is about forty years old.

4 verb stem ＋ に行く

If a person moves to another place in order to do something, we can describe their movement and its purpose this way:

The purpose of movement can either be a noun like 買い物 (shopping), or a phrase consisting of a verb, its object, and so forth. Verbs describing the purpose of a movement must be in their stem forms. Stems, as we learned in Lesson 3, are the part you get by removing ます from the verbs' present tense long forms.

```
stems:
    食べる    →    食べ（ます）
    読む     →    読み（ます）
                        etc.
```

デパートに かばんを買い に行きました。
I went to a department store to buy a bag.

メアリーさんは日本に 日本語を勉強し に来ました。
Mary has come to Japan to study Japanese.

5 Counting People

The "counter" for people is 人, but "one person" and "two people" are irregular: 一人 and 二人.

<u>ひ</u>とり （一人）	one person
<u>ふ</u>たり （二人）	two people
さんにん （三人）	three people
<u>よ</u>にん （四人）	four people
ごにん （五人）	five people
ろくにん （六人）	six people
しちにん／ななにん （七人）	seven people
はちにん （八人）	eight people
きゅうにん （九人）	nine people
じゅうにん （十人）	ten people

何人いますか。
なんにん

To count people in a class, for example, you can add 〜人 after the noun and the particle
が, and say:

> person が　Ｘ人　います
> にん

私のクラスに(は)スウェーデン人の学生が一人います。
わたし　　　　　　　　　　じん　がくせい　　ひとり
There is one Swedish student in our class.

The place expressions are often followed by には instead of に in this type of sentence.

表現ノート
ひょうげん
Expression Notes ⑧

遊ぶ ▶ 遊ぶ means "to play," "to spend time pleasantly," or "to pay a social
あそ　　あそ
call."

子供の時、よく友だちと遊びました。
こども　とき　　とも　　　あそ
When I was a child, I often played with friends.

遅くまで遊んではいけません。
おそ　　あそ
You must not play around until late.

先週の週末は東京に遊びに行きました。
せんしゅう　しゅうまつ　とうきょう　あそ　　い
I went to Tokyo to have fun last weekend.

私のうちに遊びに来てください。
わたし　　　あそ　　き
Please come and see us.

Note that "to play" as used below requires different words.

Sports: to play tennis　テニスを<u>する</u>
　　　　to play basketball　バスケットを<u>する</u>
Games: to play video games　テレビゲームを<u>する</u>
　　　　to play cards　トランプを<u>する</u>
Music instruments: to play the guitar　ギターを<u>弾く</u>

練習 Practice
れん しゅう

Ⅰ 何をしていますか
なに

A. Look at the pictures below and answer the questions. 🔊

Example:　Q：メアリーさんは何をしていますか。
なに

　　　　　　A：メアリーさんはテレビを見ています。
み

Ex.　　　　　　(1)　　　　　　(2)　　　　　　(3)

(4)　　　　　　(5)　　　　　　(6)　　　　　　(7)

(8)　　　　　　(9)　　　　　　(10)　　　　　　(11)

B. Pair Work—What were you doing at the following times yesterday? Be as specific as possible (where, with whom, and so on).

Example:　2 P.M.　→　A：午後二時ごろ何をしていましたか。
ご ご に じ　　なに

　　　　　　　　　　　　B：友だちと部屋で勉強していました。
とも　　　へ や　べんきょう

1. 6 A.M.　　　2. 8 A.M.　　　3. 10 A.M.　　　4. 12:30 P.M.

5. 6 P.M.　　　6. 8 P.M.　　　7. 11 P.M.

C. Class Activity—Let's play charades. The teacher gives a sentence card to each student. One of the students mimes the sentence. All other students guess what the person is doing and raise their hands when they recognize the action. The person that gets the most points is the winner.

Example: 田中さんは海で泳いでいます。

Ⅱ お父さんはどこに住んでいますか

A. This is Sue's family. Answer the following questions.

Example: Q：お父さんはどこに住んでいますか。

A：お父さんはニューヨークに住んでいます。

1. お姉さんはどこに住んでいますか。
2. 弟さんはアメリカに住んでいますか。
3. お母さんは何をしていますか。
4. お姉さんは何をしていますか。
5. お姉さんは結婚していますか。
6. 弟さんは結婚していますか。
7. お父さんは何歳ですか。
8. 弟さんは何歳ですか。
9. お父さんは日本の会社に勤めていますか。

Father	lives in N.Y.	works for an American company	48 years old
Mother		high school teacher	45 years old
Sister	lives in Seoul	works for a bank; married	27 years old
Brother	lives in London	student; not married	18 years old

B. Pair Work—Ask about your partner's family and fill in the blanks below.

	何歳ですか	何をしていますか	どこに住んでいますか	結婚していますか
お父さん				
お母さん				
お兄さん				
お姉さん				
弟さん				
妹さん				

Ⅲ 山田さんはやせています (Describing People)
やまだ

A. Look at the picture and answer the questions. 🔊

Example: Q：山田さんはやせていますか。
やまだ

A：はい、山田さんはやせています。
やまだ

山田　　　吉川
やまだ　　よしかわ

1. 山田さんは太っていますか。
やまだ　　ふと

2. 山田さんはＴシャツを着ていますか。
やまだ　　ティー　　き

3. 吉川さんは何を着ていますか。
よしかわ　　なに　き

4. 山田さんはジーンズをはいていますか。
やまだ

5. 吉川さんはめがねをかけていますか。
よしかわ

6. 吉川さんはかさを持っていますか。
よしかわ　　　　も

7. 山田さんは背が高いですか。
やまだ　　せ　たか

8. 吉川さんは背が低いですか。
よしかわ　　せ　ひく

9. 山田さんは髪が長いですか。
やまだ　　かみ　なが

10. 吉川さんは目が小さいですか。
よしかわ　　め　ちい

B. Look at the picture below and describe each person.

Example: 水野さんはぼうしをかぶっています。
みずの

川村
かわむら

山中
やまなか

中山　　小川　　水野
なかやま　おがわ　みずの

C. Class Activity—One student describes another student without mentioning the name. The rest of the class guesses who the student is.

Example: 髪が短いです。Ｔシャツを着ています。ジーンズをはいていません。
かみ　みじか　　　　ティー　　き

Ⅳ 大学は新しくて、きれいです
だいがく　　あたら

A. Make sentences using two adjectives. 🔊

Example:　大学 ― 新しい／きれいな　→　大学は新しくて、きれいです。
　　　　　　だいがく　あたら　　　　　　　　　　だいがく　あたら

1. 東京　　　― 大きい／にぎやかな
　　とうきょう　　おお
2. みちこさん ― きれいな／やさしい
3. たけしさん ― 背が高い／かっこいい
　　　　　　　　せ　たか
4. アパート　 ― 静かな／大きい
　　　　　　　　しず　　おお
5. 新幹線 (Bullet Train) ― 速い／便利な
　　しんかんせん　　　　　　はや　べんり
6. スーさん　 ― 頭がいい／親切な
　　　　　　　　あたま　　しんせつ
7. 私の国の人 ― 元気な／にぎやかな
　　わたし　くに　ひと　げんき

B. Looking back on your childhood, make sentences using the given cues. 🔊

Example:　my next-door neighbor ― tall & kind

　　　→　となりの人は、背が高くて、親切でした。
　　　　　　　　ひと　せ　たか　　しんせつ

1. my town　　― quiet & nice
2. my teacher ― big & scary
3. my house　 ― old & not clean
4. classes　　 ― long & not interesting
5. my friends ― kind & interesting
6. school　　 ― lively & fun
7. homework　― difficult & tough
8. myself　　 ― small & cute

C. Describe the following items using two or more adjectives.

Example:　my roommate

　　　→　私のルームメート (roommate) は親切でおもしろいです。
　　　　　わたし　　　　　　　　　　　　　　　しんせつ
　　　　　私のルームメートは親切ですが、つまらないです。
　　　　　わたし　　　　　　　　　しんせつ

1. my hometown　　　2. my country
3. my Japanese class　4. one of my family members
5. Japanese people　　6. people of my country

Ⅴ 映画を見に行きます
えいが　み　い

A. Sue is going to the following places to do the things below. Make sentences like the example. 🔊

Example:　京都 ── かぶき (Kabuki) を見る
きょうと　　　　　　　　　　　　　み

→　スーさんは京都にかぶきを見に行きます。
きょうと　　　　　　　　み　い

1. ＬＬ　　　　　── テープを聞く
エルエル　　　　　　　　　　き
2. 図書館　　　── 本を借りる
としょかん　　　　ほん　か
3. 食堂　　　　── 昼ごはんを食べる
しょくどう　　　ひる　　　　　た
4. 郵便局　　　── 切手を買う
ゆうびんきょく　きって　か
5. 公園　　　　── 写真を撮る
こうえん　　　　しゃしん　と
6. 友だちのうち ── 勉強する
とも　　　　　　　べんきょう
7. 町　　　　　── 遊ぶ
まち　　　　　　あそ
8. デパート　　── くつを買う
か
9. 高校　　　　── 英語を教える
こうこう　　　　えいご　おし
10. 喫茶店　　　── コーヒーを飲む
きっさてん　　　　　　　　の

B. For what purpose would you go to the following places?

1. コンビニに＿＿＿＿＿＿＿＿＿＿＿＿＿に行きます。
い

2. 東京に＿＿＿＿＿＿＿＿＿＿＿＿＿に行きました。
とうきょう　　　　　　　　　　　　　　　い

3. 図書館に＿＿＿＿＿＿＿＿＿＿＿＿＿に行きます。
としょかん　　　　　　　　　　　　　　い

4. 家に＿＿＿＿＿＿＿＿＿＿＿＿＿に帰ります。
いえ　　　　　　　　　　　　　　　　かえ

5. 大学に＿＿＿＿＿＿＿＿＿＿＿＿＿に来ました。
だいがく　　　　　　　　　　　　　　　き

Ⅵ この部屋に女の人が何人いますか
へや　おんな　ひと　なんにん

Pair Work─Ask your partner the following questions.

Example:　A：この部屋に女の人が何人いますか。
へや　おんな　ひと　なんにん

B：二人います。
ふたり

1. この部屋に男の人が何人いますか。
　　へや　おとこ　ひと　なんにん

2. この部屋に＿＿＿＿＿＿＿人が何人いますか。
　　へや　　　(nationality)　じん　なんにん

3. この部屋に髪が長い人が何人いますか。
　　へや　かみ　なが　ひと　なんにん

4. この部屋に元気な人が何人いますか。
　　へや　げんき　ひと　なんにん

Ⅶ まとめの練習
れんしゅう

A. Answer the following questions.

1. どこに住んでいますか。
　　す

2. 結婚していますか。
　　けっこん

3. 自転車／車を持っていますか。
　　じてんしゃ　くるま　も

4. 日本の歌を知っていますか。
　　にほん　うた　し

5. 日本語の先生は今日何を着ていますか／はいていますか。
　　にほんご　せんせい　きょうなに　き

6. 兄弟がいますか。何人いますか。
　　きょうだい　　　なんにん

7. お父さん／お母さんはどこに勤めていますか。
　　とう　　　かあ　　　　つと

8. 子供の時、自転車を持っていましたか。
　　こども　とき　じてんしゃ　も

9. 高校の時、日本語を知っていましたか。
　　こうこう　とき　にほんご　し

B. Class Activity—Show a picture of your family to the class and describe it.

体の部分
かられ　ぶ　ぶん

Parts of the Body

かみ（髪）

みみ（耳）

め（目）

はな（鼻）

くち（口）

ゆび（指）

て（手）

くび（首）

は（歯）

あたま（頭）　　かお（顔）

かた（肩）

むね（胸）

せなか（背中）

おなか

おしり

あし（足）

家族
(か ぞく)
F a m i l y

	I. Someone Else's Family	II. Own Family A: Formal Situation	B: Informal Situation
Father	お父さん (とう)	父 (ちち)	お父さん (とう)
Mother	お母さん (かあ)	母 (はは)	お母さん (かあ)
Older brother	お兄さん (にい)	兄 (あに)	お兄さん (にい)
Older sister	お姉さん (ねえ)	姉 (あね)	お姉さん (ねえ)
Younger brother	弟さん (おとうと)	弟 (おとうと)	
Younger sister	妹さん (いもうと)	妹 (いもうと)	
Husband	ご主人 (しゅじん)	主人／夫 (しゅじん) (おっと)	*(See below.)
Wife	奥さん (おく)	家内／妻 (かない) (つま)	*(See below.)
Grandfather	おじいさん	祖父 (そ ふ)	おじいさん
Grandmother	おばあさん	祖母 (そ ぼ)	おばあさん
Child	お子さん (こ)	うちの子 (こ)	

*Depending on each person, several words are used for spouses, e.g., for husband, だんな, うちの人 (ひと), and for wife, 女房 (にょうぼう), ワイフ, かみさん, and so on.

* * *

A：田中さんのお父さんは何歳ですか。　*How old is your father, Mr. Tanaka?*
(たなか) (とう) (なんさい)

B：[formal]　父は五十歳です。　*My father is 50 years old.*
(ちち) (ご じゅっさい)

　　[informal]　お父さんは五十歳です。
(とう) (ご じゅっさい)

A：田中さんのお兄さんはどこに住んでいますか。
(たなか) (にい) (す)
Where does your older brother live, Mr. Tanaka?

B：[formal]　兄は東京に住んでいます。　*My older brother lives in Tokyo.*
(あに) (とうきょう) (す)

　　[informal]　お兄さんは東京に住んでいます。
(にい) (とうきょう) (す)

Note that you can use お兄さん and お姉さん when you talk to your older brothers
(にい) (ねえ)
and sisters. The younger brothers and sisters are called by their names.

Younger brother:　お兄さん。　*Hi, Big Brother.*
(にい)

Older brother:　何？　たろう。　*What is it, Taro?*
(なに)

第8課 LESSON 8
バーベキュー Barbecue

会話 Dialogue　🔊
かい　わ

Ⅰ At school.

1	みちこ：	たけしさん、あしたみんなでバーベキューをしませんか。
2	たけし：	いいですね。だれが来ますか。
3	みちこ：	スーさんとロバートさんが来ます。メアリーさんも来ると思います。
4	たけし：	けんさんは？
5	みちこ：	けんさんはアルバイトがあると言っていました。
6	たけし：	残念ですね。何か持っていきましょうか。
7	みちこ：	何もいらないと思います。

Ⅱ Robert is cooking at the barbecue.

1	みちこ：	上手ですね。ロバートさんは料理するのが好きですか。
2	ロバート：	ええ、よく家で作ります。
3	みちこ：	何か手伝いましょうか。
4	ロバート：	じゃあ、トマトを切ってください。
		＊　　　＊　　　＊
5	ロバート：	始めましょうか。
6	みちこ：	あっ、まだ飲まないでください。
7		メアリーさんも来ると言っていましたから。
8	メアリー：	遅くなってすみません。
9	みんな：	じゃあ、乾杯！

Michiko: Takeshi, would you like to have a barbecue party tomorrow?

Takeshi: That's nice. Who will come?

Michiko: Sue and Robert will come. I think Mary will come, too.

Takeshi: How about Ken?

Michiko: Ken said he had a part-time job.

Takeshi: Too bad. Shall I bring something?

Michiko: I think nothing is needed.

Ⅱ

Michiko: You are good (at cooking). Do you like cooking, Robert?

Robert: Yes, I often cook at home.

Michiko: Shall I help you with something?

Robert: Well then, cut the tomatoes, please.

            *   *   *

Robert: Shall we start?

Michiko: Don't drink yet. Mary said that she would come.

Mary: I'm sorry for being late.

Everyone: Well then . . . Cheers!

単語
たん ご
Vocabulary

Nouns

あさって		the day after tomorrow
あめ	雨	rain
かいしゃいん	会社員	office worker
カメラ		camera
カラオケ		karaoke
くうき	空気	air
けさ	今朝	this morning
こんげつ	今月	this month
しごと	仕事	job; work; occupation
だいがくせい	大学生	college student
ディスコ		disco
てんきよほう	天気予報	weather forecast
ところ	所	place
* トマト		tomato
なつ	夏	summer
* なにか	何か	something
パーティー		party
* バーベキュー		barbecue
はし		chopsticks
ふゆ	冬	winter
ホームステイ		homestay; living with a local family
まいしゅう	毎週	every week
らいげつ	来月	next month

な-adjectives

* じょうず(な)	上手	skillful; good at . . .	（〜が）
へた(な)	下手	clumsy; poor at . . .	（〜が）
ゆうめい(な)	有名	famous	

U-verbs

あめがふる	雨が降る	it rains
あらう	洗う	to wash
* いう	言う	to say

---

* Words that appear in the dialogue

* いる		to need	（〜が）
* おそくなる	遅くなる	to be late (for . . .)	（〜に）
* おもう	思う	to think	
* きる	切る	to cut	
* つくる	作る	to make	
* もっていく	持っていく	to take (something)	

Ru-verbs

じろじろみる	じろじろ見る	to stare (at . . .) （〜を）
* はじめる	始める	to begin

Irregular Verbs

うんてんする	運転する	to drive	（〜を）
せんたくする	洗濯する	to do laundry	
そうじする	掃除する	to clean	
* りょうりする	料理する	to cook	

Adverbs and Other Expressions

ううん		uh-uh; no
うん		uh-huh; yes
* かんぱい	乾杯	Cheers! (a toast)
* ざんねん（ですね）	残念（ですね）	That's too bad.
* まだ + negative		not . . . yet
* みんなで		all (of the people) together

文法 G r a m m a r
ぶん ぼう

1 Short Forms

In this and the next lesson, we will learn a new paradigm of conjugation, which we will
call "short forms.[1]" Before we start worrying about their meaning and how they are used,
let us first see what they look like. It should be obvious why they are called short forms.
We will list the already familiar "long forms" to the right in the table below.

Present tense, affirmative	short forms	long forms
verbs:	読む[a] よ	読みます よ
い-adjectives:	かわいい[a]	かわいいです
な-adjectives:	静かだ[b] しず	静かです しず
noun ＋ です:	学生だ[b] がくせい	学生です がくせい

Present tense, negative	short forms	long forms
verbs:	読まない[c] よ	読みません よ
い-adjectives:	かわいくない[d]	かわいくありません
な-adjectives:	静かじゃない[d] しず	静かじゃありません しず
noun ＋ です:	学生じゃない[d] がくせい	学生じゃありません がくせい

The following rules summarize how short forms are constructed.

> Verbs and い-adjectives in the affirmative (a above)
> → same as their dictionary forms
> な-adjectives and noun ＋ です in the affirmative (b above)
> → replace です with だ
> い- and な-adjectives and noun ＋ です in the negative (d above)
> → replace ありません with ない

---

[1]Various names have been given to this paradigm. They include "plain forms," "informal forms," and
"direct style." Long forms, on the other hand, are often called "polite forms," "formal forms," and
"distal style."

As noted in Lesson 5, the adjective いい is irregular. Its negative short form is よくない.

Verbs in the negative need to be analyzed in more detail, because *ru-*, *u-*, and irregular verbs conjugate differently.

Negative short forms of verbs (c above)

ru-verbs: Take the final る off and add ない.

食べる　→　食べない

u-verbs: Take the final *-u* off and add *-anai*.

書く	→	書かない	作る	→ 作らない
話す	→	話さない	泳ぐ	→ 泳がない
待つ	→	待たない	呼ぶ	→ 呼ばない
死ぬ	→	死なない	買う	→ 買わない[1]
読む	→	読まない		

irregular verbs:

する　→　しない　　くる　→　こない[2]

exception:

ある　→　ない[3]

With verbs in the negative, the following three points are worth noting.

(1) The negative short forms of verbs that end with the *hiragana* う are 〜わない instead of 〜あない.[2]
(2) The vowel changes with the irregular verb くる.
(3) The verb ある in the negative is ない.

2 Uses of Short Forms

We now turn to discussion of how we utilize short forms. In this lesson, we will learn to use the short forms in the following four contexts:

- In represented, or quoted, speech ("I think . . . ," "She said . . .")
- In casual conversations, as signs of intimacy
- In making negative requests ("Please don't . . .") (See 3 on p. 157.)

---

[2]This suggests that the bases of verbs like 買う and 会う actually end with the consonant *w*. This consonant remains dormant when the base is followed by the vowel *i*, thus we have 買います, where *w* is lacking, but it surfaces with the vowel *a* following, 買わない. This mystery consonant also explains why the *te*-form of such a verb has the small つ, just like verbs whose bases obviously end with a consonant, such as とる and 待つ.

● In expressing ideas like "I like doing . . ." or "I am good at doing . . ."

(See 4 below.)

Quotations   To quote a person's utterances or thoughts, you use a clause ending with a predicate in the short form, plus と言っていました (They said ". . ."), と思います (I think that . . .), and so forth. と is a quotation particle, which does the job of both the English word "that" in indirect quotation and of quotation marks (" ") in direct quotation.

スーさんは、あした試験があると言っていました。
Sue said that there would be an exam tomorrow.

(私は)たけしさんはメアリーさんが好きだと思います。[4]
I think Takeshi likes Mary.

Casual conversations   Two people who are close friends or family members speak with short forms at the end of sentences, using them as a sign of intimacy. The use of long forms, in contrast, tends to imply the speaker's intention to "keep a proper distance" from the listener. Short forms, then, are like talking on a first name basis, while long forms are like using "Mr." and "Ms."

It may not be easy to decide when it is appropriate to switch to short forms. First of all, Japanese speakers are often very conscious of seniority. A year's difference in age may in many cases totally preclude the possibility of establishing a truly "equal" relationship.

---

[3]Note that the present tense in Sue's original utterance is preserved in Mary's report.

[4]To say that you *don't think* something is the case, it is more common in Japanese to say it like 〜ない と思います (I *think* that something is *not* the case) than 〜と思いません (I *don't think*). Therefore:

(私は)メアリーさんはたけしさんが好きじゃないと思います。
I don't think Mary likes Takeshi (=I think Mary doesn't like Takeshi.)

Second, license to use short forms is not mutual; senior partners may feel perfectly justified in using short forms while expecting their junior partners to continue addressing them with long forms. Thus if somebody who is older, say, your Japanese language professor, talks to you using short forms, they would be greatly surprised if you should return the favor.

Here are a few observations on the grammar of short forms as they are used in casual conversations.

- In the casual conversational use of short forms, question sentences do not end with the question particle か, but with rising intonation alone.
- The だ ending of な-adjectives and noun + です constructions (b in the previous section) is usually dropped.

In casual conversations, はい and いいえ are often replaced by the less formal うん and ううん.

3 ～ないでください

To request that someone refrain from doing something, one can use a negative verbal short form plus でください.

ここで写真を撮らないでください。
Please don't take pictures here.

| negative short form ＋ でください | *Please don't . . .* |

4 verb のが好きです

Short forms are used in constructions where verbs and adjectives are to be treated as nouns. Thus 私は～が好きです／きらいです can, besides describing your preference for items denoted by nouns, such as 猫, also describe your preference for activities, such as swimming, drinking coffee, and studying Japanese. Add の to a verbal short form to express the idea of "doing x."

（私は）日本語を勉強するのが好きです。
I like studying the Japanese language.

（私は）部屋を掃除するのがきらいです。
I don't like cleaning my room.

"To be good/bad at doing something" is 〜が上手です (is good at . . .) and 〜が下手です (is bad at . . .).[5]

ロバートさんは料理を作るのが上手です。
Robert is good at cooking meals.

たけしさんは英語を話すのが下手です。
Takeshi is not a good speaker of English.

| person は | activity (verb) のが | 好き きらい 上手 下手 | です。 | like doing . . . doesn't like doing . . . is good at doing . . . is poor at doing . . . |

It is a common mistake to use the *te*-form of a verb in such contexts, misled by the association between 〜ている and the verb in the *-ing* form in English.

✕ たけしさんは英語を話してが下手です。

5　が

Consider what ロバートさんは沖縄に行きました means. This sentence of course is about Robert and describes what he did. It is likely to be uttered when the topic of Robert has already been breached. Grammatically speaking, (1) the noun ロバート stands as the subject in relation to the verb 行く (he was the person who performed the going), and (2) the noun is, per the function of the particle は, presented as the topic of the sentence (*as for* Robert, he went to Okinawa).

What if we both know that somebody went to Okinawa recently, and *I* know that it was Robert, but *you* don't. I will say:

ロバートさんが沖縄に行きました。　　*ROBERT went to Okinawa.*

---

[5]To describe one's skills or lack thereof, we also often use a different set of expressions, namely, 〜がとくいです (is comfortable with . . .) and 〜がにがてです (is uncomfortable with . . .).

私は日本語を話すのがとくいです。　*I am good at/comfortable with speaking Japanese.*

This sentence means that *Robert* went to Okinawa, which in English would be uttered with an extra emphasis on the name Robert. His identity is the new piece of information provided by this sentence. It is one of the functions of the particle が to (1) present the subject of a sentence in a way such that (2) the noun will "fill in the blank on the information sheet."

The "blank on the information sheet" is a question word like だれ and 何. The above sentence will fill in the blank left out by:

だれが沖縄に行きましたか。　　　　Compare: ✕ だれは沖縄に行きましたか。
Who went to Okinawa?

As we learned in Lesson 2, a question word that is the subject of a sentence is never followed by the particle は, but always by the particle が. As we have seen, a noun that will provide the answer to such a question is also followed by the particle が.

どのクラスがおもしろいですか。
Which class is (the most) interesting?

日本語のクラスがおもしろいです。
Japanese class is.

(このクラスで)だれがめがねをかけていますか。
Who wears glasses (in this class)?

山下先生がめがねをかけています。
Professor Yamashita does.

6　何か and 何も

The word for "something" is 何か, and the word for "anything" in negative sentences is 何も.

"Some" and "any" in:		
positive statements	何か	*something*
questions	何か	*anything?*
negative statements	何も ＋ negative	*not . . . anything*

These two words are used in places where the particles は, が, and を are expected. In these contexts, they are used on their own, without the help of particles. We will learn in Lesson 10 what to do in cases where particles other than these are expected.

猫が何か持ってきました。
The cat has brought something.

猫は何か食べましたか。
Did the cat eat anything?

いいえ、猫は何も食べませんでした。
No, the cat did not eat anything.

表現ノート   Expression Notes ⑨

〜する▶ Most irregular verbs are compounds of nouns and the verb する. If you have learned an irregular verb, therefore, you have also learned a noun.

verbs	nouns	
勉強する *to study*	勉強 *study*	ex. 日本語の勉強は楽しいです。 *Japanese language study is fun.*
料理する *to cook*	料理 *cooking*	ex. ロバートさんの料理はおいしいです。 *Robert's cooking is good.*

Some of these nouns can be used as the "object" of the verb する.

私は日本語の勉強をしました。   *I studied Japanese.*
    Compare: 私は日本語を勉強しました。

たけしさんは部屋の掃除をしました。   *Takeshi cleaned his room.*
    Compare: たけしさんは部屋を掃除しました。

練習 Practice
れん しゅう

① Short Forms

A. Change the affirmatives into negatives. 🔊

Example: かく → かかない

1. みる
2. あける
3. すむ
4. かける
5. はく
6. はじめる
7. つくる
8. せんたくする
9. あらう
10. くる
11. わすれる
12. ある
13. おもう
14. もっていく
15. はいる
16. かえる
17. あめがふる

B. Change the affirmatives into negatives. 🔊

Example: たかい → たかくない
げんきだ → げんきじゃない
がくせいだ → がくせいじゃない

1. ゆうめいだ
2. あめだ
3. いそがしい
4. かわいい
5. みじかい
6. しんせつだ
7. やすい
8. きれいだ
9. たいへんだ
10. いい
11. かっこいい
12. すきだ
13. きらいだ

② Informal Speech

A. Answer the following questions in informal speech, first in the affirmative, then in the negative. 🔊

Example: Q：よく魚を食べる？
　　　　　　さかな た
A：うん、食べる。／ううん、食べない。
　　　　　た　　　　　　　　　た

1. 今日、勉強する？
きょう べんきょう
2. 今日、友だちに会う？
きょう とも あ
3. よくお茶を飲む？
ちゃ の
4. よく電車に乗る？
でんしゃ の
5. 毎日、日本語を話す？
まいにち にほんご はな
6. 毎日、テレビを見る？
まいにち み

7. あした、大学に来る？　　8. 今日、宿題がある？
　　　　だいがく　く　　　　　　　きょう　しゅくだい

9. 自転車を持っている？　　10. 来週、ディスコに行く？
　　じてんしゃ　も　　　　　　　らいしゅう　　　　い

11. 毎週、部屋を掃除する？　12. 毎日、洗濯する？
　　まいしゅう　へや　そうじ　　　　まいにち　せんたく

B. Answer the following questions in informal speech, first in the affirmative, then in the negative.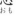

Example:　Q：元気？
　　　　　　　　　げんき
　　　　　　　A：うん、元気。／ううん、元気じゃない。
　　　　　　　　　　　げんき　　　　　　げんき

1. ひま？　　　　　　　　　　　2. 忙しい？
　　　　　　　　　　　　　　　　　いそが

3. 日本語のクラスはおもしろい？　4. 日本語のクラスは難しい？
　　にほんご　　　　　　　　　　　にほんご　　　むずか

5. この教科書はいい？　6. 先生はこわい？　　7. 料理が上手？
　　きょうかしょ　　　　せんせい　　　　　　りょうり　じょうず

8. お風呂が好き？　　　9. スポーツがきらい？　10. 今日は月曜日？
　　ふろ　す　　　　　　　　　　　　　　　　　　きょう　げつようび

Ⅲ 日本人だと思います
　　　　にほんじん　おも

A. Make a guess about Mary, using 〜と思います。
　　　　　　　　　　　　　　　　　　　おも

Example:　good at Japanese

　　　　　→　メアリーさんは日本語が上手だと思います。
　　　　　　　　　　　　　　にほんご　じょうず　おも

1. often cooks　　　　　　　　　2. drives a car
3. doesn't smoke　　　　　　　　4. listens to a Japanese language tape every day
5. doesn't go home late at night　6. doesn't drink alcohol much
7. often goes to see movies　　　8. not married
9. likes Takeshi　　　　　　　　10. busy
11. a good student　　　　　　　12. not tall
13. not scary　　　　　　　　　　14. not quiet
15. not a freshman

B. Make a guess about the person or place below and answer the following questions.

Example:　Q：この人は日本人ですか。
　　　　　　　　　ひと　にほんじん
　　　　　　　A：ええ、日本人だと思います。
　　　　　　　　　　　にほんじん　おも
　　　　　　　　　いいえ、日本人じゃないと思います。
　　　　　　　　　　　　にほんじん　　　　おも

Picture A

1. この人は会社員ですか。
2. 有名ですか。
3. ひまですか。
4. 頭がいいですか。
5. 背が高いですか。
6. 忙しいですか。
7. 結婚していますか。
8. お金をたくさん持っていますか。
9. よく食べますか。
10. よくスポーツをしますか。
11. フランス語を話しますか。

A

Picture B

1. ここは日本ですか。
2. 有名な所ですか。
3. 空気はきれいですか。
4. 暑いですか。
5. 冬は寒いですか。
6. 人がたくさん住んでいますか。
7. ここの人はよく泳ぎますか。
8. よく仕事をしますか。
9. 夏によく雨が降りますか。

B

C. Make a guess about the following things, using ～と思います.

1. the weather tomorrow
2. the next test
3. what your classmates will do tomorrow

Ⅳ メアリーさんは忙しいと言っていました
いそが　　　　　　　　い

A. Report what the following people said, using 〜と言っていました. 🔊
い

Example:　メアリー／今月は忙しいです。
こんげつ　いそが
　　→　　Q：メアリーさんは何と言っていましたか。
なん　い
　　　　　A：今月は忙しいと言っていました。
こんげつ　いそが　　　　い

メアリー

Ex.　今月は忙しいです。
こんげつ　いそが
1. 来月もひまじゃありません。
らいげつ
2. あしたは買い物をします。
か　もの
3. 京都に住んでいます。
きょうと　す

ロバート

4. ホームステイをしています。
5. お父さんは親切です。
とう　しんせつ
6. お母さんは料理が上手です。
かあ　りょうり　じょうず
7. お兄さんは大学生です。
にい　だいがくせい
8. 家族は英語を話しません。
かぞく　えいご　はな

天気予報
てんきよほう

9. あしたはいい天気です。
てんき
10. あしたは寒くありません。
さむ
11. あさっては雨が降ります。
あめ　ふ
12. あさっては寒いです。
さむ

B. Pair Work—Ask your partner the following questions. Take notes and report to the class later, using 〜と言っていました.
い

1. 週末は何をしますか。
しゅうまつ　なに
2. 日本はどうですか。
にほん
3. 日本の友だち／日本の家族はどんな人ですか。
にほん　とも　にほん　かぞく　ひと
4. どんな人が好きですか。
ひと　す

(V) 食べ<ruby>た</ruby>ないでください

What would you say when you want someone . . .

Example: not to look at your photo → 写真を見ないでください。
<ruby>しゃしん</ruby> <ruby>み</ruby>

1. not to speak English
2. not to call you
3. not to come to your house
4. not to go
5. not to smoke
6. not to sleep in class
7. not to forget
8. not to stare at you
9. not to start the class yet
10. not to be late
11. not to erase the <u>blackboard</u> yet
（こくばん）

(VI) 勉強するのが好きですか
<ruby>べんきょう</ruby> <ruby>す</ruby>

A. Tell what Mary is good/poor at, using 上手です or 下手です.
<ruby>じょう ず</ruby> <ruby>へ た</ruby>

Example: tennis (good)
→ メアリーさんはテニスが上手です。
<ruby>じょう ず</ruby>

swimming (poor)
→ メアリーさんは泳ぐのが下手です。
<ruby>およ</ruby> <ruby>へ た</ruby>

1. French (good)
2. video games (poor)
3. cooking (good)
4. making sushi (poor)
5. speaking Japanese (good)
6. taking pictures (good)
7. driving a car (good)
8. eating <u>with chopsticks</u> (good)
（はしで）
9. writing <u>love letters</u> (good)
（ラブレター）

B. Pair Work—Ask if your partner likes to do the following activities.

Example: studying
→ A：勉強するのが好きですか。
<ruby>べんきょう</ruby> <ruby>す</ruby>
B：はい、好きです／大好きです。
<ruby>す</ruby> <ruby>だい す</ruby>
いいえ、きらいです／大きらいです。
<ruby>だい</ruby>

1. eating
2. sleeping
3. singing
4. doing shopping
5. playing sports
6. studying Japanese
7. doing cleaning
8. doing laundry
9. cooking
10. taking a bath
11. driving a car
12. washing a car

* If you neither like it nor dislike it, you can use 好きでもきらいでもありません。
<ruby>す</ruby>

Ⅶ だれがイギリス人ですか
じん

A. Use the table below and answer the questions. 🔊

Example: Q：だれがイギリス人ですか。
じん

A：ロバートさんがイギリス人です。
じん

1. だれが韓国人ですか。
かんこくじん

2. だれが料理をするのが上手ですか。
りょうり　　　　　　じょうず

3. だれがいつも (always) 食堂で食べますか。
しょくどう　た

4. だれがデートをしましたか。

5. だれが犬が好きですか。
いぬ　す

Robert	British	is good at cooking	cooks often	went to Okinawa last weekend	doesn't like cats
Mary	American	is good at skiing	does not cook	had a date last weekend	likes dogs
Sue	Korean	is good at singing	cooks sometimes	went to Tokyo last weekend	likes cats
Takeshi	Japanese	is good at swimming	always eats at cafeteria	had a date last weekend	doesn't like cats

B. Pair Work—Use the table above and ask your partner questions with だれが.

Ⅷ 週末、何もしませんでした
しゅうまつ　なに

A. You went to a party but did nothing there. Make sentences using the cues. 🔊

Example: パーティーに行きましたが、(eat)
い

→ パーティーに行きましたが、何も食べませんでした。
い　　　　　　　　　　　なに　た

1. パーティーに行きましたが、(drink)
い

2. カラオケがありましたが、(sing)

3. テレビがありましたが、(watch)

4. カメラを持っていましたが、(take)
も

5. ゆみさんに会いましたが、(talk)
あ

6. パーティーに行きましたが、(do)
い

B. Answer the following questions.

Example: Q：きのうの晩ごはんは何か作りましたか。

A：はい、スパゲッティ (spaghetti) を作りました。

いいえ、何も作りませんでした。

1. けさ、何か食べましたか。
2. きのう、何か買いましたか。
3. きのう、テレビで (on TV) 何か見ましたか。
4. 今、何かいりますか。
5. 週末、何かしますか。
6. 週末、何か勉強しますか。

Ⅸ まとめの練習

A. Interview one of your classmates about any future plans and report to the class.

Example: スーさんは来年ソウルへ行くと言っていました。

B. Pair Work/Group Work—You are planning a party. Decide on the following points and fill in the chart.

いつですか	
どこでしますか	
どんなパーティーですか	
何を持っていきますか	
だれが来ますか	

C. Class Activity—Find someone who . . .

1. likes to study Japanese _____
2. hates to do cleaning _____
3. likes to sing _____
4. is poor at driving _____
5. whose mother is good at cooking _____

D. Pair Work—A and B are making plans for a one-day trip with two other friends C and D. A knows C's schedule and B knows D's schedule. Play the roles of A and B. Discuss your own and your friend's schedules using 〜と言っていました, and find out which days all four of you are available.

Example:　A：十六日はひまですか。
　　　　　　B：いいえ、買い物に行きます。十八日は、どうですか。
　　　　　　A：私は、何もしません。でも、Cさんが映画を見に行くと言っていました。
　　　　　　B：そうですか。じゃあ……

Student A

A's schedule						
16	17	18	19	20 study	21 quiz	22 party
23	24	25	26	27	28	29 part-time job

C told A that he would . . .
　18th: go to see a movie
　24th: meet friends
　26th: go to Osaka to have fun

Student B

B's schedule

16 shopping	17 work	18	19	20	21	22 tennis
23	24	25	26	27	28	29 work

D told B that she would . . .

    19th: do a part-time job

    27th: go to eat Japanese cuisine

    28th: go to Kyoto to see temples

第9課 | L E S S O N ·····················9
かぶき Kabuki

会話 かいわ D i a l o g u e 🔊

Ⅰ Mary and Takeshi are talking.

1 たけし： メアリーさんはかぶきが好きですか。

2 メアリー： かぶきですか。あまり知りません。でも、ロバートさんはおもしろかっ

3 たと言っていました。

4 たけし： かぶきの切符を二枚もらったから、見に行きませんか。

5 メアリー： ええ、ぜひ。いつですか。

6 たけし： 木曜日です。十二時から四時までです。

Ⅱ During intermission at a Kabuki theater.

1 メアリー： きれいでしたね。

2 たけし： 出ている人はみんな男の人ですよ。

3 メアリー： 本当ですか。

4 たけし： ええ。ところで、もう昼ごはんを食べましたか。

5 メアリー： いいえ、まだ食べていません。

6 たけし： じゃあ、買いに行きましょう。

Ⅲ At a concession stand.

1 たけし： すみません。お弁当を二つください。

2 店の人： はい。

3 たけし： それから、お茶を一つとコーヒーを一つ。

4 店の人： 二千八百円です。どうもありがとうございました。

I

Takeshi: Mary, do you like Kabuki?

Mary: Kabuki? I don't know it well. But Robert said it was interesting.

Takeshi: I got two tickets for Kabuki, so would you like to go to see it?

Mary: Sure. When is it?

Takeshi: On Thursday. From 12:00 to 16:00.

II

Mary: It was beautiful.

Takeshi: The people who appear are all men.

Mary: Really?

Takeshi: Yes. By the way, did you already eat lunch?

Mary: No, I haven't eaten it yet.

Takeshi: Then, shall we go to buy it?

III

Takeshi: Excuse me. Two box lunches, please.

Vendor: Here they are.

Takeshi: And then, one tea and one coffee.

Vendor: That is 2,800 yen. Thank you very much.

単語
たん ご

Ｖｏｃａｂｕｌａｒｙ

Ｎｏｕｎｓ

いいこ	いい子	good child
いろ	色	color
* おべんとう	お弁当	boxed lunch
おんせん	温泉	spa; hot spring
* かぶき		Kabuki; traditional Japanese theatrical art
ギター		guitar
くすり	薬	medicine
くすりをのむ	薬を飲む	to take medicine
コンサート		concert
こんど	今度	near future
さくぶん	作文	essay; composition
しけん	試験	exam
しんかんせん	新幹線	Shinkansen; "Bullet Train"
スキー		ski
せんげつ	先月	last month
たんご	単語	word; vocabulary
ピアノ		piano
びょうき	病気	illness; sickness

い-ａｄｊｅｃｔｉｖｅｓ

あおい	青い	blue
あかい	赤い	red
くろい	黒い	black
さびしい	寂しい	lonely
しろい	白い	white
わかい	若い	young

な-ａｄｊｅｃｔｉｖｅ

いじわる(な)	意地悪	mean-spirited

Ｕ-ｖｅｒｂｓ

おどる	踊る	to dance
おわる	終わる	(something) ends　(〜が)

* Words that appear in the dialogue

にんきがある	人気がある	to be popular
はじまる	始まる	(something) begins （〜が）
ひく	弾く	to play (a string instrument or piano)
* もらう		to get (from somebody) （*person* に *thing* を）

Ru-verbs

おぼえる	覚える	to memorize
* でる	出る	(1) to appear; to attend （〜に）
		(2) to exit （〜を）

Irregular Verbs

うんどうする	運動する	to do physical exercises
さんぽする	散歩する	to take a walk

Adverbs and Other Expressions

* 〜から		from . . .
* ぜひ	是非	by all means
* ところで		by the way
* みんな		all
* もう		already

Numbers (used to count small items)

* ひとつ	一つ	one
* ふたつ	二つ	two
みっつ	三つ	three
よっつ	四つ	four
いつつ	五つ	five
むっつ	六つ	six
ななつ	七つ	seven
やっつ	八つ	eight
ここのつ	九つ	nine
とお	十	ten

文法 G r a m m a r
ぶん ぼう

1 Past Tense Short Forms

We will now continue the discussion on short forms, which we started in the last lesson. Here we will learn the past tense paradigm of short forms.

Past tense, affirmative		compare with:
verbs:	読んだ[a] よ	読んで よ
い-adjectives:	かわいかった[b]	かわいい
な-adjectives:	静かだった[c] しず	静かだ しず
noun ＋ です:	学生だった[c] がくせい	学生だ がくせい
Past tense, negative		
verbs:	読まなかった[b] よ	読まない よ
い-adjectives:	かわいくなかった[b]	かわいくない
な-adjectives:	静かじゃなかった[b] しず	静かじゃない しず
noun ＋ です:	学生じゃなかった[b] がくせい	学生じゃない がくせい

Below is a brief discussion on the formation of past tense short forms.

> Verbs in the affirmative (a above)
> → replace て/で in *te*-forms with た/だ
>
> い-adjectives in the affirmative, and all categories in the negative (b above)
> → replace the final い with かった
>
> な-adjectives and noun ＋ です in the affirmative (c above)
> → replace だ in the present tense short forms with だった

The two irregularities that we noted earlier are observed here once again. They are:

行く → 行った   いい → よかった, よくなかった[1]
い   い

Short form predicates in the past tense can be used in the same way as the present tense forms, which we discussed in Lesson 8.

---

[1]See 行って in Lesson 6. See よかったです, よくありません, and よくありませんでした in Lesson 5.
い

● In represented, or quoted, speech

スーさんは、高校の時めがねをかけていたと言っていました。
Sue said that she wore (had worn) glasses in high school.

（私は）トムさんがやったと思います。
I think Tom did it.

● In casual conversations

晩ごはん、食べた？　　―　うん、食べた。
Have dinner yet?　　　*Uh-huh, I did.*

Note that in Japanese the tense of the original utterance is preserved when it is reported. If you are reporting somebody's utterance in which the present tense is used, you must also use the present tense inside the quote. Thus, if your friend Sue said 今、日本語を勉強しています, using the present tense, your report will be:

スーさんは日本語を勉強していると言っていました。
Sue said that she was studying Japanese.

2　Qualifying Nouns with Verbs and Adjectives

The short forms of verbs can be used to qualify nouns, much like adjectives can. In the example below, the phrase あそこで本を読んでいる (reading a book over there) is used as a qualifier for the noun 学生.[2]

あそこで本を読んでいる 学生はみちこさんです。
The student who is reading a book over there is Michiko.

The following table shows various forms of noun qualification. The phrases in the boxes qualify the noun 人 (person) to their right. Example 1 is a straightforward adjectival example. Example 2 contains a phrase describing a person's attribute (Lesson 7), example 3 has a verb in the short form (Lesson 8), and example 4 has a な-adjective, which is relational (Lesson 5).

---

[2]A qualifying phrase like this, which has a sentence-like structure of its own, is technically known as a "relative clause."

1.	おもしろい	人 (ひと)	a person	who is interesting
2.	髪が長い (かみ なが)	人 (ひと)	a person	who has long hair
3.	めがねをかけている	人 (ひと)	a person	who wears glasses
4.	猫が好きな (ねこ す)	人 (ひと)	a person	who likes cats

adjectives and verbs noun
used as qualifiers

Here are more examples of verbs used in descriptions of people.

あそこで写真を撮っている 人 (はだれですか。)
(しゃしん と) (ひと)
(Who is) the person taking pictures over there?

毎日運動をする 人 (は元気です。)
(まいにちうんどう) (ひと)（げんき）
People who do physical exercises every day (are healthy.)

たばこを吸わない 人 (が好きです。)
(す) (ひと)（す）
(I like) people who do not smoke.

去年結婚した 友だち (から手紙が来ました。)
(きょねんけっこん) (とも)（てがみ き）
(A letter came from) a friend who got married last year.

3 まだ～ていません

Consider first the following pair of sentences in English.

 Zelda has lost her key.
 Zelda lost her key.

These two sentences present the same fact, Zelda losing her key, in different ways. The first "present perfect" example describes the event as something that is connected with the present: hearing the sentence, one will understand that Zelda is still without her key. On the other hand, the second "simple past" example describes the event as something that is independent of the situation at the present moment; we do not know whether Zelda is still looking for her key or has later retrieved it.

In Japanese, past tense forms do double duty on the affirmative end of polarity, but the past tense and the ている construction share the work on the negative end. Thus in the affirmative, the past tense is used both with words like きのう (disconnected from the present) and もう ("already," connected with the present).

私はきのう宿題を<u>しました</u>。　　and　　私はもう宿題を<u>しました</u>。
I did the homework yesterday.　　　　　*I have already done the homework.*

With the negative, the past is used to talk about a finished time period like きのう, but ている is used if your intention is to talk about how things stand now ("not yet").

私はきのう宿題を<u>しませんでした</u>。　　and　　私はまだ宿題を<u>していません</u>。
I did not do the homework yesterday.　　　　*I have not done the homework yet.*

まだ〜ていません	*have not . . . yet*

This use of ている can be found both with verbs describing *changes* and with verbs describing *activities*, as defined in Lesson 7.

スーさんはまだ起きていません。　　(change)
Sue has not woken up yet.

私はまだ昼ごはんを食べていません。　(activity)
I haven't eaten lunch yet.

4　〜から

We learned in Lesson 6 that から added to a sentence means "because."

私は朝ごはんを食べませんでした。忙しかったですから。
I didn't have breakfast. (Because) I was busy.

In this lesson, we learn to incorporate the explanation clauses in the statements themselves, rather than adding them as separate sentences. You can simply transpose the "explanation＋から" sequence to the beginning of a sentence for which the explanation is offered.

(explanation) **から**、(situation)。 　　　　= (situation), *because* (explanation). 　　　　= (explanation), *therefore,* (situation).

あした試験があるから、私は今晩勉強します。
I will study this evening, because we will have an exam tomorrow.
(＝We will have an exam tomorrow, therefore, I will study this evening.)

寒かったから、出かけませんでした。
We didn't go out, because it was cold.
(＝It was cold, therefore, I didn't go out.)

Note that the resulting order of elements resembles that of a "therefore" sentence more closely than that of a "because" clause in English.

Before the conjunction から, you find both the long and short forms. Thus the から clauses in the above examples can be rewritten as あした試験がありますから and 寒かったですから.[3] The long form before から is more polite, and is frequently found in request and suggestion sentences.

かぶきの切符がありますから、一緒に見に行きましょう。
Let's go to see Kabuki. I have tickets.

---

[3]The long form before から is inappropriate when the entire sentence ends in a short form, however. Thus it is inappropriate to say：✕寒かったですから、出かけなかった。

練習 Practice

れん しゅう

① Short Forms Past

A. Verbs 🔊

(a) Change the following verbs into the past affirmatives.

Example: かく → かいた

1. はなす   2. しぬ   3. すむ   4. かける
5. いく   6. あそぶ   7. つくる   8. せんたくする
9. あらう   10. くる   11. ひく   12. まつ
13. いそぐ   14. もらう   15. おどる   16. でる

(b) Change the following verbs into the past negatives.

Example: かく → かかなかった

1. みる   2. すてる   3. すむ   4. かける
                 (to throw away)
5. はく   6. はじまる   7. つくる   8. せんたくする
9. あらう   10. くる   11. いう   12. うんどうする
13. おぼえる 14. うたう   15. かえる   16. やすむ

B. Adjectives and Nouns 🔊

(a) Change the following into the past affirmatives.

Example: たかい   → たかかった
         げんきな → げんきだった
         がくせい → がくせいだった

1. ゆうめいな   2. あめ   3. あかい   4. かわいい
5. みじかい   6. しんせつな 7. やすい   8. きれいな
9. いいてんき   10. かっこいい 11. さびしい   12. ねむい

(b) Change the following into the past negatives.

Example: たかい　　→　たかくなかった

げんきな　→　げんきじゃなかった

がくせい　→　がくせいじゃなかった

1. いじわるな　2. びょうき　　3. わかい　　　4. かわいい

5. ながい　　　6. べんりな　　7. あおい　　　8. しずかな

9. いいてんき　10. かっこいい　11. おもしろい　12. さびしい

Ⅱ Informal Speech

A. Using the cues below, make questions about yesterday in informal speech. How do you answer those questions? 🔊

Example: テレビを見る

→　Q：きのうテレビを見た？

A：うん、見た。／ううん、見なかった。

1. ピザを食べる
2. 散歩する
3. 図書館で本を借りる
4. うちを掃除する
5. うちで料理する
6. 友だちに会う
7. 単語を覚える
8. 学校に来る
9. 家族に電話をかける
10. コンピューターを使う
11. 手紙をもらう
12. 遊びに行く
13. 運動する
14. ディスコで踊る

B. Make questions about childhood in informal speech. How do you answer those questions?

Example: 元気
げんき
→ Q：子供の時、元気だった？
こども とき げんき
A：うん、元気だった。／ううん、元気じゃなかった。
げんき げんき

1. かわいい
2. 髪が長い
かみ なが
3. 背が高い
せ たか
4. 勉強が好き
べんきょう す
5. スキーが上手
じょうず
6. さびしい
7. 楽しい
たの
8. スポーツが好き
す
9. 宿題がきらい
しゅくだい
10. 頭がいい
あたま
11. 先生は親切
せんせい しんせつ
12. いじわる

Ⅲ 元気だったと思います
げんき おも

A. Make a guess about the childhoods of the people below.

Example: 元気でしたか。
げんき
→ Q：この人は子供の時、元気でしたか。
ひと こども とき げんき
A：はい、元気だったと思います。
げんき おも
いいえ、元気じゃなかったと思います。
げんき おも

(a) マドンナについて（about Madonna）

1. きれいでしたか。
2. いじわるでしたか。
3. 歌が上手でしたか。
うた じょうず
4. 頭がよかったですか。
あたま
5. 背が高かったですか。
せ たか
6. 髪が黒かったですか。
かみ くろ
7. やせていましたか。
8. ピアノを弾きましたか。
ひ
9. よく勉強しましたか。
べんきょう
10. よくお母さんを手伝いましたか。
かあ てつだ

(b) 日本語の先生について（about your Japanese teacher）

1. かわいかったですか。　　2. 学校が好きでしたか。
3. 太っていましたか。　　　4. いじわるでしたか。
5. よく遊びましたか。　　　6. 人気がありましたか。

B. Choose one classmate and guess what they were like as a child using the following characteristics.

Example: 頭がいい　→　ロバートさんは子供の時、頭がよかったと思います。

1. いい子　　　　　　2. 元気　　　　　　3. 背が高い／低い
4. 髪が長い／短い　　5. 忙しい　　　　　6. ひま
7. 静か　　　　　　　8. いじわる　　　　9. 学校が好き
10. かわいい

Ⅳ 子供の時遊んだと言っていました

A. Pair Work—Ask your partner the following questions about his/her childhood and report to the class using ～と言っていました.

Example: いじわるでしたか。
→　A：子供の時、いじわるでしたか。
　　B：はい、いじわるでした。
　　A：Bさんは、子供の時いじわるだったと言っていました。

1. 学校が好きでしたか。　　2. 頭がよかったですか。
3. 背が高かったですか。　　4. かわいかったですか。
5. めがねをかけていましたか。　6. よく何をしましたか。

B. What would these people say/have said? Make up your own quote for the following people.

Example: シュワルツェネッガーは、きのうたくさん運動したと言っていました。

Ex. シュワルツェネッガー　(1) マイケル・ジャクソン　(2) エルビス・プレスリー

(3) 友だち
とも

(4) 母（[my] mother）
はは

(5) 日本語の先生
にほんご　せんせい

Ⓥ めがねをかけている人です
ひと

A. Look at the picture below and answer the questions.

Example: 田中さん
たなか
→ 　Q：田中さんはどの人ですか。
たなか　　　ひと
　A：めがねをかけている人です。白いトレーナーを着ている人です。
ひと　　しろ　　　　　　き　ひと

1. 中村さん　2. 山口さん　3. 野村さん　4. 森さん　5. 大川さん　6. 鈴木さん
なかむら　　　やまぐち　　　のむら　　　　もり　　　おおかわ　　　すずき

B. Pair Work—One of you looks at picture A below and the other looks at picture B (p. 188). Ask each other questions and identify all the people in the picture.

Example: よしこ → A：よしこさんはどの人_{ひと}ですか。
B：テレビを見_みている人_{ひと}です。

Picture A

Ask which of the people are the following:

1. たろう
2. きょうこ
3. だいすけ
4. ようこ

C. Class Activity—Describe your classmates.

The class is divided into two groups, A and B. Each member of group A acts out something and freezes in the middle of doing so. Members of group B answer the teacher's questions, using 〜ている人_{ひと}です. Take turns when finished.

Example: Teacher：マイクさんはどの人_{ひと}ですか。
Student：車_{くるま}を運転_{うんてん}している人_{ひと}です。

Ⅵ まだ食_たべていません

A. Answer the following questions using まだ〜ていません.

Example: Q：もう昼_{ひる}ごはんを食_たべましたか。
A：いいえ、まだ食_たべていません。

1. もう切符_{きっぷ}を買_かいましたか。
2. もう宿題_{しゅくだい}をしましたか。
3. もう作文_{さくぶん}を書_かきましたか。

4. もう薬を飲みましたか。

5. もう晩ごはんを食べましたか。

6. もう新しい単語を覚えましたか。

B. Pair Work—Ask if your partner has done . . . yet.

Example: 天ぷらを食べる

→　A：もう天ぷらを食べましたか。

B：ええ、もう食べました。／いいえ、まだ食べていません。

1. 新幹線に乗る

2. 温泉に入る

3. 十課 (Lesson 10) を読む

4. かぶきを見に行く

5. ＿＿＿＿＿＿＿＿＿＿＿＿＿＿＿＿＿＿＿ を見る
　　　(a name of newly released movie)

6. ＿＿＿＿＿＿＿＿＿＿＿＿＿＿＿＿＿＿＿ を聞く
　　　(a name of newly released CD)

7. ＿＿＿＿＿＿＿＿＿＿＿＿＿＿＿＿＿＿＿ を読む
　　　(a name of current best-selling novel)

Ⅶ　天気がいいから、遊びに行きます

A. Match up the phrases to make sense.

1. 魚がきらいだから　　　　　　　・　　　　・今はひまです。

2. 試験が終わったから　　　　　　・　　　　・行きませんか。

3. 旅行に行ったから　　　　　　　・　　　　・すしを食べません。

4. コンサートの切符を二枚もらったから・　　　・急ぎましょう。

5. 天気がよくなかったから　　　　・　　　　・遊びに行きませんでした。

6. クラスが始まるから　　　　　　・　　　　・学校を休みました。

B. Complete the following sentences adding reasons.

1. _____から、お金がぜんぜんありません。
　　　　　　　　　　　　　　　　　　　　　　（かね）

2. _____から、日本語を勉強しています。
　　　　　　　　　　　　　　　　　　　　　　（にほんご）（べんきょう）

3. _____から、先週の週末は忙しかったです。
　　　　　　　　　　　　　　　　　　　　　　（せんしゅう）（しゅうまつ）（いそが）

4. _____から、きのう学校を休みました。
　　　　　　　　　　　　　　　　　　　　　　（がっこう）（やす）

Ⅷ まとめの練習
（れんしゅう）

A. Role Play—One of you is working at a fast-food restaurant. The other is a customer. Using Dialogue Ⅲ as a model, order some food and drinks from the menu below. Be sure to say how many you want.

B. Answer the following questions.

1. ピアノを弾きますか。

2. ギターを弾くのが上手ですか。

3. 踊るのが好きですか。

4. 病気の時、よく薬を飲みますか。

5. よく散歩しますか。

6. 去年の誕生日（birthday）に何かもらいましたか。
   だれに何をもらいましたか。

7. 今日、クラスは何時に始まりましたか。何時に終わりますか。

8. 犬が好きですか。

9. 子供の時、よく友だちと遊びましたか。

10. どんな色のトレーナーを持っていますか。

11. 今度の試験は難しいと思いますか。

12. あなたの国では、どんなスポーツが人気がありますか。

13. どんな色が好きですか。

Pair Work Ⓥ B.

Example: よしこ

→ A：よしこさんはどの人ですか。
B：テレビを見ている人です。

Picture B

Ask which of the people are the following:

1. ゆたか
2. じゅん
3. ちかこ
4. えり

色
いろ

C o l o r s

There are two kinds of words for colors.

Group 1: い-adjectives

黒い くろ	—————— black	白い しろ	—————— white
赤い あか	—————— red	青い あお	—————— blue
黄色い き いろ	—————— yellow	茶色い ちゃいろ	—————— brown

These words become nouns without the い.

赤いかばん
あか
red bag

赤が一番好きです。
あか　いちばん す
I like red the best.

Group 2: nouns

緑／グリーン みどり	—————— green	紫 むらさき	—————— purple
灰色／グレー はいいろ	—————— gray	水色 みずいろ	—————— light blue
ピンク	—————— pink	金色／ゴールド きんいろ	—————— gold
銀色／シルバー ぎんいろ	—————— silver		

There words need の in order to make noun phrases.

緑／グリーンのセーター
みどり
green sweater

Here are some words related to colors.

顔が青いですね。
かお　あお
You look pale.

白黒の写真
しろくろ　しゃしん
black and white picture

メアリーさんは金髪です。
きんぱつ
Mary has blonde hair.

第10課 | L E S S O N ·············· 10

冬休みの予定 Winter Vacation Plans
ふゆ やす よ てい

会 話 Dialogue
かい わ

Ⅰ Winter vacation is approaching.

1 メアリー： 寒くなりましたね。
　　　　　　さむ

2 たけし： ええ。メアリーさん、冬休みはどうしますか。
　　　　　　　　　　　　　　　ふゆやす

3 メアリー： 韓国か台湾に行くつもりですが、まだ決めていません。
　　　　　　かんこく たいわん い　　　　　　　　　　　き

4 たけし： いいですね。

5 メアリー： 韓国と台湾とどっちのほうがいいと思いますか。
　　　　　　かんこく たいわん　　　　　　　　　　おも

6 たけし： うーん、台湾のほうが暖かいと思います。でも、スーさんは韓国の食べ
　　　　　　　　　　たいわん　　　あたた　おも　　　　　　　　　　　　かんこく　た

7 　　　　　 物はおいしいと言っていましたよ。
　　　　　　もの　　　　　　い

8 メアリー： そうですか。ところで、たけしさんはどこかに行きますか。

9 たけし： どこにも行きません。お金がないから、ここにいます。
　　　　　　　　　　い　　　　　　かね

10 メアリー： そうですか。じゃあ、たけしさんにおみやげを買ってきますよ。
　　　　　　　　　　　　　　　　　　　　　　　　　　　　か

11 たけし： わあ、ありがとう。

Ⅱ At a travel agency.

1 メアリー： 大阪からソウルまで飛行機の予約をお願いします。
　　　　　　おおさか　　　　　　　　ひこうき　よやく　ねが

2 旅行会社の人：はい、いつですか。
　りょこうがいしゃ ひと

3 メアリー： 十二月十九日です。
　　　　　　じゅうに がつじゅうくにち

4 旅行会社の人：午前と午後の便がありますが……。
　りょこうがいしゃ ひと　ごぜん ごご びん

5 メアリー： 午前のをお願いします。
　　　　　　ごぜん　　ねが

6 　　　　　 クレジットカードで払ってもいいですか。
　　　　　　　　　　　　　　　はら

7 旅行会社の人：はい。
　りょこうがいしゃ ひと

8 メアリー： ソウルまでどのぐらいかかりますか。

9 旅行会社の人：一時間ぐらいです。
　りょこうがいしゃ ひと　いちじかん

I

Mary: It is getting cold.

Takeshi: Yes. Mary, what will you do at winter break?

Mary: I am planning to go to Korea or Taiwan, but I haven't decided yet.

Takeshi: That's nice.

Mary: Which do you think is better, Korea or Taiwan?

Takeshi: Mm . . . I think it is warmer in Taiwan. But Sue said that the food was delicious in
　　　　　Korea.

Mary: I see. By the way, are you going somewhere, Takeshi?

Takeshi: I won't go anywhere. I don't have money, so I will stay here.

Mary: Is that so? Then I'll buy some souvenir for you.

Takeshi: Wow, thank you.

II

Mary: I'd like to reserve a plane ticket from Osaka to Seoul.

Travel agent: When is it?

Mary: December 19.

Travel agent: We have a morning flight and an afternoon flight.

Mary: A morning flight, please. Can I use a credit card?

Travel agent: Yes.

Mary: How long does it take to Seoul?

Travel agent: About one hour.

単語
たん ご

Vocabulary

Nouns

あき	秋	fall
いしゃ	医者	doctor
えき	駅	station
おかねもち	お金持ち	rich person
かお	顔	face
きせつ	季節	season
* クレジットカード		credit card
ことし	今年	this year
サッカー		soccer
シャツ		shirt
せいかつ	生活	life; living
せかい	世界	world
ちかてつ	地下鉄	subway
てぶくろ	手袋	gloves
とこや	床屋	barber's
はる	春	spring
パンツ		pants
びよういん	美容院	beauty parlor
* びん	便	flight
ふね	船	ship; boat
やきゅう	野球	baseball
ゆうめいじん	有名人	celebrity
* よやく	予約	reservation
らいがっき	来学期	next semester
りんご		apple

い-adjectives

* あたたかい	暖かい	warm
おそい	遅い	slow; late
すずしい	涼しい	cool (weather—not used for things)
つめたい	冷たい	cold (thing/people)
ねむい	眠い	sleepy

* Words that appear in the dialogue

な-adjective

かんたん（な）	簡単	easy; simple

U-verbs

* かかる		to take (amount of time/money) (*no particle*)
とまる	泊まる	to stay (at a hotel, etc.)　（〜に）
* なる		to become
* はらう	払う	to pay

Ru-verb

* きめる	決める	to decide

Irregular Verb

れんしゅうする	練習する	to practice

Adverbs and Other Expressions

あるいて	歩いて	on foot
いちばん	一番	best
* 〜か〜		or
〜かげつ	〜か月	for . . . months
〜ご	〜後	in . . . time; after . . .
このごろ		these days
〜しゅうかん	〜週間	for . . . weeks
〜で		by (means of transportation); with (a tool)
どうやって		how; by what means
どちら		which
* どっち		which
* どのぐらい		how much; how long
〜ねん	〜年	. . . years
はやく	早く	(do something) early; fast

文法 G r a m m a r
ぶん ぽう

1 Comparison

In Japanese, adjectives have the same shape in noncomparative and comparative sentences; there is no alteration as in "great/greater." The idea of comparison is expressed by adding something to the nouns that are compared.

> A のほうが　B より[1] (property)。　=　*A is more* (property) *than B.*

エルビス・プレスリーのほうがフランク・シナトラよりかっこいいです。
Elvis Presley is more hip than Frank Sinatra.

バーブラ・ストライザンドのほうがマドンナより歌が上手です。
うた　じょうず
Barbra Streisand is a better singer than Madonna.

You can ask for another person's opinion on two things in comparative terms.

> A とB と　どっちのほう[2]が　(property)。
> =　*Between A and B, which is more* (property)?

バスと電車とどっちのほうが安いですか。
てんしゃ　　　　　　　やす
Which is cheaper, (going by) bus or (by) train?

In comparison among three or more items, the degree qualifier いちばん is used.

> [(class of items) の中で] A がいちばん (property)。
> なか
> =　*A is the most* (property) [*among* (a class of items)].

パバロッティとカレーラスとドミンゴの中で、だれがいちばん歌が上手だと思い
なか　　　　　　　　　　　　うた　じょうず　おも
ますか。
Between Pavarotti, Carreras, and Domingo, who do you think is the best singer?

---

[1]In real life, the phrases A のほうが and B より often appear in the reverse order, making it very easy to be misled into believing the opposite of what is actually said. Don't rely on the word order, therefore, to decide which item is claimed to be superior. Listen carefully for the words のほうが and より.

[2]There are several alternates for どっちのほう. They are: どちらのほう、どっち、and どちら. Any one of these can be used in question sentences seeking comparisons between two items. どっち and どっちのほう are slightly more colloquial than どちら and どちらのほう.

もちろん、パバロッティがいちばん<u>歌</u>が<u>上手</u>です。
Pavarotti is best, naturally.

Note that the words のほう and どっち are not used in statements of comparison among three or more items. Normal question words like だれ, どれ, and 何 are used instead.[3]

2   adjective/noun ＋ の

When a noun follows an adjective, and when it is clear what you are referring to, you can replace the noun with the pronoun の, "one." You can use の to avoid repetition.

私は黒い<u>セーター</u>を持っています。赤い<u>の</u>も持っています。（の＝セーター）
I have a black sweater. I have a red one, too.

安い<u>辞書</u>を買いに行きました。でもいい<u>の</u>がありませんでした。（の＝辞書）
I went to buy an inexpensive dictionary, but there were no good ones.

い-adjective な-adjective } ＋ noun	→	い-adjective な-adjective } ＋ の

Similarly, a noun following another noun can be reduced. Here, a sequence of the form "noun₁ の noun₂" will be reduced to "noun₁ の." You simply omit the second noun.

これはスーさんの<u>かばん</u>ですか。　　いいえ、それはメアリーさんの____です。
Is this Sue's <u>bag</u>?　　*No, that is Mary's____.*

アメリカの<u>アイスクリーム</u>のほうが日本の____よりおいしいです。
American <u>ice cream</u> is more delicious than Japanese <u>one</u>.

noun₁ **の** noun₂	→	noun₁ **の**_____

---

[3]The tendency is to use どれ when a list of items is presented, and to use 何 when a group is referred to collectively. Compare:

りんごとみかんとさくらんぼの中で、どれがいちばん好きですか。
Which do you like best, apples, tangerines, or cherries?
くだものの中で、何がいちばん好きですか。
What fruit do you like best?

3 ～つもりだ

つもり follows verbs in the present tense short forms to describe what a person is planning to do in the future. You can also use a verb in the negative plus つもり to describe what you are planning *not* to do, or what you do *not* intend to do.

> verb (present, short) ＋ つもりだ　　　　*(I) intend to do . . .*

（私は）週末にたけしさんとテニスをする<u>つもりです</u>。
I intend to play tennis with Takeshi this weekend.

山下先生はあした大学に<u>来ない</u>つもりです。
Professor Yamashita does not intend to come to school tomorrow.

お寺を見に行く<u>つもりでした</u>けど、天気がよくなかったから、行きませんでした。
We were planning to visit a temple, but we didn't, because the weather was not good.

4 adjective ＋ なる

The verb なる means "to become," indicating a change. なる follows nouns and both types of adjectives.

い-adjectives:	暖かい	→	暖かくなる	*to become warm/warmer*
な-adjectives:	静か(な)	→	静かになる	*to become quiet/quieter*
nouns:	会社員	→	会社員になる	*to become a company employee*

日本語の勉強が楽しくなりました。
Studying the Japanese language is fun now (though it was like torture before).

日本語の勉強が好きになりました。
I have grown fond of studying the Japanese language.

With い-adjectives, the final い is dropped and く is added, as in their negative conjugations. A common mistake is to expand the pattern of な-adjectives and nouns and use に with い-adjectives. It is wrong to say, for example, ×暖かいになる.

When an adjective is used with なる, a question arises whether the sentence describes an absolute change (ex. "it has become warm, hence it is not cold any longer") or a relative change (ex. "it has become warmer, but it is still cold"). なる sentences are ambiguous in isolation. If you want to make clear that you are talking in relative terms, you can use the pattern for comparison together with なる.

メアリーさんは<u>前より</u>日本語が上手になりました。
Mary has become better in Japanese <u>than before</u>.

5 どこかに/どこにも

In Lesson 8 we learned the Japanese expressions for "something" and "not . . . anything," 何か and 何も. As you must have noticed, these expressions are made up of the question word for things, 何, plus particles か and も. Other expressions for "some" and "any" in Japanese follow this pattern. Thus,

| *something* | 何か__ | *someone* | だれか__ | *somewhere* | どこか__ |
| *not anything* | 何__も | *not anyone* | だれ__も | *not anywhere* | どこ__も |

As we noted in Lesson 8, these words are used by themselves, where particles は, が, or を would be expected. It is, then, interesting to observe how these expressions interact with other particles, such as に, へ, and で. These particles appear in the places shown with underscores above. Let us look at some examples.

どこか<u>へ</u>行きましたか。
Did you go anywhere?

いいえ、どこ<u>へ</u>も行きませんでした。
No, I didn't go anywhere.

だれか<u>に</u>会いましたか。
Did you see anybody?

いいえ、だれ<u>に</u>も会いませんでした。
No, I didn't see anybody.

何かしましたか。
Did you do anything?

いいえ、何もしませんでした。
No, I didn't do anything.

6　で

You can use the particle で with nouns that describe the means of transportation and the instruments you use.

はしでごはんを食べます。	*We eat our meals <u>with chopsticks</u>.*
日本語で話しましょう。	*Let's talk <u>in Japanese</u>.*
バスで駅まで行きました。	*I went to the station <u>by bus</u>.*
テレビで映画を見ました。	*I saw a movie <u>on TV</u>.*

表現ノート
ひょうげん

Expression Notes ⑩

午前と午後の便がありますが……▶ We sometimes use が and けど at the end of a sentence when we want our partners to treat what we have just said as a given, common ground to build upon. These words often indicate the speaker's intention to give her partner a chance to react and speak up. By relegating the right to speak to one's partner, they also contribute to the politeness of one's utterance.

In the dialogue, the travel agent lays out the relevant information on the table; there are two flights, one leaving in the morning and another in the afternoon. が attached to her sentence indicates that she wants to build upon, and move forward with, these pieces of information. Instead of asking the obvious question, namely, どちらがいいですか, the agent chooses not to finish her sentence, and lets her customer come forward with an answer immediately.

練習 Practice
れん しゅう

① 電車のほうがバスより速いです
でんしゃ　　　　　　　　　はや

A. Look at the pictures below and answer the following questions. 📶

Example:　Q：電車とバスとどちらのほうが速いですか。
　　　　　　　　でんしゃ　　　　　　　　　　　　　　はや
　　　　　　A：電車のほうがバスより速いです。
　　　　　　　　でんしゃ　　　　　　　　　　はや

Picture (a)

1. 新幹線とバスとどちらのほうが速いですか。
　　しんかんせん　　　　　　　　　　　　はや
2. 新幹線と電車とどちらのほうが遅いですか。
　　しんかんせん　でんしゃ　　　　　　　　　おそ
3. 新幹線とバスとどちらのほうが安いですか。
　　しんかんせん　　　　　　　　　　　　やす
4. 電車とバスとどちらのほうが高いですか。
　　でんしゃ　　　　　　　　　　　　たか

Picture (b)

5. 東京と大阪とどっちのほうが大きいですか。
　　とうきょう　おおさか　　　　　　　　おお
6. 京都と大阪とどっちのほうが小さいですか。
　　きょうと　おおさか　　　　　　　　ちい

(a)

大阪	三時間　¥12,000	東京
おおさか	さんじかん	とうきょう
	六時間　¥10,000	
	ろくじかん	
	八時間　¥8,000	
	はちじかん	

Picture (c)

7. 田中さんと山田さんとどっちのほうが背が高いですか。
　　たなか　　　やまだ　　　　　　　　　　せ　たか
8. 山田さんと鈴木さんとどっちのほうが背が低いですか。
　　やまだ　　　すずき　　　　　　　　　　せ　ひく
9. 田中さんと鈴木さんとどっちのほうが若いですか。
　　たなか　　　すずき　　　　　　　　　わか
10. 山田さんと鈴木さんとどっちのほうが髪が短いですか。
　　やまだ　　　すずき　　　　　　　　　かみ　みじか

(b)

京都
きょうと
260万人
まんにん

大阪
おおさか
870万人
まんにん

東京
とうきょう
1,200万人
まんにん

(c)

田中　　　山田　　　鈴木
たなか　　やまだ　　すずき

25歳　　　20歳　　　35歳
さい　　　さい　　　さい

B. Pair Work—Make questions using the following cues and ask your partner. When you answer the questions, add reasons for your answers, if possible.

Example:　夏／冬（好き）

→　A：夏と冬とどちら（のほう）が好きですか。

　　　B：夏のほうが（冬より）好きです。

　　　　　　（or 夏も冬も好きです。／夏も冬もきらいです。）

　　　A：どうしてですか。

　　　B：泳ぐのが好きですから。

1. すし／天ぷら（おいしい）
2. 頭がいい人／かっこいい人（好き）
3. 野球／サッカー（人気がある）
4. 中国料理／日本料理（好き）
5. 船／飛行機（好き）
6. 日本の車／ドイツ (Germany) の車（いい）
7. 漢字／カタカナ（かんたん）
8. シュワルツェネッガー／スタローン（頭がいい）
9. マイケル・ジャクソン／マドンナ（お金持ち）
10. 春／秋（好き）
11. 日本の冬／あなたの国の冬（暖かい）
12. 日本の生活／あなたの国の生活（大変 or 楽しい）

Ⅱ 新幹線がいちばん速いです

A. Look at the pictures on the previous page and answer the questions below. 🔊

Example:　Q：この中で、どれがいちばん速いですか。

　　　　　A：新幹線がいちばん速いです。

Picture (a)

1. この中で、どれがいちばん遅いですか。
2. この中で、どれがいちばん安いですか。

Picture (b)

3. この中で、どこがいちばん大きいですか。
4. この中で、どこがいちばん小さいですか。

Picture (c)

5. この中で、だれがいちばん背が高いですか。
6. この中で、だれがいちばん若いですか。
7. この中で、だれがいちばん髪が長いですか。

B. Answer the following questions.

Example: 食べ物／好き
→　Q：食べ物の中で、何がいちばん好きですか。
　　A：すしがいちばん好きです。

1. 飲み物／好き　　　2. 世界の町／好き　　　3. 有名人／好き
4. 日本料理／きらい　5. 音楽／好き　　　　　6. 季節／好き
7. クラス／いい学生　8. クラス／背が高い　　9. クラス／たくさん食べる

C. Group Work—Make a group of three or four people. Ask each other questions and make as many superlative sentences as possible about the group.

Example: この中で、Aさんがいちばん若いです。
Bさんがいちばん背が高いです。
Cさんがいちばんよく遅くクラスに来ます。

D. Class Activity—First form pairs and make comparative and superlative question sentences with your partner. (You should know the answers.) Then ask questions to the class. The rest of the class answer the questions.

Example: 富士山とエベレストとどちらのほうが高いですか。
田中さんと山田さんとどちらのほうが若いですか。
クラスの中で今日だれがいちばんお金を持っていますか。
世界の国の中でどこがいちばん小さいですか。

(Ⅲ) これは私のです

A. This is a refrigerator in a dormitory. Tell whose each thing is, using の.

Example: このりんごはリーさん<u>の</u>です。

B. You are a customer. Look at the picture and tell which you want.

Example:

Store attendant：どちらのコーヒーがいいですか。

Customer：　　　熱いのをください。
　　　　　　　あつ

熱い　　冷たい
あつ　　つめ

(1) どちらの辞書がいいですか。
　　　　　じしょ

(2) どちらのかばんがいいですか。

大きい　　小さい
おお　　　ちい

高い　　安い
たか　　やす

(3) どちらの手袋がいいですか。
て ぶくろ

赤い   青い
あか   あお

(4) どちらのパンツがいいですか。

長い   短い
なが   みじか

(5) どちらのシャツがいいですか。

白い   黒い
しろ   くろ

Ⅳ 見に行くつもりです
み い

A. You are planning to do/not to do the following things next week. Tell what you will/will not do using 〜つもりです. 🔊

Example: 月曜日に本を読むつもりです。
げつよう び ほん よ

月曜日 げつよう び	Ex. to read books	(1) to practice the piano
火曜日 か よう び	(2) to do exercises	
水曜日 すいよう び	(3) to do laundry	
木曜日 もくよう び	(4) to write letters to friends	(5) not to go out
金曜日 きんよう び	(6) to eat dinner with friends	(7) not to study Japanese
土曜日 ど よう び	(8) to stay at a friend's	(9) not to go home
日曜日 にちよう び	(10) to clean a room	(11) not to get up early

B. Answer the following questions.

Example: Q：週末、映画を見に行きますか。

A：ええ、見に行くつもりです。

いいえ、見に行かないつもりです。

1. 今日の午後、勉強しますか。
2. 今晩、テレビを見ますか。
3. あさって、買い物をしますか。
4. 冬休みに旅行しますか。
5. 週末、料理を作りますか。
6. 三年後、日本にいますか。
7. 来学期も日本語を勉強しますか。

Ⓥ きれいになりました

A. Describe the following pictures.

Example: きれい → きれいになりました。

Ex. きれい (1) 眠い

(2) 元気　(3) 大きい　(4) 髪が短い

(5) ひま　(6) 暑い　(7) 涼しい

(8) 医者
いしゃ

(9) 春
はる

(10) 円が安い
えん やす

110
150

$1 =¥110 → $1 =¥150

B. Fill in the blanks with appropriate forms.

1. 掃除をしたから、部屋が＿＿＿＿＿＿＿＿なりました。
   そうじ　　　　　　　　　へや

2. 美容院／床屋に行ったから、髪が＿＿＿＿＿＿＿＿なりました。
   びよういん　どこや　い　　　　かみ

3. 円が＿＿＿＿＿＿＿＿なりました。
   えん

4. 毎日ピアノを練習しているから、＿＿＿＿＿＿＿＿なりました。
   まいにち　　　　れんしゅう

5. お酒をたくさん飲んで、顔が＿＿＿＿＿＿＿＿なりました。
   さけ　　　　　の　　　かお

6. 十一月は暖かかったですが、このごろ＿＿＿＿＿＿＿＿なりました。
   じゅういちがつ　あたた

7. 教えるのが好きだから、＿＿＿＿＿＿＿＿なるつもりです。
   おし　　　す

Ⅵ 自転車で行きます
じ てんしゃ い

A. Look at each picture and explain how to get to and from one place to another. 🔊

Example: うちから駅まで自転車で行きます。
えき　じ てんしゃ い

Ex.　　　　　　　　　(1)　　　　　　　　　(2)

Ex. 10 min. うち → 駅(えき)

(1) 40 min. うち → 学校(がっこう)

(2) 20 min. うち → バス停(てい)

(3) 1 hour うち → 会社(かいしゃ)

(4) 30 min. 横浜(よこはま) → 東京(とうきょう)

(5) 15 min. 会社(かいしゃ) → デパート

(6)   (7)   (8)

名古屋
なごや
2 hours
東京
とうきょう

日本
8 hours
ハワイ

日本
にほん
1 week
インドネシア

B. Use the same pictures and describe how long it takes. 📣

Example: うちから駅まで十分かかります。
えき　　　じゅっぷん

C. Explain how you get from your house to school.

Example: うちから南駅まで自転車で行きます。五分かかります。
みなみえき　　　じてんしゃ　い　　　　　　ごふん

南駅から西駅まで電車に乗ります。二十分かかります。
みなみえき　　にしえき　　でんしゃ　の　　　　　にじゅっぷん

西駅から学校まで歩いて行きます。十分ぐらいかかります。
にしえき　　がっこう　　ある　い　　　　　じゅっぷん

Ⅶ まとめの練習
れんしゅう

A. The chart below shows winter vacation plans for Mary and her friends. First, answer the following questions about Mary's plan.

Mary	will go to Korea with Sue	by plane	3 weeks	will stay at Sue's house	will do shopping and eat Korean foods
Robert	will go back to London	by plane	2 weeks		will meet friends
Ken	will go to Tokyo with a friend	by bullet train	3 days	will stay at a hotel	will play at Tokyo Disneyland
Tom	will go to the south pole (南極) なんきょく	by boat	2 months	doesn't know yet	will take pictures with penguins（ペンギン）
Takeshi	will go nowhere				

1. メアリーさんは今年の冬休みにどこかに行くつもりですか。
ことし　ふゆやす

2. どうやって韓国へ行きますか。だれと行きますか。
かんこく　い　　　　　　い

3. どのぐらい行きますか。
い

4. どこに泊まりますか。

5. 韓国で何をするつもりですか。

How about the others' plans? Make pairs and ask questions.

B. Pair Work—Talk about your plans for the upcoming vacation.

C. Role Play—One of you works for a travel agency and the other is a customer. Using Dialogue Ⅱ as a model, make reservations for the following tickets.

(1) From Nagoya to Los Angeles	Jan. 1	1 person	smoking seat
(2) From Tokyo to Paris	Feb. 14	1 person	window seat
(3) From Osaka to Rome	Apr. 18	2 persons	aisle seats
(4) From Tokyo to Bangkok	Aug. 20	4 persons	nonsmoking seats

smoking seat = 喫煙席 (きつえんせき) aisle seat = 通路側の席 (つうろがわ せき)
window seat = 窓側の席 (まどがわ せき) nonsmoking seat = 禁煙席 (きんえんせき)

駅 で
えき

At the Station

Types of Trains

普通 ふつう	local
急行 きゅうこう	express
特急 とっきゅう	super express

Destination

～行き い	bound for . . .
～方面 ほうめん	serving . . . areas

Types of Tickets and Seats

乗車券 じょうしゃけん	(boarding) ticket
回数券 かいすうけん	coupons
定期券 ていきけん	commuter's pass
整理券 せいりけん	vouchers; zone tickets
学割 がくわり	student discount
指定席 していせき	reserved seat
自由席 じゆうせき	general admission seat
禁煙車 きんえんしゃ	nonsmoking car
往復 おうふく	round trip
片道 かたみち	one way

Places in Stations

～番線 ばんせん	track number . . .	出口 でぐち	exit
切符売り場 きっぷうば	ticket vending area	入口 いりぐち	entrance
改札 かいさつ	gate	階段 かいだん	stairs
ホーム	platform	いちばん前 まえ	first car; front end
売店 ばいてん	kiosk	いちばん後ろ うし	last car; tail end

Miscellaneous Public Transportation Terms

乗り換え ——————— transfer
のか

次は〜 ——————— next (stop), . . .
つぎ

先発 ——————— departing first
せんぱつ

次発 ——————— departing second
じはつ

終電 ——————— last train
しゅうてん

Announcements

まもなく発車します ——————— We will be leaving soon.
はっしゃ

電車が参ります ——————— A train is arriving.
でんしゃ まい

次は〜に止まります ——————— Next (we'll stop at) . . .
つぎ と

ドアが閉まります。ご注意ください —— The doors are closing. Please be careful.
し ちゅうい

Useful Expressions

この電車は秋葉原に止まりますか。——— Does this train stop at Akihabara?
でんしゃ あきはばら と

終電は何時ですか。——————— What time is the last train?
しゅうてん なんじ

東京までの指定席を一枚お願いします。— One reserved ticket to Tokyo, please.
とうきょう していせき いちまい ねが

学割が使えますか。——————— Can I get a student discount?
がくわり つか

*　　　　　　*　　　　　　*

A：鎌倉行きの電車はどれですか。
かまくらい でんしゃ

Which one is the train bound for Kamakura?

B：二番線です。
にばんせん

Track number two.

第11課│LESSON ⋯⋯⋯⋯⋯⋯11
休みのあと After the Vacation
やす

会話 Dialogue
かい わ

Michiko and Mary meet after the vacation.

Ⓘ

1 みちこ： メアリーさん、久しぶりですね。休みはどうでしたか。
ひさ   やす

2 メアリー： すごく楽しかったです。韓国で買い物をしたり、韓国料理を食べたり
たの   かんこく か もの   かんこくりょうり た

3 しました。

4 みちこ： いいですね。私も旅行したいです。
わたし りょこう

5 メアリー： みちこさんの休みは楽しかったですか。
やす たの

6 みちこ： まあまあでした。一日だけドライブに行きましたが、毎日アルバイト
いちにち   い   まいにち

7 をしていました。

Ⅱ

1 メアリー： みちこさん、友だちを紹介します。こちらはジョンさんです。ジョンさ
とも   しょうかい

2 んは先月、日本に来ました。
せんげつ にほん き

3 ジョン： 初めまして。
はじ

4 みちこ： 初めまして、どうぞよろしく。
はじ

Ⅲ

1 みちこ： ジョンさん、出身はどこですか。
しゅっしん

2 ジョン： オーストラリアのケアンズです。

3 みちこ： そうですか。

4 ジョン： みちこさんはケアンズに行ったことがありますか。
い

5 みちこ： いいえ、ありません。

6 ジョン： 山や海があって、きれいな所ですよ。グレートバリアリーフで有名です。
やま うみ   ところ   ゆうめい

7 　　　　　みちこさんはどこの出身ですか。
8 みちこ：　長野です。今度遊びに来てください。食べ物もおいしいですよ。
9 ジョン：　ぜひ、行きたいです。

Ⅰ

Michiko: Mary, I haven't seen you for a long time. How was your vacation?

Mary: It was really fun. I went shopping, ate Korean dishes, and things like that in Korea.

Michiko: Sounds good. I want to travel, too.

Mary: Did you have a fun vacation, Michiko?

Michiko: It was okay. I went for a drive just for one day, but I was working part-time every day.

Ⅱ

Mary: Michiko, I want to introduce you to a friend of mine. This is John. He came to Japan last month.

John: How do you do?

Michiko: How do you do? Nice to meet you.

Ⅲ

Michiko: John, where are you from?

John: I am from Cairns, Australia.

Michiko: Is that so.

John: Have you been to Cairns?

Michiko: No, I haven't.

John: It has mountains and the ocean and is a beautiful place. It's famous for the Great Barrier Reef. Where are you from, Michiko?

Michiko: I am from Nagano. Please come to visit me sometime. The food is good, too.

John: By all means, I would love to.

単語
たんご
Vocabulary

🔊

Nouns

* オーストラリア		Australia
おかし	お菓子	snack; sweets
おしょうがつ	お正月	New Year's
おとこのこ	男の子	boy
おもちゃ		toy
おんなのこ	女の子	girl
がいこく	外国	foreign country
かしゅ	歌手	singer
キャンプ		camp
* こちら		this person (polite)
こんがっき	今学期	this semester
しゃちょう	社長	president of a company
じゅぎょう	授業	class
しょうらい	将来	future
* ドライブ		drive
ビール		beer
びじゅつかん	美術館	art museum
ホストファミリー		host family
みずうみ	湖	lake
* やま	山	mountain
ゆめ	夢	dream
ルームメート		roommate

U-verbs

うそをつく		to tell a lie
おなかがすく		to become hungry
かう	飼う	to own (a pet)
サボる		to cut classes
とる	取る	to take (a class); to get (a grade)
ならう	習う	to learn
のぼる	登る	to climb (*place* に)
はたらく	働く	to work

* Words that appear in the dialogue

Ru-verbs

つかれる	疲れる	to get tired
やめる		to quit

Irregular Verbs

けんかする		to have a fight; to quarrel
* しょうかいする	紹介する	to introduce (*person* に *person* を)
ダイエットする		to go on a diet
ちこくする	遅刻する	to be late (for an appointment)
りゅうがくする	留学する	to study abroad (*place* に)

Adverbs and Other Expressions

あと	後	after (an event) (*event* の)
* しゅっしん	出身	coming from (*place* の)
* すごく		very
そして		and then
* 〜だけ		just . . . ; only . . .
〜てん	〜点	. . . points
* ひさしぶり	久しぶり	it has been a long time
* まあまあ		okay; so-so
もっと		more

文法 Grammar
ぶん ぼう

1 ～たい

You can use a verb stem (the verb form that goes before ます) ＋たいです to describe your hope or aspiration.

今度の週末は、映画を見<u>たい</u>です。 *or* 映画が見<u>たい</u>です。
こんど しゅうまつ えいが み えいが み
I want to see a film this weekend.

いつか中国に行き<u>たい</u>です。
ちゅうごく い
I want to go to China someday.

verb stem ＋ たいです	*I want to do . . .*

As you can see in the first example above, having たい attached to a verb slightly affects the composition of the sentence. A verb that takes the particle を can have either the particle を or が when it is followed by たい. Particles other than を remain the same.

The combination of a verb and たい conjugates as an い-adjective. Here are examples of negative and past tense たい sentences.

あの人にはもう会い<u>たくありません</u>。
ひと あ
I don't want to see that person any more.

セーターが買い<u>たかった</u>から、デパートに行きました。
か い
I went to a department store, because I wanted to buy a sweater.

If your wish is one you have entertained for some time, that is, if you "have wanted to," you can use たいと思っています instead of たいです.
おも

たいです sentences are not usually used to describe wishes held by others. Somebody else's wishes are usually reported in Japanese either as quotations, observations, or guesses. To quote somebody, saying that she wants to do something, you can use と言っていました
い
with たい.

メアリーさんはトイレに行き<u>たい</u>と言っていました。
い い
Mary said she wanted to go to the bathroom.

To describe your observation to the effect that somebody wants to do something, you must use a special verb たがっている instead of たい. If a verb takes the particle を, the derived verb たがっている will retain the を, unlike たい, with which we had a choice between the particles が and を.

メアリーさんはコーヒーを飲みたがっています。
(It seems) Mary wants to drink coffee.

The verb たがっている, which comes from the dictionary form たがる, indicates "I think that she wants to, because of the way she is behaving." We will have more to say about this type of sentence in Lesson 14.

I want to . . . /Do you want to . . . ?	*They want to . . .*
• verb stem ＋ たいです	• verb stem ＋ たがっています
• たい conjugates as an い-adjective	• たがる conjugates as an *u*-verb
• が or を	• を only

2　〜たり〜たりする

You already know that you can connect two clauses with the *te*-form of predicates, as in:

大阪で買い物をして、韓国料理を食べます。
In Osaka, I will do some shopping and eat Korean food.

This sentence, however, tends to suggest that shopping and dining are *the only* activities you plan to perform in Osaka. If you want to avoid such implications and want to mention activities or events just *as exemplars*, thus leaving room for other things which are left unsaid, you can use a special predicate form 〜たり〜たりする.

大阪で買い物をしたり、韓国料理を食べたりします。
In Osaka, I will do such things as shopping and eating Korean dishes.

(activity A) たり　(activity B) たりする	*do such things as A and B*

To get the たり form of a predicate, you just add り to the past tense short form of a predicate. (Thus we have したり for the verb する, whose past tense is した, and 食べたり for 食べる, past tense 食べた.) Note that the helping verb する at the end of the sentence indicates the tense of the sentence. You can change a 〜たり〜たりする sentence into the past tense, or incorporate it in a bigger sentence, by working on the helping verb part.

週末は、勉強したり、友だちと話したり<u>しました</u>。
I studied and talked with my friends, among other things, over the weekend.

踊ったり、音楽を聞いたり<u>する</u>のが好きです。
I like dancing, listening to music, and so forth.

3 ～ことがある

The past tense short form of a verb ＋ ことがある describes that you did something, or something happened, in earlier times.

ヨーロッパに行った<u>ことがありますか</u>。 ― はい、行った<u>ことがあります</u>。
Have you ever been to Europe? *Yes, I have.*

たけしさんは授業を休んだ<u>ことがありません</u>。
Takeshi has never been absent from classes (in his life).

verb (past, short) ＋ ことがある	*have the experience of . . .*

4 noun A や noun B

や connects two nouns, as does と. や suggests that the things referred to are proposed as examples, and that you are not citing an exhaustive list.

A や B	*A and B, for example*

京都や奈良に行きました。
I went to Kyoto and Nara (for example, and may have visited other places as well).

表現ノート
ひょうげん

は in negative sentences▶ In negative sentences, you often find the particle は where you expect が or を. Observe the reply sentences in the following dialogues:

Q：山下先生はテレビを見ますか。 *Do you watch TV, Prof. Yamashita?*
A：いいえ、テレビは見ません。 *No, I don't.*

Q：コーヒーが飲みたいですか。 *Do you want to have a cup of coffee?*
A：いいえ、コーヒーは飲みたくありません。 *No, I don't.*

を and が, respectively, would not be ungrammatical in the above examples. Many Japanese speakers, however, find the は versions more natural.

The rule of thumb is that negative Japanese sentences tend to contain at least one は phrase. If you add 私は to the sentences above, therefore, the need for は is already fulfilled, and Japanese speakers feel much less compelled to use は after テレビ and コーヒー.

は may also follow particles like で and に.

英語では話したくありません。 *I don't want to speak in English.*
広島には行ったことがありません。 *I have never been to Hiroshima.*

だけ▶ You can add だけ to numbers to talk about having just that many items. だけ implies that you have something up to the amount needed, but not more than that.

私はその人に一回だけ会ったことがあります。
I have met that person just once.
一つだけ質問があります。 *I have just one question.*
三十分だけ寝ました。 *I slept for just thirty minutes.*

だけ suggests that you can live with that few, though the number admittedly could have been higher. We will learn another word in Lesson 14, namely, しか, which means "only" in the sense that you do not have enough of.

に▶ You can use the particle に to indicate the occasion on which you do something.

晩ごはんにサラダを食べました。 *I ate salad at dinner.*

に can also indicate the role you want something to play.

おみやげに絵葉書を買いました。 *I bought a postcard as a souvenir.*

ドライブ▶ドライブ is used when you go somewhere by car for pleasure. To say "to have a drive" or "to go for a drive," use ドライブに行く or ドライブする.

> 湖までドライブに行きました／ドライブしました。
> *I went for a drive to the lake.*

When you simply want to say "to drive a car" (not necessarily for pleasure), use 運転する instead.

> 日本で車を運転したことがありますか。
> *Have you ever driven a car in Japan?*

夢▶夢, like the English word "dream," has two meanings. One is the dream you have while sleeping; the others the dream that you wish would come true. To say "I have a dream," in Japanese, you use the verb 見る for sleeping dreams, and 持っている or ある for your visions.

> ゆうべこわい夢を見ました。   *I had a scary dream last night.*
> 夢を持っています／夢があります。   *I have a dream.*
> あなたの将来の夢は何ですか。   *What is your future dream?*

には▶ The particle は often follows the particle に in sentences describing a place in terms of the things that are found there.

> 東京には大きいデパートがたくさんあります。
> *There are lots of big department stores in Tokyo.*

> 私の大学にはいい日本語の先生がいます。
> *We have a good Japanese teacher in my college.*

These sentences would be okay without は, but there is a subtle difference between the versions with and without は. The は sentences are *about* the places; they answer questions (either explicitly asked, or implicit) like "What is Tokyo like?"

The sentences without は after に, on the other hand, are answers to a question like "Where do you find good teachers of Japanese?"

See the grammar note discussing the difference between が and は in Lesson 8. In the case of the particle に, the contrast is between the simple に and the combination には. (See also the grammar note on counting people in Lesson 7.)

練習 Practice
れん しゅう

Ⅰ ハンバーガーが食べたいです

A. Change the following phrases into 〜たい sentences. 🔊

Example: ハンバーガーを食べる
た

（はい）　　→　ハンバーガーが食べたいです。
た

（いいえ）　→　ハンバーガーが食べたくありません。
た

1. 湖に行く　（はい）
みずうみ い

2. 日本語のテープを聞く　（はい）
にほんご き

3. 旅行をする　（はい）
りょこう

4. ゆっくり休む　（いいえ）
やす

5. 会社の社長になる　（いいえ）
かいしゃ しゃちょう

6. 日本で働く　（はい）
にほん はたら

7. 車を買う　（はい）
くるま か

8. 日本に住む　（いいえ）
にほん す

9. 留学する　（はい）
りゅうがく

10. 山に登る　（いいえ）
やま のぼ

B. Pair Work—Ask if your partner wants to do the things above. When you answer, give reasons as in the example.

Example:　A：ハンバーガーが食べたいですか。
た

B：はい、食べたいです。おなかがすいていますから。
た

いいえ、食べたくありません。さっき食べましたから。
た た

C. Change the following phrases into 〜たい sentences in the past tense. 🔊

Example:

おもちゃの電車で遊ぶ
でんしゃ あそ

（はい）　　→　子供の時、おもちゃの電車で遊びたかったです。
こども とき でんしゃ あそ

（いいえ）　→　子供の時、おもちゃの電車で遊びたくありませんでした。
こども とき でんしゃ あそ

1. テレビを見る　（はい）
み

2. 飛行機に乗る　（はい）
ひこうき の

3. お風呂に入る　（いいえ）
ふろ はい

4. 犬を飼う　（はい）
いぬ か

5. 学校をやめる　（いいえ）
がっこう

6. 魚を食べる　（いいえ）
さかな た

7. 男の子／女の子と話す　（いいえ）
おとこ こ おんな こ はな

8. ピアノを習う　（いいえ）
なら

9. 車を運転する　（はい）
   <ruby>車<rt>くるま</rt></ruby><ruby>運転<rt>うんてん</rt></ruby>

10. 有名になる　（はい）
    <ruby>有名<rt>ゆうめい</rt></ruby>

11. ミッキー・マウスに会う　（はい）
    <ruby>会<rt>あ</rt></ruby>

D. Pair Work—Ask if your partner wanted to do the things above during their childhood.

E. Pair Work—Ask your partner the following questions and report the answers as in the example.

Example:　A：けんさんは何が食べたいですか。
　　　　　　　　　　<ruby>何<rt>なに</rt></ruby>　<ruby>食<rt>た</rt></ruby>

　　　　　　B：ピザが食べたいです。
　　　　　　　　　　<ruby>食<rt>た</rt></ruby>

　　　→　A：けんさんはピザが食べたいと言っていました。
　　　　　　　　　　　　　　　<ruby>食<rt>た</rt></ruby>　　　<ruby>言<rt>い</rt></ruby>

　　　　　けんさんはピザを食べたがっています。
　　　　　　　　　　　　　　<ruby>食<rt>た</rt></ruby>

1. 昼ごはんに何が食べたいですか。
   <ruby>昼<rt>ひる</rt></ruby>　<ruby>何<rt>なに</rt></ruby><ruby>食<rt>た</rt></ruby>

2. 何がいちばん買いたいですか。
   <ruby>何<rt>なに</rt></ruby>　<ruby>買<rt>か</rt></ruby>

3. どこにいちばん行きたいですか。
   　　　　　　<ruby>行<rt>い</rt></ruby>

4. だれにいちばん会いたいですか。
   　　　　　　<ruby>会<rt>あ</rt></ruby>

5. 何が習いたいですか。
   <ruby>何<rt>なに</rt></ruby>　<ruby>習<rt>なら</rt></ruby>

6. 今週の週末、何がしたいですか。
   <ruby>今週<rt>こんしゅう</rt></ruby>　<ruby>週末<rt>しゅうまつ</rt></ruby><ruby>何<rt>なに</rt></ruby>

7. 何がしたくありませんか。
   <ruby>何<rt>なに</rt></ruby>

8. 子供の時、何になりたかったですか。
   <ruby>子供<rt>こども</rt></ruby>　<ruby>時<rt>とき</rt></ruby><ruby>何<rt>なに</rt></ruby>

9. 将来、何になりたいですか。
   <ruby>将来<rt>しょうらい</rt></ruby>　<ruby>何<rt>なに</rt></ruby>

10. 今学期の後、何がしたいですか。
    <ruby>今学期<rt>こんがっき</rt></ruby>　<ruby>後<rt>あと</rt></ruby>　<ruby>何<rt>なに</rt></ruby>

Additional Vocabulary——職業 (Occupations)
<ruby>職業<rt>しょくぎょう</rt></ruby>

さっか（作家）	writer	ジャーナリスト	journalist
けいさつかん（警察官）	police officer	しゅふ（主婦）	housewife
はいゆう（俳優）	actor/actress	じょゆう（女優）	actress
かんごし（看護師）	nurse	しょうぼうし（消防士）	firefighter
べんごし（弁護士）	lawyer		
やきゅうせんしゅ（野球選手）	baseball player		
だいとうりょう（大統領）	president of a country		

F. Complete the following sentences.

1. 今日はいい天気だから、＿＿＿＿＿＿＿＿＿＿＿＿たいです。
   きょう　　　　てんき

2. あしたは休みだから、＿＿＿＿＿＿＿＿＿＿＿＿たいです。
   　　　やす

3. 疲れたから、＿＿＿＿＿＿＿＿＿＿＿＿たくありません。
   つか

4. 田中さんはいじわるだから、一緒に＿＿＿＿＿＿＿＿たくありません。
   たなか　　　　　　　　　いっしょ

5. 高校の時、もっと＿＿＿＿＿＿＿＿＿＿＿たかったです。
   こうこう　とき

⑪ 掃除したり、洗濯したりします
そうじ　　　せんたく

A. Tell what the following people did on the weekend using 〜たり〜たりする.

Example:　ジョン: saw temples in Kyoto, went to a museum, etc.

→　ジョンさんはお寺を見たり、美術館に行ったりしました。
　　　　　　　　てら　み　　　びじゅつかん　い

1. たけし: went camping, went for a drive, etc.

2. きょうこ: made sweets, read books at home, etc.

3. スー: went to Osaka to have fun, went to eat, etc.

4. けん: cleaned his room, did laundry, etc.

5. ロバート: met friends, watched videos, etc.

6. 山下先生: went to a hot spring, rested, etc.
   やましたせんせい

B. Look at the pictures and make your own sentences using 〜たり〜たりする.

C. Pair Work—Ask your partner the following questions. When you answer, use 〜たり〜たりする as in the example.

Example:　A：日本で何をしたいですか。
　　　　　　B：日本のお菓子を食べたり、富士山 (Mt. Fuji) に登ったりしたいです。

1. 週末よく何をしますか。
2. デートの時、何をしますか。
3. あなたの国ではお正月に何をしますか。
4. 子供の時、よく何をしましたか。
5. 日本で何をしますか／しましたか。
6. 冬休み／夏休みに何をしましたか。
7. クラスで何をしてはいけませんか。
8. 今度の週末、何をするつもりですか。
9. 何をするのが好きですか／きらいですか。

Ⅲ 有名人に会ったことがありますか

A. The following are what John has or hasn't done. Make the sentences using 〜ことがある.

Example:　○ eat tempura　→　天ぷらを食べたことがあります。
　　　　　　✕ go to Tokyo　→　東京に行ったことがありません。

1. ○ eat sushi
2. ○ study French
3. ○ work at a restaurant
4. ✕ go to Hiroshima
5. ✕ write love letters
6. ○ sleep in class
7. ○ climb Mt. Fuji
8. ✕ drive a car in Japan
9. ✕ see Japanese movies

B. Pair Work—Make questions using 〜ことがある and ask your partner.

Example:　日本のお酒を飲む
　　　→　A：日本のお酒を飲んだことがありますか。
　　　　　B：はい、あります。
　　　　　A：どうでしたか。
　　　　　B：おいしかったです。

1. ダイエットをする　　　2. テストで0点を取る
3. 英語を教える　　　　　4. 有名人に会う
5. カラオケに行く　　　　6. ふぐ (blowfish) を食べる
7. 中国語を勉強する　　　8. 新幹線に乗る
9. うそをつく　　　　　 10. 日本料理を作る
11. 遅刻する　　　　　　 12. 授業をサボる
13. 友だち／ルームメート／ホストファミリーとけんかする
14. 留学する

Ⅳ すしや天ぷらをよく食べます

Pair Work—Ask your partner the following questions. When you answer, use ～や～ as in the example.

Example:　A：どんな日本料理をよく食べますか。
　　　　　B：すしや天ぷらをよく食べます。

1. どんなスポーツをよく見ますか。
2. どんな音楽が好きですか。
3. どんな料理をよく作りますか。
4. あなたの大学の食堂には、どんな食べ物がありますか。
5. あなたの大学には、どこの国の人がいますか。
6. 外国に行ったことがありますか。どこですか。
7. 今、どんな授業を取っていますか。
8. 俳優 (actors) の中で、だれが好きですか。
9. 歌手の中で、だれが好きですか。

Ⅴ まとめの練習
ⓥ れんしゅう

A. Talk about your dream for the future or what it was when you were a child.

1. あなたの夢は何ですか。
   ゆめ　なん

   Example: 私は将来、お金持ちになりたいです。そして、いろいろな国に行き
   わたし しょうらい　かね も　　　　　　　　　　　　　　　　　くに　い
   たいです。

2. 子供の時の夢は何でしたか。
   こども　とき　ゆめ　なん

   Example: 子供の時、歌手になりたかったです。
   こども　とき　か しゅ

B. Class Activity—Find someone who . . .

1. has seen celebrities _____

2. has never used chopsticks _____

3. wants to live in Japan in the future _____

4. wanted to be a star（スター）as a child _____

5. wants to cut classes tomorrow _____

6. doesn't want to go out today _____

C. Class Activity—Bring pictures of your hometown and describe it.

Example:

私はニューヨークの出身です。ニューヨークはとても大きくてにぎやかです。
わたし　　　　　　　　　しゅっしん　　　　　　　　　　　　　　　　　おお

きれいな公園や有名な美術館やたくさんの劇場 (theater) があります。
こうえん ゆうめい びじゅつかん　　　　　げきじょう

よくミュージカルを見たり、公園で散歩したりしました。
み　　こうえん さん ぽ

夏休みに帰って、友だちに会いたいです。
なつやす　かえ　　とも　あ

日本語のクラスで
にほんご

In the Japanese Class

Useful Expressions

どちらでもいいです。———— Both are fine.

同じです。———————— Same thing.
おな

だいたい同じです。———— More or less the same.
おな

ちょっと違います。———— A little different.
ちが

使えません。———————— Can't use it.
つか

間違っています。———— It's wrong.
まちが

手をあげてください。———— Raise your hand.
て

読んできてください。———— Read it before coming to class.
よ

宿題を出してください。———— Hand in the homework.
しゅくだい だ

教科書を閉じてください。———— Close the textbook.
きょうかしょ と

となりの人に聞いてください。———— Ask the person sitting next to you.
ひと き

やめてください。———— The time is up. Please stop.

今日はこれで終わります。———— That's it for today.
きょう お

しつもんが
ありますか

Useful Vocabulary

宿題————————homework
しゅくだい

しめきり————deadline

練習————————exercise
れんしゅう

意味————————meaning
いみ

発音————————pronunciation
はつおん

文法————————grammar
ぶんぽう

質問————————question
しつもん

答————————answer
こたえ

例————————example
れい

かっこ————( )

まる————○ (correct)

ばつ————× (wrong)

くだけた言い方————colloquial expression
い かた

かたい言い方————bookish expression
い かた

ていねいな言い方——polite expression
い かた

方言————————dialect
ほうげん

標準語————standard Japanese
ひょうじゅんご

たとえば————for example

ほかに————anything else

〜番————number . . .
ばん

〜ページ————page number . . .

〜行目————line number . . .
ぎょうめ

二人ずつ————two people each
ふたり

第12課 LESSON 12

病気 Feeling Ill
びょう き

会話 Dialogue
かい わ

🔊

Ⓘ Mary and Michiko are talking at school.

1 みちこ： メアリーさん、元気がありませんね。
げん き

2 メアリー： うーん。ちょっとおなかが痛いんです。
いた

3 みちこ： どうしたんですか。

4 メアリー： きのう友だちと晩ごはんを食べに行ったんです。たぶん食べすぎたん
とも ばん た い た

5 だと思います。
おも

6 みちこ： 大丈夫ですか。
だいじょう ぶ

7 メアリー： ええ。心配しないでください。……ああ、痛い。
しんぱい いた

8 みちこ： 病院に行ったほうがいいですよ。
びょういん い

Ⅱ At a hospital.

1 メアリー： 先生、のどが痛いんです。きのうはおなかが痛かったんです。
せんせい いた いた

2 医 者： ああ、そうですか。熱もありますね。かぜですね。
い しゃ ねつ

3 メアリー： あの、もうすぐテニスの試合があるので、練習しなくちゃいけないん
しあい れんしゅう

4 ですが……。

5 医 者： 二三日、運動しないほうがいいでしょう。
い しゃ に さんにち うんどう

6 メアリー： わかりました。

7 医 者： 今日は薬を飲んで、早く寝てください。
い しゃ きょう くすり の はや ね

8 メアリー： はい、ありがとうございました。

9 医 者： お大事に。
い しゃ だい じ

Ⅰ

Michiko: You don't look well, Mary.

Mary: Um . . . I have a little stomachache.

Michiko: What's the matter?

Mary: I went out to have dinner with my friend yesterday. I think maybe I ate too much.

Michiko: Are you all right?

Mary: Yes. Don't worry about it. Oh, it hurts.

Michiko: You had better go to a hospital.

Ⅱ

Mary: Doctor, I have a sore throat. I had a stomachache yesterday.

Doctor: I see. You have a fever, too. It is just a cold.

Mary: Well, I will have a tennis tournament soon, so I have to practice, though . . .

Doctor: You had better not exercise for a couple of days.

Mary: I understand.

Doctor: Take medicine and go to bed early tonight.

Mary: Yes. Thank you so much.

Doctor: Take care.

単語
Vocabulary

Nouns

	あし	足	leg; foot
	いみ	意味	meaning
*	おなか		stomach
*	かぜ	風邪	cold
	かのじょ	彼女	girlfriend
	かれ	彼	boyfriend
	きおん	気温	temperature (weather—not used for things)
	くもり	曇り	cloudy weather
*	しあい	試合	match; game
	ジュース		juice
	せいじ	政治	politics
	せいせき	成績	grade (on a test, etc.)
	せき		cough
*	のど		throat
	は	歯	tooth
	はな	花	flower
	はれ	晴れ	sunny weather
	ふく	服	clothes
	ふつかよい	二日酔い	hangover
	プレゼント		present
	ホームシック		homesickness
	もの	物	thing (concrete object)
	ゆき	雪	snow
	ようじ	用事	business to take care of

い-adjectives

	あまい	甘い	sweet
*	いたい	痛い	hurt; painful
	おおい	多い	there are many . . .
	せまい	狭い	narrow; not spacious
	つごうがわるい	都合が悪い	inconvenient; to have a scheduling conflict
	わるい	悪い	bad

* Words that appear in the dialogue

な-adjective

すてき(な)	素敵	fantastic

U-verbs

かぜをひく	風邪をひく	to catch a cold
きょうみがある	興味がある	to be interested (in . . .) (*topic* に)
なくす		to lose
* ねつがある	熱がある	to have a fever
のどがかわく	のどが渇く	to become thirsty

Ru-verbs

せきがでる	せきが出る	to cough
わかれる	別れる	to break up; to separate (*person* と)

Irregular Verbs

きんちょうする	緊張する	to get nervous
* しんぱいする	心配する	to worry

Adverbs and Other Expressions

いつも		always
* おだいじに	お大事に	Get well soon.
* げんきがない	元気がない	don't look well
* たぶん	多分	probably; maybe
できるだけ		as much as possible
* 〜でしょう		probably; . . . , right?
〜ど	〜度	. . . degrees (temperature)
* にさんにち	二三日	for two to three days
* 〜ので		because . . .
はじめて	初めて	for the first time
* もうすぐ		very soon; in a few moments/days

文法 G r a m m a r
ぶん ぼう

1　～んです

There are two distinct ways to make a statement in Japanese. One way is to simply report the facts as they are observed. This is the mode of speech that we have learned so far. In this lesson, we will learn a new way: the mode of *explaining* things.

A *report* is an isolated description of a fact. When you are late for an appointment, you can already report in Japanese what has happened, バスが来ませんでした. This sentence, however, does not have the right apologetic tone, because it is not offered as an explanation for anything. If you want to mention the busses failing to run on time as an excuse for being late, you will need to use the *explanation* mode of speech, and say:

バスが来なかったんです。　　　*(As it happens,) the bus didn't come.*

An explanation has two components, one that is explicitly described in the sentence (the bus not coming), and another, which is implied, or explained, by it (you being late for the appointment). The sentence-final expression んです serves as the link between what the sentence says and what it accounts for. Compare:

あしたテストがあります。　*I have an exam tomorrow.* (a simple observation)

あしたテストがあるんです。*I have an exam tomorrow. (So I can't go out tonight.)*

トイレに行きたいです。　　*I want to go to the bathroom.* (declaration of one's wish)

トイレに行きたいんです。　*I want to go to the bathroom. (So tell me where it is.)*

んです goes after the short form of a predicate. The predicate can be either in the affirmative or in the negative, either in the present tense or in the past tense. んです itself is invariant and does not usually appear in the negative or the past tense forms.[1] In writing, it is more common to find のです instead of んです.

成績がよくないんです。(in response to the question, "Why do you look so upset?")
せいせき
(As a matter of fact) My grade is not good.

---

[1] In casual exchanges, んです appears in its short form, んだ. In casual questions, んですか is replaced by の. We will examine these further in Lesson 15.

試験が終わったんです。(explaining to a person who has caught you smiling)
しけん　お
The exam is over. (That's why I'm smiling.)

When it follows a noun or a な-adjective, な comes in between.

	report sentences	explanation sentences
な-adjective:	静かです しず	静かなんです しず
noun:	学生です がくせい	学生なんです がくせい

You can use んです in questions to invite explanations and further clarifications from the person you are talking to. It is very often used together with question words, such as どうして (why) and どうした (what has happened).

Q：どうして彼と別れたんですか。
　　　かれ　わか
Why did you break up with your boyfriend? (You've got to tell me.)

A：彼、ぜんぜんお風呂に入らないんです。
　　かれ　　　　ふろ　はい
Oh, him. He never takes a bath. (That's a good enough reason, isn't it?)

Q：どうしたんですか。
What happened? (You look shattered.)

A：猫が死んだんです。[2]
　　ねこ　し
My cat died. (That should explain how I look today.)

You can also use んです to provide an additional comment on what has just been said.

A：とてもいい教科書ですね。
　　　　　　　きょうかしょ
That's a great textbook that you are using.

B：ええ。私の大学の先生が書いたんです。
　　　　わたし　だいがく　せんせい　か
You bet. The professors at my university wrote it (for your information).

---

[2]A どうしたんですか question is best answered by a んです sentence with the subject marked with the particle が rather than は, as in this example. See Lesson 8 for a related discussion.

2 〜すぎる

Verb stems may be followed by the helping verb すぎる, which means "too much," or "to excess." すぎる conjugates as a regular *ru*-verb.

食べ<u>すぎて</u>はいけません。	*You must not eat too much.*
早く起き<u>すぎました</u>。	*I got up too early.*

すぎる can also follow い- and な-adjective bases (the parts which do not change in conjugations); you drop the い and な at the end of the adjectives and then add すぎる.

（高い）	この本は高<u>すぎます</u>。	*This book is too expensive.*
（親切な）	あの人は親切<u>すぎます</u>。	*That person is too nice.*

3 〜ほうがいいです

ほうがいいです "it is better (for you) to do . . ." is a sentence-final expression that you can use to give advice. When you suggest an activity with ほうがいいです, you are giving a very specific piece of advice; namely, that it is advisable to do it, and if one does not follow the advice, there is a danger or a problem.

ほうがいいです is peculiar in that it follows different tense forms, depending on whether the advice given is in the affirmative or the negative. When the advice is in the affirmative, ほうがいいです generally follows the past tense short form of a verb. When the advice is in the negative, however, the verb is in the *present* tense short form.

もっと野菜を<u>食べた</u>ほうがいいですよ。	*You'd better eat more vegetables.*
授業を<u>休まない</u>ほうがいいですよ。	*It is better not to skip classes.*

4 〜ので

You can use ので to give the reason for the situation described in the balance of the sentence. Semantically, ので is just like から. Stylistically, ので sounds slightly more formal than から.

(reason) ので (situation)。	(situation), *because* (reason).	

いつも日本語で話す<u>ので</u>、日本語が上手になりました。
My Japanese has improved, because I always speak Japanese.

宿題がたくさんあった<u>ので</u>、きのうの夜、寝ませんでした。
I did not sleep last night, because I had a lot of homework.

The reason part of a sentence ends in a short form predicate. When ので follows a な-adjective or a noun, な comes in between, as it did with the explanatory predicate んです.

その人はいじわる<u>な</u><u>ので</u>、きらいです。
I do not like that person, because he is mean.

今日は日曜日<u>な</u><u>ので</u>、銀行は休みです。
Banks are closed, because today is a Sunday.

5　～なくちゃいけません

We use なくちゃいけません[3] to say that it is necessary to do something, or "must."

来週テストがあるから、たくさん勉強し<u>なくちゃいけません</u>。
I have to study a lot, because there will be an exam next week.

なくちゃ means "if you do not do . . ." and いけません roughly means "you cannot go"; なくちゃいけません therefore means "you cannot go not doing . . ." with the double negatives giving rise to the affirmative sense of the mandate. To form a なくちゃいけません sentence, we substitute ない in the negative short form of a verb with なくちゃ.

verb	short negative	"must"
食べる	食べ<u>ない</u>	食べ<u>なくちゃいけません</u>
言う	言わ<u>ない</u>	言わ<u>なくちゃいけません</u>
する	し<u>ない</u>	し<u>なくちゃいけません</u>
くる	こ<u>ない</u>	こ<u>なくちゃいけません</u>

いけません is grammatically the negative long form of a verb in the present tense. You can change なくちゃいけません to なくちゃいけませんでした (past tense) to say you *had to*, and to なくちゃいけない (the short form, present tense) in casual speech and before elements like んです.

---

[3]In writing and in very formal speech, なく<u>ては</u>いけません is more common than なく<u>ちゃ</u>いけません.

けさは、六時に起きなくちゃいけませんでした。(long form, past)
I had to get up at six this morning.

毎日、練習しなくちゃいけないんです。(short form, present)
(The truth is,) I must practice every day.

6 ～でしょう

We use the sentence-final expression でしょう (probably) when we are making a guess or a prediction. でしょう follows verbs and い-adjectives in short forms, in the affirmative and in the negative.[4]

(verb)

あしたは雨が降るでしょう。 　　　　　　 *It will probably rain tomorrow.*
　　　降らないでしょう。 　　　　　　 *It will probably not rain tomorrow.*

(い-adjective)

北海道は寒いでしょう。 　　　　　　 *It is probably cold in Hokkaido.*
　　　寒くないでしょう。 　　　　　　 *It is probably not cold in Hokkaido.*

でしょう may also follow な-adjective bases and nouns. Note that でしょう goes directly after these elements; we do not use ×～なでしょう, ×～のでしょう, or ×～だでしょう.

(な-adjective)

山下先生は魚が好きでしょう。 　　　　 *Professor Yamashita probably likes fish.*
　　　好きじゃないでしょう。 　　　　 *Professor Yamashita probably doesn't like fish.*

(noun)

あの人はオーストラリア人でしょう。 　 *That person is probably an Australian.*
　　　オーストラリア人じゃないでしょう。 *That person is probably not an Australian.*

---

[4] でしょう may also follow predicates in the past tense. We will, however, concentrate on the present tense examples in this lesson.

でしょう sentences can be turned into questions (〜でしょうか), which can be used to invite another person's opinion or guess.

日本語と韓国語と、どっちのほうが難しいでしょうか。
Which would you say is more difficult, Japanese or Korean?

The short form of でしょう is だろう. You can use it to cautiously phrase a prediction or an analysis.

たけしさんは興味があるだろうと思います。
I think Takeshi would be interested in it.

In casual exchanges, you can use でしょう (with the question intonation, and most often pronounced as somewhat shorter でしょ) when you want to check if your partner agrees that you have the correct understanding about what you have just said.

ジョン、中国語がわかるでしょ？ これ、読んで。
John, you understand Chinese, right? Can you read this for me?

練習 Practice

れん しゅう

① どうしたんですか

A. You are in the following situations. Explain them using 〜んです.

Example: 頭が痛いです
あたま いた
→ Q：どうしたんですか。
A：頭が痛いんです。
あたま いた

(1) 彼から電話が
かれ でんわ
ありました

(2) プレゼントを
もらいました

(3) あしたは休みです
やす

(4) きのうは
誕生日でした
たんじょうび

(5) テストが難しく
むずか
ありませんでした

(6) のどが痛いです
いた

(7) かぜをひきました

(8) 切符をなくしました
きっぷ

(9) あしたテストがあります

(10) せきが出ます
で

(11) 彼女と別れました
かのじょ　わか

B. Respond to the comments using 〜んです.

Example:

すてきな車ですね。
くるま

My father's　→　父のなんです。
ちち

(1)

きれいな花ですね。
はな

I received them
from my friend.

(2)

新しい靴ですね。
あたら　　くつ

Italian ones

(3)

すてきなセーター
ですね。

My mother made it.

(4)

いいかばんですね。

It was cheap.

(5)

かっこいい彼ですね。
かれ

kind

C. Pair Work—Your partner has said something nice about what you have. Respond using 〜んです.

Example:　B：すてきな時計ですね。
　　　　　　　A：友だちにもらったんです。

D. Pair Work—Make up dialogues asking for reasons.

Example:　I went to Tokyo last week.

→　A：先週東京に行きました。
　　B：どうして東京に行ったんですか。
　　A：母がアメリカから来たんです。

1. I am very tired.
2. I have no money.
3. It is not convenient today.（都合が悪い）
4. I want to marry my boyfriend/girlfriend.
5. I am going to Japan to study.
6. He speaks Chinese very well.（中国語が上手です）
7. I don't want to watch that movie.

Ⅱ 食べすぎました

A. Describe the following pictures using 〜すぎる. Use "verb ＋ すぎる" for (1) through (4) and "adjective ＋ すぎる" for (5) through (10). 🔊

Example:

→　作りすぎました。

→　この部屋はせますぎます。

(1)   (2)   (3)

(4)   (5)   (6)   (7)

(8)   (9)   (10)

B. Look at the verbs below. Think about the results of over doing these things and make sentences as in the example.

Example: 食べる → 食べすぎたから、おなかが痛いんです。

1. 飲む
2. 勉強する
3. コンピューターを使う
4. 本を読む
5. テニスをする
6. 甘い物を食べる
7. 歌を歌う
8. 緊張する

Ⅲ 薬を飲んだほうがいいです
くすり の

A. Using the cues below, give advice to a friend who has a headache. Decide if you should use the affirmative or the negative. 🔊

Example: 薬を飲む → B：頭が痛いんです。
くすり の　　　　　　　あたま いた

A：薬を飲んだほうがいいですよ。
くすり の

1. 早く寝る　　　　2. 遊びに行く　　　　3. 病院に行く
はや ね　　　　　　　あそ い　　　　　　びょういん い

4. 仕事を休む　　　5. うちに帰る　　　　6. 運動する
し ごと やす　　　　　　　かえ　　　　　　うんどう

B. Pair Work—Give advice to your partner in the following situations, using 〜ほうがいい.

Example: 日本語が上手になりたい
に ほん ご じょう ず

→ B：日本語が上手になりたいんです。
に ほん ご じょう ず

A：日本人の友だちを作ったほうがいいですよ。
に ほん じん とも つく

できるだけ英語を話さないほうがいいですよ。
えい ご はな

1. ホームシックだ　　　2. やせたい　　　　　3. 友だちとけんかした
とも

4. お金がない　　　　　5. 成績が悪い　　　　6. 二日酔いだ
かね　　　　　　　　せいせき わる　　　　　ふつか よ

7. 歯が痛い　　　　　　8. 教科書をなくした　9. いつも授業に遅刻する
は いた　　　　　　きょうか しょ　　　　　じゅぎょう ち こく

C. Pair Work—You are a health counselor. Someone who hasn't been feeling well is at your office. Ask the following questions. Complete this form first, then give your advice using 〜ほうがいい.

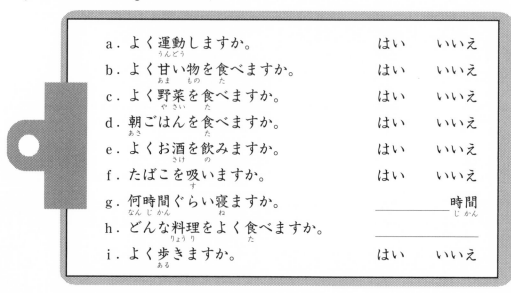

a. よく運動しますか。　　　　　　　　　はい　　いいえ
うんどう

b. よく甘い物を食べますか。　　　　　　はい　　いいえ
あま もの た

c. よく野菜を食べますか。　　　　　　　はい　　いいえ
や さい た

d. 朝ごはんを食べますか。　　　　　　　はい　　いいえ
あさ た

e. よくお酒を飲みますか。　　　　　　　はい　　いいえ
さけ の

f. たばこを吸いますか。　　　　　　　　はい　　いいえ
す

g. 何時間ぐらい寝ますか。　　　　　　　_____時間
なん じ かん ね　　　　　　　　　　　　じ かん

h. どんな料理をよく食べますか。　　　　_____
りょう り た

i. よく歩きますか。　　　　　　　　　　はい　　いいえ
ある

ⅣⅤ いい天気なので、散歩します

A. Connect the two sentences using 〜ので. 🔊

Example: いい天気です／散歩します
→ いい天気なので、散歩します。

1. 安いです／買います
2. あの映画はおもしろくありません／見たくありません
3. 今週は忙しかったです／疲れています
4. 病気でした／授業を休みました
5. 彼女はいつも親切です／人気があります
6. 政治に興味がありません／新聞を読みません
7. あしたテストがあります／勉強します
8. のどがかわきました／ジュースが飲みたいです
9. 歩きすぎました／足が痛いです

B. Make sentences using the cues below as reasons, according to the example.

Example: かぜをひきました → かぜをひいたので、授業を休みました。

1. お金がありません
2. おなかがすいています
3. ホームシックです
4. 用事があります
5. 単語の意味がわかりません
6. 疲れました

C. Fill in the blanks with appropriate words.

1. _____ので、中国に行きたいです。

2. _____ので、人気があります。

3. _____ので、かぜをひきました。

4. _____ので、別れました。

5. _____ので、日本に住みたくありません。

6. _____ので、遅刻しました。

7. _____ので、緊張しています。

Ⓥ 七時に起きなくちゃいけません
しち じ お

A. Look at Tom's schedule and make sentences, according to the example. 🔊

Example: 7:00 A.M.／起きる → トムさんは七時に起きなくちゃいけません。
お しち じ お

7:00 A.M.	Ex. 起きる お
8:00 A.M.	(1) うちを出る で
9:00 A.M.	(2) 授業に出る じゅぎょう で
1:00 P.M.	(3) 山下先生に会う やましたせんせい あ
2:00 P.M.	(4) 英語を教える えいご おし
3:00 P.M.	(5) LLに行って、テープを聞く エルエル い き
5:00 P.M.	(6) うちに帰る かえ
6:00 P.M.	(7) ホストファミリーと晩ごはんを食べる ばん た
8:00 P.M.	(8) 宿題をする しゅくだい
9:00 P.M.	(9) お風呂に入る ふ ろ はい
10:00 P.M.	(10) 薬を飲む くすり の
11:00 P.M.	(11) うちに電話をかける でんわ

B. Pair Work—Invite the partner to do the following things together. Turn down the invitation and give an explanation using 〜なくちゃいけない。

Example: play tennis

→ A：あしたの朝、一緒にテニスをしませんか。
あさ いっしょ

B：ちょっと都合が悪いんです。あしたは授業に出なくちゃいけ
つ ごう わる じゅぎょう で
ないんです。

1. do homework   2. eat lunch   3. drink coffee
4. study in the library   5. go to karaoke

C. Answer the following questions.

1. 日本語の授業で何をしなくちゃいけませんか。
2. 日本で外国人は何をしなくちゃいけませんか。
3. かっこよくなりたいんです。何をしなくちゃいけませんか。
4. 友だちが遊びに来ます。何をしなくちゃいけませんか。
5. あしたは初めてのデートです。何をしなくちゃいけませんか。
6. 子供の時、何をしなくちゃいけませんでしたか。

Ⅵ あしたは晴れでしょう

A. Here is tomorrow's weather forecast (天気予報). Play the role of a meteorologist and tell the weather forecasts for each city. 🔊

Examples:　Tokyo/snow

→　東京はあした雪でしょう。

temperature in Tokyo/around 2℃

→　東京の気温は、二度ぐらいでしょう。

city	weather		temperature
Tokyo	Ex. snow		Ex. around 2℃
Sydney	(1) sunny	(2) hot	(3) around 30℃
Hong Kong	(4) rain	(5) cool	(6) around 18℃
Rome	(7) cloudy	(8) warm	(9) around 20℃

B. Pair Work—Play the role of a meteorologist. Predict the weather for your favorite city. The other person fills in the blanks. Switch roles and do the same thing.

city	weather	temperature

Ⅶ まとめの練習
れんしゅう

A. Using Dialogue Ⅰ as a model, make skits in the following situations.

　　—Your friend looks sad.
　　—Your friend looks happy.

B. Pair Work—A and B are deciding when they can play tennis together. Play the role of A and B. Discuss your schedules and find the day on which both of you are available. Refer to p. 245 for B's schedule.

　　Example:　A：来週の月曜日に一緒にテニスをしませんか。
　　　　　　　　　らいしゅう　げつよう び　いっしょ
　　　　　　　　B：来週の月曜日はちょっと都合が悪いんです。英語を教えなくちゃ
　　　　　　　　　らいしゅう　げつよう び　　　　　　　つ ごう　わる　　　　えい ご　　おし
　　　　　　　　　いけないんです。日曜日はどうですか。
　　　　　　　　　　　　　　　　にちよう び

　　　　　A's schedule

Sunday	go shopping
Monday	
Tuesday	read books
Wednesday	
Thursday	
Friday	meet friends
Saturday	

C. Role Play—Visiting a Doctor's Office

Using Dialogue Ⅱ as a model, act the role of a doctor or a patient.

Doctor—Fill out the medical report on p. 245 and give advice to the patient.

Patient—Describe the symptoms you have and answer the doctor's questions.

Sex: ☐ Male ☐ Female

Age:

Symptoms: ☐ Sore throat

☐ Headache

☐ Stomachache

☐ Any other pain

☐ Cough

☐ Fever

☐ Allergy（アレルギー）

☐ Others

Pair Work Ⅶ B.

Example: A：来週の月曜日に一緒にテニスをしませんか。
らいしゅう げつようび いっしょ

B：来週の月曜日はちょっと都合が悪いんです。英語を教えなくちゃ
らいしゅう げつようび つごう わる えいご おし
いけないんです。日曜日はどうですか。
にちようび

B's schedule

Sunday	
Monday	teach English
Tuesday	
Wednesday	clean rooms, do laundry, etc.
Thursday	
Friday	
Saturday	practice karate

健康と病気
けん こう びょう き
H e a l t h   a n d   I l l n e s s

At the Reception of the Clinic

Patient: すみません、初めてなんですが。
はじ
Excuse me, this is my first visit.

Receptionist: はい、保険証を見せてください。
ほけんしょう み
OK. Please show me your health insurance certificate.

この紙に名前と住所を書いてください。
かみ なまえ じゅうしょ か
Please fill in your name and address on this paper.

* * *

Patient: これは何の薬ですか。
なん くすり
What kinds of medicine are these?

Receptionist: 痛み止めです。食後に飲んでください。
いた ど しょくご の
These are painkillers. Please take one after meals.

Patient: わかりました。
I see.

Receptionist: お大事に。
だいじ
Please take care.

Useful Expressions for Illness（病気）and Injuries（けが）
びょう き

下痢です。————————I have diarrhea.
げ り
便秘です。————————I am constipated.
べん ぴ
生理です。————————I have my period.
せい り
花粉症です。———————I have hay fever.
か ふんしょう
（〜に）アレルギーがあります。——I have an allergy to . . .

虫歯があります。—————I have a bad tooth.
むし ば
くしゃみが出ます。————I sneeze.
で
鼻水が出ます。————I have a runny nose.
はなみず で
背中がかゆいです。————My back itches.
せ なか
発疹があります。—————I have rashes.
はっしん

めまいがします。─────────── I feel dizzy.

吐きました。─────────── I threw up.
は

気分が悪いです。─────────── I am not feeling well.
き ぶん わる

やけどをしました。─────────── I burned myself.

足の骨を折りました。─────────── I broke my leg.
あし ほね お

けがをしました。─────────── I hurt myself.

Useful Vocabulary

● 医者（Doctor's office）
いしゃ

内科─────── physician
ない か

皮膚科─────── dermatologist
ひ ふ か

外科─────── surgeon
げ か

産婦人科─────── obstetrician and gynecologist
さん ふ じん か

整形外科─────── orthopedic surgeon
せいけい げ か

眼科─────── ophthalmologist
がん か

歯科─────── dentist
し か

耳鼻科─────── otorhinolaryngologist; ENT doctor
じ び か

● その他（Miscellaneous）
た

抗生物質─────── antibiotic
こうせいぶっしつ

レントゲン─────── X-ray

手術─────── operation
しゅじゅつ

注射─────── injection
ちゅうしゃ

体温計─────── thermometer
たいおんけい

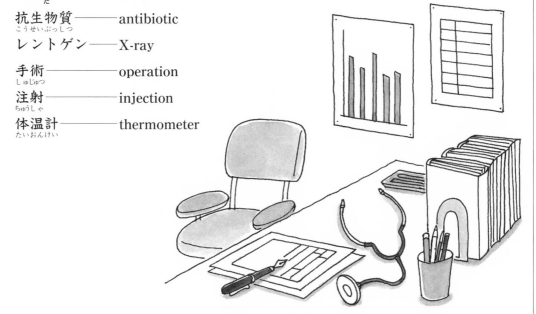

読み書き編
よかへん

読み書き編 ●もくじ

第 9 課 **スーさんの日記** Sue's Diary —————————————— 292

午 後 前 名 白 雨 書 友 間 家 話 少 古 知 来

第 10 課 **かさじぞう** The Folktale *Kasajizo* ————————— 298

住 正 年 売 買 町 長 道 雪 立 自 夜 朝 持

第 11 課 **友だち募集** Looking for Friends —————————— 304

手 紙 好 近 明 病 院 映 画 歌 市 所 勉 強 有 旅

第 12 課 **七 夕** Tanabata Festival ——————————————— 310

昔 々 神 早 起 牛 使 働 連 別 度 赤 青 色

第1課 だい いっ か | L E S S O N ·············1

ひらがな Hiragana

あ *a*	い *i*	う *u*	え *e*	お *o*
か *ka*	き *ki*	く *ku*	け *ke*	こ *ko*
さ *sa*	し *shi*	す *su*	せ *se*	そ *so*
た *ta*	ち *chi*	つ *tsu*	て *te*	と *to*
な *na*	に *ni*	ぬ *nu*	ね *ne*	の *no*
は *ha*	ひ *hi*	ふ *fu*	へ *he*	ほ *ho*
ま *ma*	み *mi*	む *mu*	め *me*	も *mo*
や *ya*		ゆ *yu*		よ *yo*
ら *ra*	り *ri*	る *ru*	れ *re*	ろ *ro*
わ *wa*				を *o*
ん *n*				

(Refer to "Japanese Writing System" on pages **18-22** for more details.)

① Hiragana Practice

A. Choose the correct *hiragana*.

1. *yo* ま よ
2. *ho* は ほ
3. *me* ぬ め
4. *su* む す
5. *ki* さ き
6. *chi* さ ち
7. *ta* た に
8. *ro* ろ る
9. *e* え ん

B. Match the words.

Person's name		Place name	
1. たなか ・	・Akai	9. さっぽろ・	・Gifu
2. やまもと・	・Nakamura	10. きょうと・	・Beppu
3. あかい ・	・Takahashi	11. かなざわ・	・Sapporo
4. はしもと・	・Tanaka	12. おおさか・	・Osaka
5. たかはし・	・Morikawa	13. ながさき・	・Kyoto
6. なかむら・	・Sakuma	14. ぎふ ・	・Kanazawa
7. もりかわ・	・Yamamoto	15. べっぷ ・	・Nagasaki
8. さくま ・	・Hashimoto	16. ちば ・	・Chiba

C. What's wrong with the *hiragana* below? Rewrite the correct *hiragana*.

(1) ほ (2) む (3) き (4) ʃ (5) あ

D. Write as many *hiragana* as possible which contain the following parts.

(1)

(2)

(3)

(4)

(5)

(6)

E. Put the *hiragana* in the right order to make sense.

Example: だともち → <u>ともだち</u>

1. わんで ___ ___ ___

2. ごいえ ___ ___ ___

3. んほに ___ ___ ___

4. えなま ___ ___ ___

5. んせせい ___ ___ ___ ___

6. がだいく ___ ___ ___ ___

=====================================

Ⅱ Reading Practice

Read what the following people are saying and answer the questions.

かいしゃいんです。

たなか ゆうこ

だいがくせいです。せんもんは れきしです。

はらだ りょう

かとう　やすお

だいがくいんせいです。せんもんは けいざいです。

きたの　ひろみ

こうこうの さんねんせいです。

やまだ　まこと

だいがくせいです。せんもんは にほんごです。

1. Who is an office worker?　_____

2. Whose major is Japanese?　_____

3. Who is a high school student?　_____

4. What is Harada's major?　_____

Ⅲ Writing Practice

You received a letter from a Japanese friend. Read it and write a letter introducing yourself.

はじめまして、まえかわみちこです。

にほんじんです。

わたしはだいがくのいちねんせいです。

せんもんはえいごです。

どうぞよろしくおねがいします。

*どうぞよろしくおねがいします is
more polite than どうぞよろしく.

カタカナ Katakana

ア *a*	イ *i*	ウ *u*	エ *e*	オ *o*
カ *ka*	キ *ki*	ク *ku*	ケ *ke*	コ *ko*
サ *sa*	シ *shi*	ス *su*	セ *se*	ソ *so*
タ *ta*	チ *chi*	ツ *tsu*	テ *te*	ト *to*
ナ *na*	ニ *ni*	ヌ *nu*	ネ *ne*	ノ *no*
ハ *ha*	ヒ *hi*	フ *fu*	ヘ *he*	ホ *ho*
マ *ma*	ミ *mi*	ム *mu*	メ *me*	モ *mo*
ヤ *ya*		ユ *yu*		ヨ *yo*
ラ *ra*	リ *ri*	ル *ru*	レ *re*	ロ *ro*
ワ *wa*				ヲ *o*
ン *n*				

(Refer to "Japanese Writing System" on pages **22-24** for more details.)

① Katakana Practice

A. Choose the correct *katakana*.

1. *o*   オ   ア   2. *nu*   ヌ   メ   3. *sa*   テ   サ

4. *shi*   シ   ツ   5. *ku*   ワ   ク   6. *ma*   マ   ム

7. *ru*   レ   ル   8. *ho*   モ   ホ   9. *yu*   エ   ユ

B. Match the following words and pictures.

1. (　) オレンジジュース   7. (　) サンドイッチ
2. (　) フライドポテト   8. (　) ステーキ
3. (　) ケーキ   9. (　) スパゲッティ
4. (　) サラダ   10. (　) ピザ
5. (　) チョコレートパフェ   11. (　) トースト
6. (　) コーヒー   12. (　) レモンティー

(a)

(b)

(c)

(d)

(e)

(f)

(g)

(h)

(i)

(j)

(k)

(l)

C. Match each country with its capital city.

Countries		Capital Cities
1. マレーシア	•	・オタワ
2. オランダ	•	・ワシントン DC
3. アメリカ	•	・ニューデリー
4. エジプト	•	・アムステルダム
5. オーストラリア	•	・クアラルンプール
6. スウェーデン	•	・ブエノスアイレス
7. インド	•	・キャンベラ
8. アルゼンチン	•	・カイロ
9. カナダ	•	・ストックホルム

D. Word Search—Find the following country names in the box of *katakana*.

ベトナム (Vietnam)

シンガポール (Singapore)

チェコ (Czech)

アメリカ (America)

スウェーデン (Sweden)

エクアドル (Ecuador)

メキシコ (Mexico)

ブラジル (Brazil)

ボスニア (Bosnia)

オランダ (Holland)

インドネシア (Indonesia)

カナダ (Canada)

ルワンダ (Rwanda)

タイ (Thailand)

オーストラリア (Australia)

イ	ン	ド	ネ	シ	ア	イ	ル	ワ	ン	ダ
コ	ウ	モ	リ	ブ	ク	ロ	ク	マ	チ	コ
オ	ー	ス	ト	ラ	リ	ア	ネ	コ	ェ	イ
ラ	タ	ウ	ナ	ジ	ア	メ	キ	シ	コ	ヌ
ン	ヌ	ェ	メ	ル	ヒ	リ	ネ	ズ	ミ	ベ
ダ	キ	ー	ク	ヘ	ル	カ	ナ	ダ	ラ	ト
カ	モ	デ	ジ	ビ	ボ	ス	ニ	ア	ク	ナ
ワ	シ	ン	ガ	ポ	ー	ル	パ	ン	ダ	ム
タ	イ	ゴ	リ	ラ	エ	ク	ア	ド	ル	メ

E. Put the *katakana* in the right order to make sense.

Example: キケー → ケーキ

1. トノー ___ ___ ___

2. ニュメー ___ ___ ___ ___

3. ンペ ___ ___

4. ンジーズ ___ ___ ___ ___

5. プテー ___ ___ ___

6. レーナトー ___ ___ ___ ___ ___

Ⅱ Name Tags

Write your name in the box below and make your own name tag.

Example: マイケル・ジョーダン

マイケル・ジョーダン

Ⅲ Reading Practice

Mary wrote about the things below. Find out which item she wrote about.

1. ( ) これは わたしの ぼうしじゃ ありません。
   キャシーさんの ぼうしです。
   ニューヨークヤンキースの ぼうしです。

2. (　　) これは わたしの じてんしゃです。
　　　　 オーストラリアの じてんしゃです。
　　　　 たかいです。

3. (　　) これは ミシェルさんの じしょです。
　　　　 スペインごの じしょじゃありません。
　　　　 フランスごの じしょです。

4. (　　) これは ジャクソンさんの くつです。
　　　　 にほんの くつじゃありません。
　　　　 イタリアの くつです。

(a)　(b)　(c)　(d)

(e)　(f)　(g)　(h)

¥50,000　　¥8,000

Ⅳ Writing Practice

Write about the things you or your classmates own. Use Mary's sentences in Ⅲ as a model.

第3課 | L E S S O N 3
まいにちのせいかつ Daily Life

001	一 (one)	イチ イッ ひと	一（イチ）one　一時（イチジ）one o'clock 一年生（イチネンセイ）first-year student 一分（イップン）one minute　一つ（ひとつ）one
			(1) 一
002	二 (two)	ニ ふた	二（ニ）two　二時（ニジ）two o'clock 二年生（ニネンセイ）second-year student 二つ（ふたつ）two　二日間（ふつかカン）two days
			(2) 一 二
003	三 (three)	サン みっ	三（サン）three　三時（サンジ）three o'clock 三年生（サンネンセイ）third-year student 三つ（みっつ）three
			(3) 一 二 三
004	四 (four)	よん よ よっ シ	四（よん）four　四時（よジ）four o'clock 四年生（よネンセイ）fourth-year student 四つ（よっつ）four　四月（シガツ）April
			(5) 丨 冂 �四 四
005	五 (five)	ゴ いつ	五（ゴ）five　五時（ゴジ）five o'clock 五つ（いつつ）five
			(4) 一 丆 五 五
006	六 (six)	ロク ロッ むっ	六（ロク）six　六時（ロクジ）six o'clock 六百（ロッピャク）six hundred 六分（ロップン）six minutes　六つ（むっつ）six
			(4) 丶 亠 宀 六
007	七 (seven)	シチ なな	七（シチ／なな）seven　七時（シチジ）seven o'clock 七つ（ななつ）seven
			(2) 一 七
008	八 (eight)	ハチ ハッ やっ	八（ハチ）eight　八時（ハチジ）eight o'clock 八百（ハッピャク）eight hundred 八歳（ハッサイ）eight years old　八つ（やっつ）eight
			(2) ノ 八

009	九 (nine)	キュウ ク ここの	九（キュウ）nine　　九時（クジ）nine o'clock 九歳（キュウサイ）nine years old　　九つ（ここのつ）nine
			(2) ノ 九
010	十 (ten)	ジュウ ジュッ　とお	十（ジュウ）ten　　十時（ジュウジ）ten o'clock 十歳（ジュッサイ）ten years old　　十（とお）ten
			(2) 一 十
011	百 (hundred)	ヒャク ピャク ビャク	百（ヒャク）hundred　　三百（サンビャク）three hundred 六百（ロッピャク）six hundred 八百（ハッピャク）eight hundred
			(6) 一 ア ア 百 百 百
012	千 (thousand)	セン ゼン	千（セン）thousand　　三千（サンゼン）three thousand 八千（ハッセン）eight thousand
			(3) ノ 二 千
013	万 (ten thousand)	マン	一万（イチマン）ten thousand 十万（ジュウマン）one hundred thousand 百万（ヒャクマン）one million
			(3) 一 ナ 万
014	円 (yen; circle)	エン	百円（ヒャクエン）one hundred yen 円（エン）circle
			(4) 丨 冂 冂 円
015	時 (time)	ジ とき	一時（イチジ）one o'clock 子供の時（こどものとき）in one's childhood 時々（ときどき）sometimes　　時計（トケイ）watch
			(10) 丨 冂 日 日 旷 旷 旷 旷 時 時

(In this chart, *katakana* indicates the *on'yomi* [pronunciation originally borrowed from Chinese] and *hiragana* indicates the *kun'yomi* [native Japanese reading].)

① 漢字の練習 (Kanji Practice)
かんじ　　　れんしゅう

A. Read the price of the following items in kanji and write it in numbers.

Example: チョコレート　　(1) ハンカチ　　　　　(2) せんす

百五十円　　　　　　　六百五十円　　　　　千八百円

（¥ 150 ）　　　　　　（¥_____）　　　　（¥_____）

(3) きもの　　　　　(4) テレビ　　　　　　(5) マンション

七十一万四千円　　　　十二万三千円　　　　三千九百万円

（¥_____）　　　　（¥_____）　　　　（¥_____）

B. Write the following prices in kanji.

Example:　¥5,420　→　　五千四百二十円

1. ¥30 _____　　　2. ¥140 _____　　　3. ¥251 _____

4. ¥6,070 _____　　　　5. ¥8,190 _____

6. ¥42,500 _____　　　　7. ¥168,000 _____

8. ¥3,200,000 _____　　9. ¥57,000,000 _____

Ⅱ まいにちのせいかつ

An international exchange student writes about his daily routine. Read the passage to find out about his schedule and fill in the blanks below.

> わたしはまいにち七時におきます。うちであさごはんをたべます。八時にだいがくへいきます。九時ににほんごをべんきょうします。十二時半(はん)にだいがくでひるごはんをたべます。ときどきコーヒーをのみます。四時にとしょかんでほんをよみます。六時ごろうちへかえります。十時にテレビをみます。十二時ごろねます。

7:00	_____
( )	go to the university
9:00	_____
( )	eat lunch
4:00	_____
6:00	_____
( )	watch TV
( )	_____

Ⅲ 書く練習 (Writing Practice)
か れんしゅう

Write about your daily routine. Use the above passage as a model.

第4課 | L E S S O N ⋯⋯⋯⋯4
メアリーさんのしゅうまつ Mary's Weekend

016	日 (day; sun)	ニ ニチ び ひ ニッ	日本（ニホン）Japan　　日曜日（ニチヨウび）Sunday 毎日（マイニチ）every day　　母の日（ははのひ）Mother's Day 日記（ニッキ）diary　　三日（ミッカ）three days
			(4) 丨 冂 月 日
017	本 (book; basis)	ホン もと	本（ホン）book　　日本（ニホン）Japan 日本語（ニホンゴ）Japanese language 山本さん（やまもとさん）Mr./Ms. Yamamoto
			(5) 一 十 才 木 本
018	人 (person)	ジン ひと ニン	日本人（ニホンジン）Japanese people 一人で（ひとりで）alone　　この人（このひと）this person 三人（サンニン）three people
			(2) ノ 人
019	月 (moon; month)	ゲツ ガツ つき	月曜日（ゲツヨウび）Monday　　一月（イチガツ）January 月（つき）moon
			(4) 丿 刀 月 月
020	火 (fire)	カ ひ	火曜日（カヨウび）Tuesday 火（ひ）fire
			(4) 丶 丷 少 火
021	水 (water)	スイ みず	水曜日（スイヨウび）Wednesday　　水（みず）water
			(4) 亅 才 水 水
022	木 (tree)	モク き	木曜日（モクヨウび）Thursday 木（き）tree
			(4) 一 十 才 木
023	金 (gold; money)	キン かね	金曜日（キンヨウび）Friday お金（おかね）money
			(8) ノ 人 𠆢 合 仐 全 金 金

024	土 (soil)	ド つち	土曜日（ドヨウび）Saturday 土（つち）soil
			⑶　一　十　土
025	曜 (weekday)	ヨウ	日曜日（ニチヨウび）Sunday
			⒅　｜　冂　冃　日　日¹　日²　日³　日⁴　日⁵　旦　町　畊　曙　曙　曙　曜　曜
026	上 (up)	うえ ジョウ	上（うえ）top; above 上手な（ジョウズな）good at 屋上（オクジョウ）rooftop
			⑶　｜　上　上
027	下 (down)	した カ	下（した）under 地下鉄（チカテツ）subway　　下手な（へたな）poor at
			⑶　一　丁　下
028	中 (middle)	なか チュウ　ジュウ	中（なか）inside　　中国（チュウゴク）China 中学（チュウガク）junior high school 一年中（イチネンジュウ）all year around
			⑷　｜　口　口　中
029	半 (half)	ハン	三時半（サンジハン）half past three 半分（ハンブン）half
			⑸　、　ソ　ⴼ　半　半

(In this chart, *katakana* indicates the *on'yomi* and *hiragana* indicates the *kun'yomi*.)

Ⅰ 漢字の練習 (Kanji Practice)
かんじ　れんしゅう

A. Match the kanji with the English equivalents.

1. 水曜日 ・　　　　　・ Sunday
2. 金曜日 ・　　　　　・ Monday
3. 日曜日 ・　　　　　・ Tuesday
4. 月曜日 ・　　　　　・ Wednesday
5. 土曜日 ・　　　　　・ Thursday
6. 木曜日 ・　　　　　・ Friday
7. 火曜日 ・　　　　　・ Saturday

B. Look at the picture and choose the appropriate kanji for the blanks.

| 上 | 下 | 中 |

1. レストランはビルの＿＿＿です。
   (building)
2. 日本語学校はレストランの＿＿＿です。
   ご がっこう
3. スーパーはレストランの＿＿＿です。

Ⅱ おかあさんへのメモ

メアリーさんはおかあさんにメモをかきました。
Read the memo and answer the questions.

1. メアリーさんはきょうなにをしますか。
2. うちでばんごはんをたべますか。
3. 何時ごろかえりますか。
   なん

おかあさんへ
きょうは ともだちと だい
がくで べんきょうします。
うちで ばんごはんを
たべません。
九時半ごろ かえります。

十月二十一日
メアリー

Ⅲ メアリーさんのしゅうまつ

Read the following passage about Mary's weekend.

金曜日に日本人のともだちとこうえんにいきました。こうえんでともだちとはなしました。それから、レストランへいきました。たくさんたべました。

土曜日は一人でおてらへいきました。たくさんみせがありました。みせでおまんじゅうをかいました。

日曜日はおそくおきました。おかあさんもおそくおきました。わたしはあさテレビをみました。それから、おかあさんとひるごはんをたべました。ごごは日本語をべんきょうしました。本もよみました。

みせ　store
おまんじゅう　sweet bun
おそく　late

Arrange the following activities in the order Mary did.

( ) → ( ) → ( ) → ( ) → ( )

1. studied Japanese　　2. bought sweet buns　　3. went to a restaurant
4. watched TV　　5. went to a park

Ⅳ 書く練習 (Writing Practice)

A. You are going out. Write a memo to someone in your house, telling when you will be back and whether you will have dinner at home.

B. Write about your weekend.

第5課 LESSON 5
りょこう Travel

#	Kanji	Readings	Words	Stroke order
030	山 (mountain)	やま / サン	山 (やま) mountain / 富士山 (フジサン) Mt. Fuji	(3) 丨 凵 山
031	川 (river)	かわ / がわ	川 (かわ) river / 小川さん (おがわさん) Mr./Ms. Ogawa	(3) ノ 丿 川
032	元 (origin)	ゲン	元気な (ゲンキな) fine	(4) 一 二 テ 元
033	気 (spirit)	キ	元気な (ゲンキな) fine　天気 (テンキ) weather / 電気 (デンキ) electricity	(6) ノ 一 亠 气 気 気
034	天 (heaven)	テン	天気 (テンキ) weather / 天国 (テンゴク) heaven	(4) 一 二 チ 天
035	私 (I; private)	わたし / シ	私 (わたし) I / 私立大学 (シリツダイガク) private university	(7) 一 二 千 禾 禾 私 私
036	今 (now)	いま / コン	今 (いま) now　今日 (きょう) today / 今晩 (コンバン) tonight	(4) ノ 人 今 今
037	田 (rice field)	た だ	田中さん (たなかさん) Mr./Ms. Tanaka / 山田さん (やまださん) Mr./Ms. Yamada / 田んぼ (たんぼ) rice field	(5) 丨 冂 田 田 田

038	女 (woman)	おんな ジョ	女の人 （おんなのひと） woman 女性 （ジョセイ） woman
			⑶ く 女 女
039	男 (man)	おとこ ダン	男の人 （おとこのひと） man 男性 （ダンセイ） man
			⑺ 丨 冂 冂 田 田 田 男 男
040	見 (to see)	み ケン	見る （みる） to see 見物 （ケンブツ） sightseeing
			⑺ 丨 冂 月 月 目 貝 見
041	行 (to go)	い コウ ギョウ	行く （いく） to go 銀行 （ギンコウ） bank 一行目 （イチギョウめ） first line
			⑹ ′ ク 彳 彳 行 行
042	食 (to eat)	た ショク	食べる （たべる） to eat 食べ物 （たべもの） food 食堂 （ショクドウ） cafeteria
			⑼ ノ 人 入 今 今 今 食 食 食
043	飲 (to drink)	の イン	飲む （のむ） to drink 飲み物 （のみもの） drink 飲酒運転 （インシュウンテン） drunken driving
			⑿ ノ 人 入 今 今 今 食 食 飣 飲 飲 飲

(In this chart, *katakana* indicates the *on'yomi* and *hiragana* indicates the *kun'yomi*.)

Ⅰ 漢字の練習 (Kanji Practice)
かん じ　れんしゅう

A. Using the parts below, make up the correct kanji.

Example:　目　→　見

1. 艮　　2. 欠　　3. ム　　4. 二　　5. 力

6. 气　　7. 人　　8. 良　　9. メ　　10. 田

B. Match the following sentences with the pictures.

1. (　　) えいがを見ます。　　　2. (　　) コーヒーを飲みます。

3. (　　) ハンバーガーを食べます。　4. (　　) 男の人と女の人がいます。

5. (　　) 山と川があります。　　　6. (　　) 今日はいい天気です。

7. (　　) 銀行に行きます。
ぎんこう

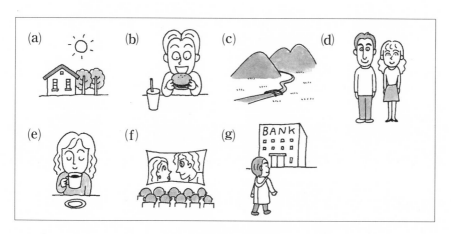

C. Match the kanji with the reading.

1. (　　) 一日　　2. (　　) 二日　　3. (　　) 三日　　4. (　　) 四日

5. (　　) 五日　　6. (　　) 六日　　7. (　　) 七日　　8. (　　) 八日

9. (　　) 九日　　10. (　　) 十日　　11. (　　) 二十日

(a) いつか　(b) ここのか　(c) ついたち　(d) とおか　(e) なのか　(f) はつか

(g) ふつか　(h) みっか　(i) むいか　(j) ようか　(k) よっか

Ⅱ りょこうのはがき

A. Match the following *katakana* words with the English equivalents.

1. コーヒー ・   ・cake
2. コンサート・   ・coffee
3. ウィーン ・   ・cafe
4. カフェ ・   ・classical
5. クラシック・   ・concert
6. ケーキ ・   ・Vienna

B. ようこさんはみちこさんにはがきをかきました。

Read the postcard below. Write T for the things she did or does and write F for the things she didn't or doesn't do in Vienna.

1. (   ) see an old castle   2. (   ) go to see a ballet
3. (   ) take pictures   4. (   ) drink beer at the cafe
5. (   ) enjoy sweets   6. (   ) eat at McDonald's

みちこさんへ
元気ですか。私は今ウィーンにいます。ここはちょっとさむいです。ウィーンはとてもきれいなまちです。
　きのうはおしろを見ました。ふるかったですが、とてもきれいでした。たくさんしゃしんをとりました。よるはクラシックのコンサートに行きました。よかったです。
　ウィーンにはカフェがたくさんあります。まいにちカフェでコーヒーを飲みます。ケーキも食べます。とてもおいしいです。
　四日にかえります。また日本であいましょうね。
　　　　　　　　山田 ようこ

〒305-0836
つくば市山中42-5
山川みちこさま
Japan

〜さま　Mr./Ms. (used in letter writing)　おしろ　castle
が　but　よる　night　また　again

C. ロバートさんもはがきをかきました。

Read the postcard below and answer the following questions in Japanese.

1. ロバートさんは今どこにいますか。

2. どんな天気ですか。

3. きのうは なにをしましたか。

4. 今日は なにをしましたか。だれとしましたか。

5. おきなわの食べものはどうですか。

みちこさん、お元気ですか。今、私はおきなわにいます。ここはちょっとあついですが、いい天気です。きのうはともだちといっしょにうみでおよぎました。今日は日本人の男の人と女の人と山に行きました。たいへんでしたが、とてもきれいでした。まいにちたのしいです。おきなわの食べものもだいすきです。では、お元気で。

十月九日

ロバート・スミス

つくば市山中
四二一五

山川 みちこさま

305-0836

山 mountain　　たいへん tough
では、お元気で　Take care.

Ⅲ 書く練習 (Writing Practice)
か　　れんしゅう

The following are your Japanese friends' addresses in your pocket notebook.
Copy their addresses on the postcards and write about your vacation.

名前 なまえ	住　　所 じゅう　　しょ	
今中ゆみ	〒753-0041	山口市東山36-8 やまぐち し ひがしやま
上田一男 うえ だ かず お	〒112-0002	文京区小石川7-7 ぶん きょう く　こ いしかわ

第6課 LESSON 6
私のすきなレストラン My Favorite Restaurant

044	東 (east)	ひがし トウ	東（ひがし）east　　東口（ひがしぐち）east exit 東京（トウキョウ）Tokyo
			(8) 一 厂 厅 厅 百 申 東 東
045	西 (west)	にし セイ　サイ	西（にし）west　　西口（にしぐち）west exit 北西（ホクセイ）northwest 関西（カンサイ）Kansai region
			(6) 一 厂 厅 厉 西 西
046	南 (south)	みなみ ナン	南（みなみ）south　　南口（みなみぐち）south exit 南東（ナントウ）southeast
			(9) 一 十 广 内 内 南 南 南 南
047	北 (north)	きた ホク　ホッ	北（きた）north　　北口（きたぐち）north exit 東北（トウホク）Tohoku region 北海道（ホッカイドウ）Hokkaido
			(5) ｜ ナ 扌 北 北
048	口 (mouth)	ぐち くち　コウ	北口（きたぐち）north exit 口（くち）mouth　　人口（ジンコウ）population
			(3) 丨 冂 口
049	出 (to exit)	で だ　シュッ シュツ	出る（でる）to exit　　出口（でぐち）exit 出す（だす）to take something out 出席（シュッセキ）attendance　　輸出（ユシュツ）export
			(5) 丨 屮 屮 出 出
050	右 (right)	みぎ ウ　ユウ	右（みぎ）right 右折（ウセツ）right turn 左右（サユウ）right and left
			(5) ノ ナ オ 右 右
051	左 (left)	ひだり サ	左（ひだり）left 左折（サセツ）left turn
			(5) 一 ナ 才 左 左

052	分 (minute; to divide)	フン　プン ブン	五分（ゴフン）five minutes 十分（ジュップン）ten minutes 自分（ジブン）oneself　　半分（ハンブン）half
			(4) ノ　八　分　分
053	先 (ahead)	セン さき	先生（センセイ）teacher 先週（センシュウ）last week　　先に（さきに）ahead
			(6) ノ　ﾉ　ｔ　生　先　先
054	生 (birth)	セイ う　ショウ	学生（ガクセイ）student　　先生（センセイ）teacher 生まれる（うまれる）to be born 一生に一度（イッショウにイチド）once in a life time
			(5) ノ　ﾉ　牛　牛　生
055	大 (big)	ダイ　おお タイ	大学生（ダイガクセイ）college student 大きい（おおきい）big 大変な（タイヘンな）tough　　大人（おとな）adult
			(3) 一　ナ　大
056	学 (learning)	ガク ガッ　まな	大学（ダイガク）university　　学生（ガクセイ）student 学校（ガッコウ）school　　学ぶ（まなぶ）to study
			(8) 丶　ﾞ　ﾞﾞ　ﾉﾞ　ﾝﾞ　学　学　学
057	外 (outside)	ガイ そと	外国（ガイコク）foreign country 外国人（ガイコクジン）foreigner 外（そと）outside
			(5) ノ　ク　タ　列　外
058	国 (country)	コク　ゴク くに	外国（ガイコク）foreign country 中国（チュウゴク）China 国（くに）country
			(8) 丨　冂　冂　冃　用　国　国　国

(In this chart, *katakana* indicates the *on'yomi* and *hiragana* indicates the *kun'yomi*.)

Ⅰ 漢字の練習 (Kanji Practice)

A. Combine the following kanji and make compound words. You can use the same kanji more than once.

Example: 外 + 国 → 外国

気　生　外　先　学　天　日　国　今　大

B. Indicate where each place is located on the map.

1. (　　) レストラン・アルデンテ：えきの中にあります。南口のそばです。
2. (　　) ロイヤルホテル：えきの東口を出て、まっすぐ五分ぐらいです。
3. (　　) 山下先生のうち：北口を出て、右へ十分ぐらいです。
4. (　　) こうえん：西口をまっすぐ十五分ぐらい行ってください。
5. (　　) 大学：北口を出て、左へ十分ぐらい行ってください。

えき	station
出る	to exit
まっすぐ	straight

Ⅱ でんごんばん (Bulletin Board)

Look at the bulletin board on the next page and answer the questions.

1. If you want to buy a bicycle, who are you going to contact?
2. Where will the party be held? Are you going to bring anything?
3. How do you get to the concert hall?
4. What can you do for the winter break (from December to January)?

ホームステイ プログラム

東北のまちでホームステイをしませんか。
とうほく
十二月二十八日(日)〜一月三日(土)
きれいな山と川のそばです。

えいごをおしえてください。

日本人の大学生です。

９３１−２６８２
ようこ

セール!! じてんしゃ

¥20,000

あたらしいです。
でんわしてください。
（よる７時〜11時）

山田　597-1651

ハロウィーンパーティー

ところ：山下先生のうち
じかん：６時〜
ともだちをつれてきてもいいですよ！
飲みものをもってきてください。

イタリアンレストラン
マンジャーレ

ランチスペシャル
1,200 円
Ａセット（サラダ・コーヒー）
Ｂセット（パン・コーヒー）

ギターコンサート

９月12日(金)
６：30〜

西コンサートホール
（西駅３出口を出て左へ３分）
えき

Ⅲ 私のすきなレストラン

Mary writes about her favorite restaurant. Read the passage and answer the questions.

私のすきなレストラン

　私のすきなレストランは、イタリアりょうりのマンジャーレです。えきの南口を出て、右へ五分ぐらいです。ちいさいレストランです。シェフはイタリア人のアントニオさんです。アントニオさんはとてもおもしろい人です。アントニオさんのりょうりはとてもおいしいです。私はよくマンジャーレに行きます。マンジャーレでワインを飲んで、ピザを食べます。アイスクリームもおいしいです。ここでいつもたくさん食べます。りょうりはやすいですから。外国人もたくさんきます。みなさんもきてください。

りょうり	cooking
いつも	always
みなさん	everyone

A. Where is the restaurant?

B. Circle the food or drink the writer has at the restaurant.

> ピザ　　スパゲッティ　　アイスクリーム
>
> ワイン　　ビール　　ステーキ

C. Choose the correct answer.

1. マンジャーレは $\begin{Bmatrix} 大きい \\ ちいさい \end{Bmatrix}$ レストランです。

2. マンジャーレは $\begin{Bmatrix} たかい \\ やすい \end{Bmatrix}$ です。

3. アントニオさんは $\begin{Bmatrix} おもしろい \\ つまらない \end{Bmatrix}$ 人です。

4. マンジャーレに外国人が $\begin{Bmatrix} きます。 \\ きません。 \end{Bmatrix}$

Ⅳ 書く練習 (Writing Practice)
か　　れんしゅう

A. You are organizing a party. Write a flyer about the party. Be sure to include: what kind of party it is, what time it starts, where it is held, what to bring, how to get there, and so on.

B. Write about your favorite restaurant.

第7課 | L E S S O N ⋯⋯⋯⋯7
メアリーさんのてがみ Mary's Letter

059	京 (capital)	キョウ	東京（トウキョウ）Tokyo　　京子（キョウこ）Kyoko 京都（キョウト）Kyoto
			⑻ ′ 亠 亡 古 古 亨 京 京
060	子 (child)	こ シ	子ども（こども）child　　京子（キョウこ）Kyoko 女の子（おんなのこ）girl　　男の子（おとこのこ）boy 電子メール（デンシメール）e-mail
			⑶ 了 了 子
061	小 (small)	ちい ショウ	小さい（ちいさい）small 小学校（ショウガッコウ）elementary school 小学生（ショウガクセイ）elementary school student
			⑶ 亅 小 小
062	会 (to meet)	あ　カイ	会う（あう）to meet　　会社（カイシャ）company 会社員（カイシャイン）office worker
			⑹ ノ 人 亼 会 会 会
063	社 (company)	シャ ジャ	会社（カイシャ）company 神社（ジンジャ）shrine
			⑺ ` ラ ネ ネ ネ 社 社
064	父 (father)	ちち　とう フ	父（ちち）father　　お父さん（おとうさん）father 父母（フボ）father and mother
			⑷ ′ ハ グ 父
065	母 (mother)	はは　かあ ボ	母（はは）mother　　お母さん（おかあさん）mother 母語（ボゴ）mother tongue
			⑸ ㄴ 夗 夘 母 母
066	高 (high)	たか　コウ	高い（たかい）expensive; high 高校（コウコウ）high school 高校生（コウコウセイ）high school student
			⑽ ′ 亠 亠 古 古 声 高 高 高 高

067	校	コウ (school)	学校（ガッコウ）school　　高校（コウコウ）high school 高校生（コウコウセイ）high school student 中学校（チュウガッコウ）junior high school
			⑽　一　十　オ　オ　オ　村　村　校　校
068	毎	マイ (every)	毎日（マイニチ）every day 毎週（マイシュウ）every week 毎晩（マイバン）every night
			⑹　ノ　ケ　と　与　与　毎
069	語	ゴ (word)	日本語（ニホンゴ）Japanese (language) 英語（エイゴ）English (language)
			⒁　丶　ニ　ニ　ミ　言　言　言　言　訂　訳　語　語　語　語
070	文	ブン (sentence)	文学（ブンガク）literature 作文（サクブン）composition 文字（モジ）letter; character
			⑷　丶　亠　ナ　文
071	帰	かえ キ (to return)	帰る（かえる）to return 帰国（キコク）going home
			⑽　丿　リ　リ　リ　リ　リ　尸　尸　帰　帰
072	入	はい いり　い ニュウ (to enter)	入る（はいる）to enter　　入口（いりぐち）entrance 入れる（いれる）to put something in 輸入（ユニュウ）import
			⑵　ノ　入

(In this chart, *katakana* indicates the *on'yomi* and *hiragana* indicates the *kun'yomi*.)

Ⅰ 漢字の練習
かん じ れんしゅう

A. Fill in the blanks with the appropriate kanji.

1. 日本＿＿＿学　高＿＿＿三年生　＿＿＿と母
   ねん

   | 父 | 文 | 校 |

2. ＿＿＿日、＿＿＿は六時におきます。

   | 母 | 毎 |

3. 日本＿＿＿はよくおふろに＿＿＿ります。

   | 人 | 入 |

4. 東＿＿＿に行きました。食べものは＿＿＿かったです。

   | 京 | 高 |

B. Which new kanji from this lesson include the *katakana* below?

Example:　エ　→　左

1. ヨ →　　　2. ネ →　　　3. ム →　　　4. ロ →

C. What's wrong with the kanji below? Rewrite the correct kanji.

1.　母　　　2.　高　　　3.　卓

4.　話　　　5.　帰　　　6.　杦

Ⅱ メアリーさんのてがみ

京子さんは今アリゾナにすんでいます。メアリーさんは京子さんにてがみをかきました。

京子さんへ

京子さん、お元気ですか。アリゾナはあついですか。日本はすこしさむいです。今、私は日本のかぞくと大学のそばにすんでいます。ここは小さくて、しずかなまちです。

私のかぞくは四人です。みんなとてもしんせつで、たのしいです。お父さんは会社につとめています。いそがしくて、毎日おそく帰ります。お母さんはとてもおもしろい人です。いっしょによくはなします。いもうとは高校生です。らいねん大学ですから、よくべんきょうします。毎日学校から帰って、すぐじゅくへ行きます。日本の高校生はたいへんですね。おにいさんは東京の大学に行っていますから、あまり会いません。

私は今、日本語と日本文学のクラスをとっています。テニスクラブにも入っています。とてもおもしろいです。

京子さんはいつ日本に帰りますか。とてもいましょうね。たのしみにしています。日本で会いましょうね。たのしみにしています。からだに気をつけてください。

十一月三日

メアリー・ハート

すこし　　　a little
みんな　　　all
〜から　　　from . . .
じゅく　　　cram school
文学　　　　literature
とる　　　　to take (a class)
（〜を）たのしみにする
　　　　　　to look forward (to)
からだに気をつける
　　　　　　to take care of oneself

Summarize what Mary wrote about the following topics in Japanese.

1. Japan: _____

2. Her town: _____

3. Father: _____

4. Mother: _____

5. Sister: _____

6. Brother: _____

7. School: _____

Ⅲ 書く練習
か　　　れんしゅう

A. Write about the following topics.

1. 日本は／私の国は_____

　_____

2. 私のまちは_____

　_____

3. かぞくは_____

　_____

4. ともだちは_____

　_____

B. Write letters to your Japanese friends. Describe your town, host family, friends, and so on.

第8課 LESSON 8

日本の会社員 Japanese Office Workers

073	員 (member)	イン	会社員（カイシャイン）office worker 店員（テンイン）store clerk
			⑽ 丶 冖 口 口 尸 月 月 目 冒 員 員
074	新 (new)	あたら　シン	新しい（あたらしい）new　　新聞（シンブン）newspaper 新幹線（シンカンセン）Bullet Train
			⒀ 丶 亠 七 立 立 辛 辛 亲 亲 亲 新 新 新
075	聞 (to listen)	き　ブン	聞く（きく）to listen　　新聞（シンブン）newspaper
			⒁ 丨 冂 冂 門 門 門 門 門 門 門 聞 聞 聞
076	作 (to make)	つく サク	作る（つくる）to make 作文（サクブン）composition 作品（サクヒン）artistic piece
			⑺ 丿 亻 亻 乍 乍 作 作
077	仕 (to serve)	シ	仕事（シごと）job
			⑸ 丿 亻 亻 仕 仕
078	事 (thing)	ごと こと　ジ	仕事（シごと）job 事（こと）thing　　火事（カジ）fire 食事（ショクジ）meal
			⑻ 一 亠 亖 彐 彐 写 写 事
079	電 (electricity)	デン	電車（デンシャ）train　　電気（デンキ）electricity 電話（デンワ）telephone
			⒀ 一 亠 雨 雨 雨 雨 雨 雷 雷 雷 電
080	車 (car)	くるま　シャ	車（くるま）car　　電車（デンシャ）train 自転車（ジテンシャ）bicycle
			⑺ 一 亠 亣 亘 百 亘 車

081	休 (to rest)	やす キュウ	休む（やすむ）to be absent; to rest 休み（やすみ）holiday; absence 休日（キュウジツ）holiday
			⑹ ノ イ 仁 什 休 休
082	言 (to say)	い ゲン	言う（いう）to say 言語学（ゲンゴガク）linguistics
			⑺ ` 一 二 言 言 言 言
083	読 (to read)	よ ドク	読む（よむ）to read 読書（ドクショ）reading books
			⑭ ` ㇕ ㇇ ㇒ 言 言 言 言 計 計 誹 誹 読 読
084	思 (to think)	おも シ	思う（おもう）to think 不思議な（フシギな）mysterious
			⑼ ㇑ 口 冊 冊 田 甲 思 思 思
085	次 (next)	つぎ ジ	次（つぎ）next 次女（ジジョ）one's second daughter
			⑹ ` ㇀ ㇉ ㇏ 次 次
086	何 (what)	なに なん	何（なに）what　何時（なんジ）what time 何人（なんニン）how many people
			⑺ ノ イ 仁 仃 仃 何 何

(In this chart, *katakana* indicates the *on'yomi* and *hiragana* indicates the *kun'yomi*.)

① 漢字の練習
かんじ れんしゅう

A. Using the parts below, make up as many kanji as possible.

Example: 乂 → 文 父

1. 言　　2. 木　　3. 日　　4. 田　　5. イ　　6. 口

B. Match the following phrases with an appropriate verb.

1. 新聞を　・　　　　　・作る
2. ラジオを・　　　　　・休む
3. 仕事を　・　　　　　・読む
4. 日本語はおもしろいと・　・する
5. カレーを・　　　　　・思う
6. 電車に　・　　　　　・聞く
7. クラスを・　　　　　・のる

② 日本の会社員

A. 留学生のマークさんはアンケートを作って、日本人の会社員に聞きました。
りゅう
Read the following questionnaire.

```
              アンケート
  1. 仕事のストレスがありますか。
        □はい        □いいえ
  2. よく残業をしますか。
       ざんぎょう
        □よくする   □ときどきする   □ぜんぜんしない
  3. 仕事の後、何をしますか。
       あと
  4. 休みはたいてい何をしますか。
```

| アンケート | questionnaire | 残業（ざんぎょう） | overtime work |
| ストレス | stress | 〜の後（〜のあと） | after . . . |

B. How would you answer the above questions?

C. マークさんはアンケートについてレポートを書きました。
   Read the report below and answer the questions.

日本の会社員

マーク・テイラー

　日本の会社員は、電車の中で、ときどき新聞を読んでいますが、たいていみんな寝（ね）ています。みんなとても疲（つか）れていると思います。私はアンケートを作って、会社員十人に聞きました。

　まず、「仕事のストレスがありますか」と聞きました。九人は「はい」と答（こた）えました。「仕事が大変（たいへん）で、休みがあまりない」と言っていました。次に、「よく残業（ざんぎょう）をしますか」と聞きました。三人は「よく残業（ざんぎょう）をする」と言っていました。五人は「ときどき残業（ざんぎょう）をする」と言っていました。次に「仕事の後（あと）、何をしますか」と聞きました。六人は「お酒（さけ）を飲みに行く」と言っていました。二人は「カラオケに行く」と言っていました。最後（さいご）に「休みはたいてい何をしますか」と聞きました。七人は「疲（つか）れているから、家（いえ）にいる」と言っていました。

　日本の会社員はたくさん仕事をして、ストレスもあります。だから、休みは何もしません。アンケートをして、日本の会社員はとても大変（たいへん）だと思いました。

〜について	about; regarding to	答える（こたえる）	to answer
疲れている（つかれている）	to be tired	次に	secondly
まず	first of all	最後に（さいごに）	lastly

1. どうしてマークさんはアンケートをしましたか。

2. 何人いましたか。

   (a) 仕事のストレスがある。 …… _____ 人

   (b) よく残業をする。 …… _____ 人
       ざんぎょう

   (c) ときどき残業をする。 …… _____ 人
         ざんぎょう

   (d) 仕事の後、お酒を飲む。 …… _____ 人
         あと さけ

   (e) 休みの日は出かけない。 …… _____ 人

Ⅲ 書く練習
   か れんしゅう

Make a questionnaire and ask several people the questions. Then, write a report based on the result.

第9課｜LESSON·····················9
スーさんの日記 Sue's Diary
にっき

087	午 (noon)	ゴ	午前（ゴゼン）A.M.　　午後（ゴゴ）P.M.; in the afternoon 午前中（ゴゼンチュウ）in the morning
			⑷ 丿 と 午 午
088	後 (after)	ゴ あと うし	午後（ゴゴ）P.M.; in the afternoon 〜の後（のあと）after . . .　　後で（あとで）later 後ろ（うしろ）back; behind　　最後に（サイゴに）lastly
			⑼ 丿 勹 彳 彳 犭 彳 彳 後 後
089	前 (before)	まえ ゼン	前（まえ）before; front　　午前（ゴゼン）A.M. 名前（なまえ）name
			⑼ 丶 丷 丷 广 广 并 首 首 前 前
090	名 (name)	な メイ	名前（なまえ）name 有名な（ユウメイな）famous　　名刺（メイシ）name card
			⑹ 丿 夕 夕 夕 名 名
091	白 (white)	しろ ハク	白い（しろい）white 白紙（ハクシ）blank sheet
			⑸ 丿 亻 白 白 白
092	雨 (rain)	あめ ウ	雨（あめ）rain 雨期（ウキ）rainy season
			⑻ 一 厂 冂 币 币 雨 雨 雨
093	書 (to write)	か ショ	書く（かく）to write 辞書（ジショ）dictionary
			⑽ 一 一 � 聿 聿 聿 書 書 書 書
094	友 (friend)	とも ユウ	友だち（ともだち）friend 親友（シンユウ）best friend　　友人（ユウジン）friend
			⑷ 一 ナ 方 友

095	間 (between)	カン　あいだ	時間（ジカン）time　　二時間（ニジカン）two hours 間（あいだ）between　　人間（ニンゲン）human being 一週間（イッシュウカン）one week
			⑿ 丨 丨 丨 丨 丨 門 門 門 間 間 間 間
096	家 (house)	いえ　　カ	家（いえ）house 家族（カゾク）family 家（うち）house; home
			⑽ 丶 宀 宀 宀 宀 宀 宇 家 家 家
097	話 (to speak)	はな　はなし　　ワ	話す（はなす）to speak　　話（はなし）talk; story 電話（デンワ）telephone 会話（カイワ）conversation
			⒀ 丶 二 二 三 言 言 言 訂 訂 訐 訐 話 話
098	少 (little)	すこ　　すく　ショウ	少し（すこし）little 少ない（すくない）few　　少々（ショウショウ）a little
			⑷ 丿 丿 小 少
099	古 (old)	ふる　　コ	古い（ふるい）old (for things) 中古（チュウコ）secondhand
			⑸ 一 十 十 古 古
100	知 (to know)	し　　チ	知る（しる）to know 知人（チジン）acquaintance
			⑻ 丿 ㇒ 匕 チ 矢 矢 知 知
101	来 (to come)	く　きこ　　ライ	来る（くる）to come　　来ます（きます）to come 来ない（こない）not to come 来週（ライシュウ）next week
			⑺ 一 ㄈ 曱 巫 平 来 来

(In this chart, *katakana* indicates the *on'yomi* and *hiragana* indicates the *kun'yomi*.)

Ⅰ 漢字の練習

A. Fill in the blanks with the appropriate kanji.

1. この＿＿＿＿いTシャツは五＿＿＿＿円でした。

百　白

2. ＿＿＿＿さいケーキを＿＿＿＿し食べました。

小　少

3. 一時＿＿＿＿テープを＿＿＿＿きました。

聞　間

4. 日本＿＿＿＿を＿＿＿＿します。

話　語

B. Choose the most appropriate word for each blank.

1. はじめまして。私の＿＿＿＿＿はキムです。

名前　午前

2. 毎日たいてい＿＿＿＿＿＿七時ごろおきます。

午後　午前

3. このきものは古いから、＿＿＿＿＿＿きものをかいます。

大きい　新しい

4. 今日はいい＿＿＿＿＿だった。でも、あしたは＿＿＿＿＿がふると思う。

元気　天気　白　雨

5. メアリーのお父さんを＿＿＿＿＿＿いますか。

帰って　知って

Ⅱ スーさんの日記

十一月二十五日（土）　雨

　今日はあさから雨がふっていた。午前中は友だちに手紙を書いて、一時間ぐらい音楽を聞いた。昼ごろメアリーの家へ行った。白くて、大きい家だった。メアリーのホストファミリーの山本さんに会った。お父さんはせが高くて、やせている人だった。家で晩ごはんを食べた。お母さんは「何もありませんが」と言っていたが、たくさんご

ちそうがあった。晩ごはんはとてもおいしかった。お母さんはとて
も料理が上手だと思う。晩ごはんの後、いろいろな話をした。そし
て、きれいなきものをもらった。お母さんは少し古いと言っていた
が、とてもきれいだ。メアリーのホストファミリーはとてもしんせ
つで楽しかった。

日記（にっき）	diary	いろいろな	various
午前中	in the morning	話をする	to have a talk
ホストファミリー	host family	そして	and
ごちそう	excellent food		

A. Put the following pictures in the right order according to Sue's diary.

(　) → (　) → (　) → (　) → (　)

(a)

(b)

(c)

(d)

(e)

B. Mark T if the following statements are true. Mark F if not true.

1. (　) スーさんは古いきものをもらった。
2. (　) お父さんはせがひくくて、やせている。
3. (　) 晩ごはんは何もなかった。
   　　　ばん
4. (　) スーさんはお母さんの料理が好きだ。
   　　　　　　　　　　　　りょうり　す
5. (　) 天気がよくなかった。
6. (　) メアリーさんのホストファミリーの名前は山田だ。

C. スーさんはメアリーさんのホストファミリーに手紙を書きました。
   　　　　　　　　　　　　　　　　　　　　　てがみ
   Read the following letter.

山本さま

　先日はどうもありがとうございました。
とても たのしかったです。りょうではあまり
日本のりょうりを食べませんが、お母さん
のりょうりはとてもおいしかったです。
それから、きものをありがとうございました。
とてもきれいなきものですね。
　どうぞかんこくに来てください。私は
ソウルのおもしろいところを知っています
から、あんないします。

　　十一月 二十八日
　　　　　　スー・キム

先日（せんじつ）　the other day
りょう　　　　　　dormitory
あんないする　　　to show someone around

ⅢＩ 書く練習
れんしゅう

A. What did you do yesterday? Write a journal.

B. Write a thank-you letter to someone.

Useful Expressions for Letters and Cards:

いろいろおせわになりました。(Thank you for everything.)

体に気をつけてください。(Please take care of yourself.)
からだ

お会いできるのを楽しみにしています。(I am looking forward to seeing you.)
たの

～おめでとう(ございます)。(Congratulations on . . .)

おたんじょうびおめでとう。(Happy Birthday)

第10課 LESSON 10
かさじぞう The Folktale *Kasajizo*

102	住 (to live)	す ジュウ	住む（すむ）to live 住所（ジュウショ）address
			(7) ノ イ イ 仁 什 住 住
103	正 (right)	ショウ ただ	お正月（おショウガツ）New Year 正しい（ただしい）right
			(5) 一 丁 下 正 正
104	年 (year)	ネン とし	三年生（サンネンセイ）third-year student 来年（ライネン）next year　今年（ことし）this year 年（とし）year
			(6) ノ ノ 匕 仁 年 年
105	売 (to sell)	う バイ	売る（うる）to sell 売店（バイテン）stand; stall
			(7) 一 十 土 声 声 売
106	買 (to buy)	か	買う（かう）to buy 買い物（かいもの）shopping
			(12) 丶 冂 四 四 罒 罒 罒 胃 胃 胃 買 買
107	町 (town)	まち チョウ	町（まち）town 北山町（きたやまチョウ）Kitayama town 町長（チョウチョウ）mayor of a town
			(7) 丨 冂 冂 田 田 町 町
108	長 (long)	なが チョウ	長い（ながい）long 長男（チョウナン）one's first son
			(8) 丨 厂 F F 乢 長 長 長
109	道 (way)	みち ドウ	道（みち）way; road 書道（ショドウ）calligraphy　柔道（ジュウドウ）judo 北海道（ホッカイドウ）Hokkaido
			(12) 丶 丷 丷 严 芦 芦 首 首 首 道 道

110	雪 (snow)	ゆき セツ (snow)	雪（ゆき）snow 新雪（シンセツ）new snow ⑾ 一 ｢ 戸 币 雨 雨 雨 雪 雪 雪
111	立 (to stand)	た リツ (to stand)	立つ（たつ）to stand 国立大学（コクリツダイガク）national university 私立高校（シリツコウコウ）private high school ⑸ 丶 亠 亍 立 立
112	自 (self)	ジ (self)	自分（ジブン）oneself 自動車（ジドウシャ）automobile 自転車（ジテンシャ）bicycle ⑹ 丶 ⺅ 冂 白 自 自
113	夜 (night)	よる よ ヤ (night)	夜（よる）night 夜中（よなか）midnight　　今夜（コンヤ）tonight ⑻ 丶 亠 广 广 广 夜 夜 夜
114	朝 (morning)	あさ チョウ (morning)	朝（あさ）morning　　今朝（けさ）this morning 朝食（チョウショク）breakfast ⑿ 一 十 土 吉 吉 直 車 卓 朝 朝 朝
115	持 (to hold)	もつ ジ (to hold)	持つ（もつ）to hold　　持ってくる（もってくる）to bring 所持品（ショジヒン）belongings ⑼ 一 十 扌 扌 扩 持 拝 持 持

(In this chart, *katakana* indicates the *on'yomi* and *hiragana* indicates the *kun'yomi*.)

① 漢字の練習
かんじ　　れんしゅう

A. Add strokes to the kanji below and turn them into new kanji from this lesson.

Example: 二 → 立

1. 上 →　　2. 田 →　　3. 雨 →　　4. 月 →

5. 白 →　　6. 土 →　　7. 員 →　　8. 自 →

B. Write each antonym in kanji.

1. 買う　　⇔ _____　　2. すわる　⇔ _____

3. みじかい ⇔ _____　　4. 夜　　　⇔ _____

C. Fill in the blanks with the appropriate kanji from the list, and add *hiragana* where necessary.

売　雪　住　買　長　立　持

1. 町で_____をしました。
　　　　shopping

2. かさを_____ていますか。
　　　　have

3. 本屋では本を_____ています。
　や
　　(are) sell(ing)

4. よく_____がふります。
　　snow

5. おじいさんの話は_____。
　　　was long

6. アパートに_____でいます。
　　　live

7. 私の後ろに女の人が_____。
　　　was standing

ⓘ かさじぞう

A. Answer the following questions.

1. 日本ではお正月に何をすると思いますか。

2. (Picture 1) これはおじぞうさんです。何だと思いますか。

3. (Picture 2) このおじいさんとおばあさんがこの話の主人公 (main characters) です。どんな人だと思いますか。どんな生活をしていると思いますか。
しゅじんこう
かつ

1 2

B. Read the Japanese folktale "かさじぞう" on pp. 302-3.

C. Put the following pictures in the right order.

( ) → ( ) → ( ) → ( ) → ( ) → ( )

(a)   (b)   (c)

(d)   (e)   (f)

ました。
うちに帰って、おじいさんはおばあさんにおじぞうさんの話をしました。
おばあさんは「おじいさん、いいことをしましたね。」と言いました。
その夜おそく、おじいさんはだれかの声（こえ）を聞きました。
「おじいさん、おじいさん。」
おじいさんは戸（と）を開（あ）けて、びっくりしました。六人のおじぞうさんが立っていました。おじぞうさんはお正月のおもちをたくさん持っていました。
お正月の朝になりました。おじいさんとおばあさんはおもちをたくさん食べました。二人はとてもしあわせでした。

むかしむかし	once upon a time
かさ	bamboo hat
お正月	New Year's
年	year
おもち	rice cake
売る	to sell
かなしい	sad
山道	mountain road
じぞう	guardian deity of children
雪	snow
〜に〜をかぶせる	to put (a hat) on a person's head
自分	oneself
とる	to take off
いいこと	good deed
声（こえ）	voice
戸（と）	door
びっくりする	to be surprised
しあわせな	happy

D. Mark T if the following statements are true. Mark F if not true.

1. (　　) おじいさんとおばあさんはお金持ちだった。
2. (　　) だれもおじいさんのかさを買わなかった。
3. (　　) おじいさんはおじぞうさんにかさを売った。
4. (　　) 雪の中でおじいさんはおじぞうさんを六つ見た。
5. (　　) おじいさんは新しいかさを六つ持っていた。
6. (　　) おばあさんはおじいさんの話を聞いて、かなしくなった。
7. (　　) おじぞうさんはお金をたくさん持ってきた。
8. (　　) おじいさんとおばあさんのお正月はとてもよかった。

かさじぞう

　むかしむかし、山の中におじいさんとおばあさんが住んでいました。おじいさんとおばあさんはうちでかさを作っていました。あしたはお正月です。新しい年がはじまります。でも、おじいさんとおばあさんはお金（かね）がなかったから、お正月のおもちもありませんでした。二人はかさを売って、おもちを買うつもりでした。

　おじいさんはかさを持って、町に売りに行きました。でも、だれもかさを買いませんでした。おじいさんはかなしくなりました。おじいさんは長い山道（みち）を歩（ある）いて帰りました。雪がたくさんふっていました。

　「あっ！おじぞうさんだ！」雪の中におじぞうさんが六つ立っていました。おじいさんは「おじぞうさん、さむくありませんか。」と聞きました。おじぞうさんは何も言いませんでした。

　「どうぞかさを使（つか）ってください。」おじいさんはおじぞうさんのあたまの上にかさをかぶせました。

　「一つ、二つ、三つ、四つ、五つ」かさは五つでした。一人のおじぞうさんはかさがありませんでした。おじいさんは自分のかさをとりました。「このかさは古いですが、どうぞ。」と言って、おじぞうさんにかぶせ

Ⅲ 書く練習（れんしゅう）

Choose one topic from the list below and write a story about it. For example: What do people do on these days? Do you have good memories? Do you know unusual tales about these days?

クリスマス	お正月	ハロウィーン	誕生日（たんじょうび）(Birthday)
感謝祭（かんしゃさい）(Thanksgiving Day)	13日の金曜日		

第11課 LESSON 11

友だち募集 Looking for Friends
ぼ しゅう

116	手 (hand)	て シュ	手紙（てがみ）letter　　歌手（カシュ）singer 手（て）hand　　手話（シュワ）sign language 上手な（ジョウズな）good at
			(4) 一　二　三　手
117	紙 (paper)	がみ かみ シ	手紙（てがみ）letter　　紙（かみ）paper 和紙（ワシ）Japanese paper
			(10) く　乡　幺　乡　乡　糸　糸　糸　紅　紙
118	好 (favorite; to like)	す コウ この	好きな（すきな）to like 好意（コウイ）good will　　好み（このみ）liking; taste
			(6) く　夕　女　女　好　好
119	近 (near)	ちか キン	近く（ちかく）nearby　　近所（キンジョ）neighborhood 最近（サイキン）recently 中近東（チュウキントウ）the Middle and Near East
			(7) 一　ア　斤　斤　斤　沂　近
120	明 (bright)	あか メイ	明るい（あかるい）cheerful; bright 明日（あした）tomorrow 説明（セツメイ）explanation
			(8) 丨　冂　日　日　日　明　明　明
121	病 (ill; sick)	ビョウ	病院（ビョウイン）hospital　　病気（ビョウキ）illness 重病（ジュウビョウ）serious illness 急病（キュウビョウ）sudden illness
			(10) 丶　一　广　广　广　疒　疒　病　病　病
122	院 (institution)	イン	病院（ビョウイン）hospital 大学院（ダイガクイン）graduate school 美容院（ビヨウイン）beauty parlor
			(10) ﾌ　�3　阝　阝　阝　阼　阼　阼　阼　院
123	映 (to reflect)	エイ うつ	映画（エイガ）movie 映画館（エイガカン）movie theater 映る（うつる）to be reflected
			(9) 丨　冂　日　日　日　日　昍　映　映

124	画	ガ カク (picture)	映画（エイガ）movie 画家（ガカ）painter　計画（ケイカク）plan (8) 一 厂 厂 币 币 币 画 画
125	歌	うた　カ (to sing)	歌う（うたう）to sing　歌（うた）song 歌手（カシュ）singer 国歌（コッカ）national anthem (14) 一 厂 厂 可 可 可 哥 哥 哥 哥 歌 歌 歌
126	市	シ いち (city)	川口市（かわぐちシ）Kawaguchi city 市役所（シヤクショ）city hall　市長（シチョウ）mayor 市場（いちば）market (5) 、 一 广 方 市
127	所	ところ　ジョ どころ　ショ (place)	いろいろな所（いろいろなところ）various places 近所（キンジョ）neighborhood 台所（ダイどころ）kitchen　住所（ジュウショ）address (8) 一 ラ ラ 戸 戸 所 所 所
128	勉	ベン つと (to make efforts)	勉強する（ベンキョウする）to study 勉める（つとめる）to try hard 勤勉な（キンベンな）diligent (10) ' ク ケ 在 各 各 免 免 勉 勉
129	強	キョウ　つよ ゴウ (strong)	勉強する（ベンキョウする）to study 強い（つよい）strong 強情な（ゴウジョウな）obstinate (11) フ ュ 弓 弓 弘 弘 弘 弘 強 強 強
130	有	ユウ あ (to exist)	有名な（ユウメイな）famous 有料（ユウリョウ）toll; fee 有る（ある）to exist (6) ノ ナ ナ 冇 有 有
131	旅	リョ たび (travel)	旅行（リョコウ）travel 旅館（リョカン）inn 一人旅（ひとりたび）traveling alone (10) 、 ㇒ ㇒ 方 扩 扩 ㇒ 㫃 旅 旅

(In this chart, *katakana* indicates the *on'yomi* and *hiragana* indicates the *kun'yomi*.)

Ⅰ 漢字の練習
かんじ れんしゅう

A. Combine the parts below to form the new kanji from this lesson.

B. Put one kanji in each box to make compunds.

(1)

歌	
	紙

(2)

	く
所	

(3)

有	
	前

(4)

	院
気	

Ⅱ 友だち募集
ぼ しゅう

A. 質問に答えてください。(Answer the following questions.)
しつもん こた

1. あなたの国には友だち募集の雑誌がありますか。
   #### ぼ しゅう ざっ し

2. あなたは雑誌で友だちを募集したことがありますか。友だちを募集している人
   #### ざっ し ぼ しゅう ぼ しゅう
   に手紙を書いたことがありますか。

B. 雑誌の「友だち募集」を読みましょう。
ざっ し ぼ しゅう

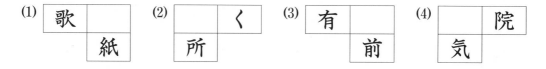

友だちになってください

大学三年生です。専門はフランス文学
です。スポーツが大好きで、休みの日に
せんもん
は、テニスをしたり、サッカーをしたり
しています。カラオケにもよく行きま
す。今度いっしょに遊びませんか。
こんど あそ

水野　裕子（20歳／女）
みず の ゆうこ はたち

手紙ください！

会社員です。川口市に住んでいます。
アウトドアが好きで、休みの日は車で
近くの山や川に行きます。将来は外国
しょうらい
の山に登りたいと思っています。山に
のぼ
登るのが好きな人、手紙ください。
のぼ

松本　明（23歳／男）
まつもと あきら さい

彼女募集！
かのじょ ぼしゅう
20歳から25歳ぐらいで、明るくて、や
はたち さい あか
さしくて、たばこを吸わない人。髪が
す かみ
長い人が好きです。ぼくは病院に勤め
なが つと
ています。趣味はドライブと映画です。
しゅみ
会って、いろいろ話しましょう。
あ はな

中村　ひろし
なかむら
（26歳／男）
さい

いっしょにバンドをやりませんか

ロックが好きな女の子です。ギターを
ひくのが好きで、将来は歌手になりた
しょうらい
いと思っています。私といっしょにバン
ドをやりませんか。それからコン
サートにもいっしょに行きましょう！

岡田　香
おか だ かおり
（18歳／女）
さい

～募集（ぼしゅう）	looking for . . .	川	river
女（おんな）	woman	彼女（かのじょ）	girlfriend
男（おとこ）	man	明るい	cheerful
アウトドア	outdoor activities	趣味（しゅみ）	hobby
近く	near place	バンド	band

C. 次の人はだれですか。その人の名前を書いてください。

　1. The person who is 18 years old　　　　　　（　　　　　　　　）さん

　2. The person who is a college student　　　　（　　　　　　　　）さん

　3. The person who likes movies　　　　　　　（　　　　　　　　）さん

　4. The person who likes climbing mountains　（　　　　　　　　）さん

　5. The person who is looking for a girlfriend　（　　　　　　　　）さん

D. 質問に答えてください。
しつもん こた

　1. 水野さんはどんなスポーツをしますか。
みず の

　2. 水野さんの専門は何ですか。
みず の せんもん

　3. 中村さんはどんな人が好きですか。
なかむら

　4. 松本さんは車を運転しますか。
まつもと うんてん

5. 岡田さんは何になりたいと思っていますか。

6. あなたはどの人に手紙を書きたいですか。どうしてですか。

E. 雑誌を見て、カレンさんは松本さんに手紙を書きました。手紙を読んで、質問に答えてください。

松本　明　様

　　はじめまして。雑誌を見ました。私も川口市に住んでいます。近所ですね。私はカナダ人の留学生です。一月に日本に来ました。今、日本語や日本文化を勉強しています。私もアウトドアが大好きで、山に登ったり、つりをしたりするのが好きです。旅行も好きです。外国は、シンガポールやニュージーランドに行ったことがあります。日本では、まだあまり旅行していませんが、これからいろいろな所に行くつもりです。古いお寺や神社を見たいと思っています。日本の有名な祭りも見たいです。スポーツはバスケットが好きです。日本人の友だちをたくさん作って、日本語でいろいろなことを話したいと思っています。よかったら、お返事ください。

　　三月二十一日

　　　　　　　　　　　　　　　　　　　　　カレン・ミラー

近所	neighborhood	神社（じんじゃ）	shrine
文化（ぶんか）	culture	祭り（まつり）	festival
つり	fishing	お返事（おへんじ）	reply

1. カレンさんはいつ日本に来ましたか。

2. カレンさんは何をするのが好きですか。

3. カレンさんは日本でどこに行きたいと思っていますか。

Ⅲ 書く練習
れんしゅう

A. 友だち募集の手紙を書きましょう。
ぼ しゅう

B. Ⅱ-B のどの人と友だちになりたいですか。その人に手紙を書きましょう。

第12課 L E S S O N ·············· 12
七夕 Tanabata Festival
たな ばた

132	昔	むかし (ancient times)	昔（むかし）old times 昔話（むかしばなし）old tale
			(8) 一 十 卄 昔 芊 芋 昔 昔
133	々	(symbol of repetition of a kanji)	昔々（むかしむかし）once upon a time 人々（ひとびと）people 時々（ときどき）sometimes　色々な（いろいろな）various
			(3) ノ 久 々
134	神	かみ　ジン シン (God)	神さま（かみさま）God　神社（ジンジャ）shrine 神道（シントウ）Shinto religion
			(9) `ヽ ラ ネ ネ ネ 初 祁 和 神
135	早	はや ソウ (early)	早い（はやい）early 早起きする（はやおきする）to get up early 早朝（ソウチョウ）early morning
			(6) ノ 口 日 日 旦 早
136	起	お キ (to get up)	起きる（おきる）to get up 起こす（おこす）to wake someone up 起立する（キリツする）to stand up
			(10) 一 十 土 キ キ キ 走 走 起 起 起
137	牛	うし ギュウ (cow)	牛（うし）cow 牛乳（ギュウニュウ）milk　牛肉（ギュウにく）beef
			(4) ノ ヒ 二 牛
138	使	つか シ (to use)	使う（つかう）to use 大使（タイシ）ambassador 使用中（ショウチュウ）"Occupied"
			(8) ノ イ 仁 仁 仁 佢 使 使
139	働	はたら ばたら　ドウ (to work)	働く（はたらく）to work 共働き（ともばたらき）both husband and wife working for a living　労働（ロウドウ）labor
			(13) ノ イ 仁 仁 仁 佢 信 信 俥 俥 働 働

140	連 (to link)	つ レン (to link)	連れて帰る （つれてかえる）to take home 国連 （コクレン）United Nations 連休 （レンキュウ）consecutive holidays
			(10) 一 ㇀ 厂 厂 肎 亘 亘 車 車 連 連
141	別 (to separate)	わか　ベツ (to separate)	別れる （わかれる）to separate　　別に （ベツに）not in particular　　特別な(トクベツな)special　　差別(サベツ) discrimination　　別々に （ベツベツに）separately
			(7) 丶 ㇁ �口 口 号 另 別 別
142	度 (time; degrees)	ド (time; degrees)	一度 （イチド）once　　今度 （コンド）near future 温度 （オンド）temperature 三十度 （サンジュウド）30 degrees
			(9) 丶 亠 广 广 庐 庐 庐 度 度
143	赤 (red)	あか セキ (red)	赤 （あか）red color　　赤い （あかい）red 赤ちゃん(あかちゃん)baby　　赤道(セキドウ) the equator 赤十字 （セキジュウジ）the Red Cross
			(7) 一 十 土 ㇏ 赤 赤 赤
144	青 (blue)	あお セイ (blue)	青 （あお）blue color　　青い （あおい）blue 青年 （セイネン）youth
			(8) 一 十 丰 主 青 青 青 青
145	色 (color)	いろ シキ　ショク (color)	色 （いろ）color 色々な （いろいろな）various　　景色 （ケシキ）scenery 特色 （トクショク）characteristic
			(6) ㇁ ㇄ 夕 夕 名 色

(In this chart, *katakana* indicates the *on'yomi* and *hiragana* indicates the *kun'yomi*.)

① 漢字の練習
かん じ　れんしゅう

A. Match the reading, kanji, and translation.

Example:　むかし　　・　　・早・　　　・ to use

　1. はや(い)　　・　　・青・　　　・ cow

　2. お(きる)　　・　　・昔・　　　・ to get up

　3. つか(う)　　・　　・牛・　　　・ early

　4. わか(れる)　・　　・色・　　　・ color

　5. あか　　　　・　　・赤・　　　・ ancient times

　6. あお　　　　・　　・起・　　　・ to separate

　7. いろ　　　　・　　・別・　　　・ blue

　8. うし　　　　・　　・使・　　　・ red

B. Which new kanji from this lesson include the *katakana* below?

　1. マ →　　　2. ネ →　　　3. カ →　　　4. ヌ →

C. Which new kanji from this lesson shares the same component as each pair of kanji below?

Example:　朝　前 → 青

　1. 住　仕　　　2. 道　近　　　3. 万　旅

② 七夕
たな　ばた

A. 絵 (picture) を見てください。これは何だと思いますか。七夕の日に作ります。
え

B. 七夕の話を読みましょう。

七月七日は七夕です。これは七夕の話です。

昔々、天に神さまが住んでいました。娘が一人いて、名前はおりひめでした。おりひめはとてもまじめで、毎日、朝早く起きてはたを織っていました。

ある日、神さまは思いました。「おりひめはもう大人だ。結婚したほうがいいだろう。」

神さまはまじめな男の人を見つけました。天の川の向こうに住んでいる人で、名前はひこぼしでした。ひこぼしは牛を使って、畑で働いていました。

おりひめとひこぼしは結婚しました。二人はとても好きになりました。いつもいっしょにいて、ぜんぜん働きませんでした。

神さまは怒りました。でも二人は仕事をしませんでした。

神さまはとても怒って、おりひめを家に連れて帰りました。二人は別れなくてはいけませんでした。おりひめはひこぼしに会いたくて、毎日泣いていました。

神さまは二人がかわいそうだと思って、言いました。

「おりひめ、ひこぼし、あなたたちは一年に一度だけ会ってもいい。それは七月七日の夜だ。おりひめ、あなたはその日、天の川の向こうに行ってもいい。でも、朝までに帰らなくちゃいけない。」

一年に一度、七夕の夜におりひめとひこぼしは会います。二人の願いはかなうのです。

この日、私たちは赤や青などいろいろな色のたんざくに願いを書きます。七夕の日の願いはかなうと人々は言います。ある子供は「いい成績を取りたい」と書きます。ある人は「すてきな人に会いたい」と書きます。あなたは七夕の日にどんな願いを書きますか。

天	the heavens; the sky	怒る（おこる）	to get angry
神さま	God	連れて帰る	to take back
娘（むすめ）	daughter	泣く（なく）	to cry
まじめな	serious	かわいそうな	pitiful
はたを織る（おる）	to weave	一年に一度	once a year
ある〜	one ...（ある日　one day）	〜までに	by ...
大人（おとな）	adult	願い（ねがい）	wish
見つける	to find	かなう	to be realized
天の川（あまのがわ）	the Milky Way	私たち	we
向こう（むこう）	the other side; over there	〜など	and so forth
牛	cow	たんざく	strip of fancy paper
畑（はたけ）	farm	人々	people

C. 質問に答えてください。

1. おりひめはどんな人ですか。

2. ひこぼしはどんな人ですか。

3. どうして神さまは怒りましたか。

4. 七月七日におりひめは何をしますか。

5. どうして私たちは七夕の日にたんざくに願いを書きますか。

6. 神さまはやさしい人だと思いますか。どうしてですか。

Ⅲ 書く練習

あなたの願いを五つ書いてください。どうしてその願いを書きましたか。理由 (reason) も書いてください。

巻末
かん　まつ

あいうえお　かきくけこ　さしすせそ　たちつてと　なにぬねの　はひふへほ　まみむめも　やゆよ　らりるれろ　わをん

さくいん1 Japanese-English

各項目の表示は以下の内容を示す。
Items at the end of each entry indicate the following:
会…… 会話・文法編
(Conversation and Grammar section)
読…… 読み書き編
(Reading and Writing section)
G…… あいさつ (Greetings)
(s)…… 課末コラム (Supplement)
Ⅰ・Ⅱ・Ⅲ……問題番号（読み書き編）
(number of excercise in the Reading and Writing section)

あ

あいだ　間　between　会L4
あう　会う　to meet; to see (a person)　会L4
アウトドア　outdoor activities　読L11-Ⅱ
あおい　青い　blue　会L9, 会L9(s)
あかい　赤い　red　会L9, 会L9(s)
あかるい　明るい　cheerful　読L11-Ⅱ
あき　秋　fall　会L10
あける　開ける　to open (something)　会L6
あさ　朝　morning　会L3
あさごはん　朝御飯　breakfast　会L3
あさって　the day after tomorrow　会L4(s), 会L8
あし　足　leg; foot　会L7(s), 会L12
アジアけんきゅう　アジア研究　Asian studies　会L1
あした　tomorrow　会L3, 会L4(s)
あそこ　over there　会L2
あそぶ　遊ぶ　to play; to spend time pleasantly　会L6
あたたかい　暖かい　warm　会L10
あたま　頭　head　会L7(s)
あたまがいい　頭がいい　bright; smart; clever　会L7
あたらしい　新しい　new　会L5
あつい　暑い　hot (weather)　会L5
あつい　熱い　hot (objects)　会L5
（〜の)あと　後　after (an event)　会L11, 読L8-Ⅱ
あとで　後で　later on　会L6
あなた　you　会L4
あに　兄　(my) older brother　会L7(s)
あね　姉　(my) older sister　会L7, 会L7(s)

あの　um . . .　会L1
あの　that . . . (over there)　会L2
アパート　apartment　会L7
あまい　甘い　sweet　会L12
あまのがわ　天の川　the Milky Way　読L12-Ⅱ
あまり ＋ negative　not much　会L3
あめ　雨　rain　会L8
あめがふる　雨が降る　it rains　会L8
アメリカ　U.S.A.　会L1, 会L2
あらう　洗う　to wash　会L8
ありがとう　Thank you.　会G
ありがとうございます　Thank you. (polite)　会G
ある　there is . . .　会L4
ある〜　one . . .　読L12-Ⅱ
あるいて　歩いて　on foot　会L10
アルバイト　part-time job　会L4
あれ　that one (over there)　会L2
アンケート　questionnaire　読L8-Ⅱ
あんないする　案内する　to show someone around　読L9-Ⅱ

い

いい　good　会L3
いいえ　No.; Not at all.　会G
いいこ　いい子　good child　会L9
いいこと　good deed　読L10-Ⅱ
いう　言う　to say　会L8
いえ　家　home; house　会L3
〜いき　〜行き　bound for . . .　会L10(s)
イギリス　Britain　会L1, 会L2
いく　行く　to go　会L3
いくら　how much　会L2
いしゃ　医者　doctor　会L1, 会L10
いじわる(な)　意地悪　mean-spirited　会L9
いす　chair　会L2(s)
いそがしい　忙しい　busy (people/days)　会L5
いそぐ　急ぐ　to hurry　会L6
いたい　痛い　hurt; painful　会L12
いただきます　Thank you for the meal. (before eating)　会G
いちがつ　一月　January　会L4(s)
いちじ　一時　one o'clock　会L1, 会L1(s)
いちじかん　一時間　one hour　会L4

あいうえお　かきくけこ　さしすせそ　たちつてと　なにぬねの　はひふへほ　まみむめも　やゆよ　らりるれろ　わをん

いちねんせい　一年生　first-year student　会L1
いちねんにいちど　一年に一度　once a year
　　　　　　　　読L12-Ⅱ
いちばん　一番　best　会L10
いちばんうしろ　一番後ろ　last car; tail end
　　　　　　　　会L10(s)
いちばんまえ　一番前　first car; front end
　　　　　　　　会L10(s)
いつ　when　会L3
いつか　五日　the fifth day of a month　会L4(s)
いっさい　一歳　one year old　会L1(s)
いっしょに　一緒に　together　会L5
いつつ　五つ　five　会L9
いってきます　I'll go and come back.　会G
いってらっしゃい　Please go and come back.　会G
いっぷん　一分　one minute　会L1(s)
いつも　always　会L12, 読L6-Ⅲ
いぬ　犬　dog　会L4
いま　今　now　会L1
いみ　意味　meaning　会L11(s), 会L12
いもうと(さん)　妹(さん)　younger sister　会L1,
　　　　　　　　会L7, 会L7(s)
いらっしゃいませ　Welcome (to our store)　会L2
いりぐち　入口　entrance　会L10(s)
いる　(a person) is in . . . ; stays at . . .　会L4
いる　to need　会L8
いろ　色　color　会L9
いろいろな　various　読L9-Ⅱ

ううん　uh-uh; no　会L8
うえ　上　on　会L4
うし　牛　cow　読L12-Ⅱ
うしろ　後ろ　back　会L4
うそをつく　to tell a lie　会L11
うた　歌　song　会L7
うたう　歌う　to sing　会L7
うち　home; house; my place　会L3
うちのこ　うちの子　(my) child　会L7(s)
うちのひと　うちの人　husband　会L7(s)
うみ　海　sea　会L5
うる　売る　to sell　読L10-Ⅱ
うん　uh-huh; yes　会L8
うんてんする　運転する　to drive　会L8
うんどうする　運動する　to do physical exercises
　　　　　　　　会L9

エアログラム　aerogramme　会L5(s)
えいが　映画　movie　会L3
えいご　英語　English (language)　会L1
ええ　yes　会L1
えき　駅　station　会L10, 読L6-Ⅰ
LL (エルエル)　language lab　会L3
～えん　～円　. . . yen　会L2
えんぴつ　鉛筆　pencil　会L2, 会L2(s)

おいしい　delicious　会L2
おうふく　往復　round trip　会L10(s)
おおい　多い　there are many . . .　会L12
おおきい　大きい　large　会L5
オーストラリア　Australia　会L1, 会L11
おかあさん　お母さん　mother　会L1, 会L2,
　　　　　　　　会L7(s)
おかえりなさい　Welcome home.　会G
おかし　お菓子　snack; sweets　会L11
おかね　お金　money　会L6
おかねもち　お金持ち　rich person　会L10
おきる　起きる　to get up　会L3
おくさん　奥さん　wife　会L7(s)
おこさん　お子さん　child　会L7(s)
おこる　怒る　to get angry　読L12-Ⅱ
おさけ　お酒　sake; alcohol　会L3
おじいさん　grandfather　会L7(s)
おしえる　教える　to teach; to instruct　会L6
おしょうがつ　お正月　New Year's　会L11,
　　　　　　　　読L10-Ⅱ
おしり　buttocks　会L7(s)
おしろ　お城　castle　読L5-Ⅱ
おそい　遅い　slow; late　会L10
おそく　遅く　(do something) late　会L6, 読L4-Ⅲ
おそくなる　遅くなる　to be late (for)　会L8
おだいじに　お大事に　Get well soon.　会L12
おちゃ　お茶　green tea　会L3
おっと　夫　husband　会L7(s)
おてあらい　お手洗い　restroom　会L2
おてら　お寺　temple　会L4
おとうさん　お父さん　father　会L1, 会L2, 会L7(s)
おとうと(さん)　弟(さん)　younger brother
　　　　　　　　会L1, 会L7, 会L7(s)
おとこ　男　man　読L11-Ⅱ

あいうえお　かきくけこ　さしすせそ　たちつてと　なにぬねの　はひふへほ　まみむめも　やゆよ　らりるれろ　わをん

あいうえお **かきくけこ** さしすせそ たちつてと なにぬねの はひふへほ まみむめも やゆよ らりるれろ わをん

かようび 火曜日 Tuesday 会L4, 会L4(s)

カラオケ karaoke 会L8

〜から because . . . 会L6

〜から from . . . 会L9, 読L7-II

からだにきをつける 体に気をつける
　　to take care of oneself 読L7-II

かりる 借りる to borrow 会L6

かれ 彼 boyfriend 会L12

かわ 川 river 読L11-II

かわいい cute 会L7

かわいそうな pitiful 読L12-II

がんか 眼科 ophthalmologist 会L12(s)

かんこく 韓国 Korea 会L1, 会L2

かんじ 漢字 kanji; Chinese character 会L6

かんたん(な) 簡単 easy; simple 会L10

かんぱい 乾杯 Cheers! (a toast) 会L8

きいろい 黄色い yellow 会L9(s)

きおん 気温 temperature (weather) 会L12

きく 聞く to listen; to hear 会L3

きく 聞く to ask 会L5

きせつ 季節 season 会L10

きた 北 north 会L6(s)

ギター guitar 会L9

きっさてん 喫茶店 cafe 会L2

きって 切手 postal stamps 会L5, 会L5(s)

きっぷ 切符 ticket 会L5

きっぷうりば 切符売り場 ticket vending area
　　　　　　　　会L10(s)

きのう 昨日 yesterday 会L4, 会L4(s)

きめる 決める to decide 会L10

キャンプ camp 会L11

きゅうこう 急行 express 会L10(s)

きゅうさい 九歳 nine years old 会L1(s)

きゅうふん 九分 nine minutes 会L1(s)

きょう 今日 today 会L3, 会L4(s)

きょうかしょ 教科書 textbook 会L6

きょうだい 兄弟 brothers and sisters 会L7

きょうみがある 興味がある to be interested (in)
　　　　　　　　会L12

〜ぎょうめ 〜行目 line number . . . 会L11(s)

きょねん 去年 last year 会L4, 会L4(s)

きらい(な) 嫌い disgusted with; to dislike 会L5

きる 着る to put on (clothes above your waist)
　　会L7

きる 切る to cut 会L8

きれい(な) beautiful; clean 会L5

きんいろ 金色 gold 会L9(s)

ぎんいろ 銀色 silver 会L9(s)

きんえんしゃ 禁煙車 nonsmoking car 会L10(s)

ぎんこう 銀行 bank 会L2

きんじょ 近所 neighborhood 読L11-II

きんちょうする 緊張する to get nervous 会L12

きんぱつ 金髪 blonde hair 会L9(s)

きんようび 金曜日 Friday 会L4, 会L4(s)

くうき 空気 air 会L8

くがつ 九月 September 会L4(s)

くじ 九時 nine o'clock 会L1(s)

くすり 薬 medicine 会L9

くすりをのむ 薬を飲む to take medicine 会L9

くだけたいいかた くだけた言い方
　　colloquial expression 会L11(s)

ください(〜を) Please give me . . . 会L2

くち 口 mouth 会L7(s)

くつ 靴 shoes 会L2

くに 国 country; place of origin 会L7

くび 首 neck 会L7(s)

くもり 曇り cloudy weather 会L12

〜ぐらい about (approximate measurement)
　　　　会L4

クラス class 会L4

グリーン green 会L9(s)

くる 来る to come 会L3

くるま 車 car 会L7

グレー gray 会L9(s)

クレジットカード credit card 会L10

くろい 黒い black 会L9, 会L9(s)

けいざい 経済 economics 会L1, 会L2

けが injury 会L12(s)

げか 外科 surgeon 会L12(s)

けさ 今朝 this morning 会L8

けしゴム 消しゴム eraser 会L2(s)

けす 消す to turn off; to erase 会L6

けっこうです 結構です That would be fine.;
　　　　　　　That wouldn't be necessary. 会L6

けっこんする 結婚する to get married 会L7

げつようび 月曜日 Monday 会L4, 会L4(s)

あいうえお　かきくけこ　さしすせそ　たちつてと　なにぬねの　はひふへほ　まみむめも　やゆよ　らりるれろ　わをん

けんかする　to have a fight; to quarrel　会L11
げんき（な）　元気　healthy; energetic　会L5
げんきがない　元気がない　don't look well　会L12
げんぞう　現像　development　会L5(s)

こ

～ご　～語　language　会L1
～ご　～後　in . . . time; after . . .　会L10
こうえん　公園　park　会L4
こうくうびん　航空便　airmail　会L5(s)
こうこう　高校　high school　会L1
こうこうせい　高校生　high school student　会L1
こうせいぶっしつ　抗生物質　antibiotic　会L12(s)
こうたくあり　光沢あり　glossy finish　会L5(s)
こうたくなし　光沢なし　mat finish　会L5(s)
こえ　声　voice　読L10-II
コーヒー　coffee　会L3
ゴールド　gold　会L9(s)
ごがつ　五月　May　会L4(s)
こくさいかんけい　国際関係　international relations　会L1
こくばん　黒板　black board　会L2(s)
ここ　here　会L4
ごご　午後　P.M.　会L1
ここのか　九日　the ninth day of a month　会L4(s)
ここのつ　九つ　nine　会L9
ごさい　五歳　five years old　会L1(s)
ごじ　五時　five o'clock　会L1(s)
ごしゅじん　ご主人　husband　会L7(s)
ごぜん　午前　A.M.　会L1
ごぜんちゅう　午前中　in the morning　読L9-II
こたえ　答　answer　会L11(s)
こたえる　答える　to answer　読L8-II
ごちそう　excellent food　読L9-II
ごちそうさま　Thank you for the meal. (after eating)　会G
こちら　this person (polite)　会L11
こづつみ　小包　parcel　会L5(s)
ことし　今年　this year　会L4(s), 会L10
こども　子供　child　会L4
この　this . . .　会L2
このごろ　these days　会L10
ごはん　御飯　rice; meal　会L4
ごふん　五分　five minutes　会L1(s)
ごめんなさい　I'm sorry.　会L4
～ごろ　at about　会L3
これ　this one　会L2

こわい　怖い　frightening　会L5
こんがっき　今学期　this semester　会L11
こんげつ　今月　this month　会L4(s), 会L8
コンサート　concert　会L9
こんしゅう　今週　this week　会L4(s), 会L6
こんど　今度　near future　会L9
こんにちは　Good afternoon.　会G
こんばん　今晩　tonight　会L3
こんばんは　Good evening.　会G
コンビニ　convenience store　会L7
コンピューター　computer　会L1, 会L2

さ

サーフィン　surfing　会L5
～さい　～歳　. . . years old　会L1, 会L1(s)
さいごに　最後に　lastly　読L8-II
さいふ　財布　wallet　会L2
さかな　魚　fish　会L2
さくぶん　作文　essay; composition　会L9
さけ　酒　sake; alcohol　会L3
サッカー　soccer　会L10
さっき　a little while ago　会L4
ざっし　雑誌　magazine　会L3
さびしい　寂しい　lonely　会L9
サボる　to cut classes　会L11
～さま　～様　Mr./Ms. . . .　読L5-II
さむい　寒い　cold (weather)　会L5
さようなら　Good-bye.　会G
さらいげつ　再来月　the month after next　会L4(s)
さらいしゅう　再来週　the week after next　会L4(s)
さらいねん　再来年　the year after next　会L4(s)
～さん　Mr./Ms. . . .　会L1
さんがつ　三月　March　会L4(s)
ざんぎょう　残業　overtime work　読L8-II
さんさい　三歳　three years old　会L1(s)
さんじ　三時　three o'clock　会L1(s)
さんじゅっぷん　三十分　thirty minutes　会L1(s)
ざんねんですね　残念ですね　That's too bad.　会L8
さんふじんか　産婦人科　obstetrician and gynecologist　会L12(s)
さんぷん　三分　three minutes　会L1(s)
さんぽする　散歩する　to take a walk　会L9

し

～じ　～時　o'clock　会L1
しあい　試合　match; game　会L12

あいうえお　かきくけこ　さしすせそ　たちつてと　なにぬねの　はひふへほ　まみむめも　やゆよ　らりるれろ　わをん

しあがり　仕上がり　date/time something is ready　会L5(s)

しあわせな　幸せな　happy　読L10-II

ジーンズ　jeans　会L2

しか　歯科　dentist　会L12(s)

しがつ　四月　April　会L4(s)

～じかん　～時間　hour　会L4

しけん　試験　exam　会L9

しごと　仕事　job; work; occupation　会L1, 会L8

じしょ　辞書　dictionary　会L2, 会L2(s)

しずか(な)　静か　quiet　会L5

じぞう　guardian deity of children　読L10-II

した　下　under　会L4

しちがつ　七月　July　会L4(s)

しちじ　七時　seven o'clock　会L1(s)

しっています　知っています　I know　会L7

しつもん　質問　question　会L11(s)

していせき　指定席　reserved seat　会L10(s)

じてんしゃ　自転車　bicycle　会L2

しぬ　死ぬ　to die　会L6

じはつ　次発　departing second　会L10(s)

じびか　耳鼻科　otorhinolaryngologist; ENT doctor　会L12(s)

じぶん　自分　oneself　読L10-II

しみんびょういん　市民病院　Municipal Hospital　会L6

しめきり　deadline　会L11(s)

しめる　閉める　to close (something)　会L6

じゃあ　then . . . ; if that is the case, . . .　会L2

しゃしん　写真　picture; photograph　会L4

しゃちょう　社長　president of a company　会L11

シャツ　shirt　会L10

じゅういちがつ　十一月　November　会L4(s)

じゅういちじ　十一時　eleven o'clock　会L1(s)

じゅういちにち　十一日　the eleventh day of a month　会L4(s)

じゅういっさい　十一歳　eleven years old　会L1(s)

じゅういっぷん　十一分　eleven minutes　会L1(s)

じゅうがつ　十月　October　会L4(s)

～しゅうかん　～週間　for . . . weeks　会L10

じゅうきゅうふん　十九分　ninteen minutes　会L1(s)

じゅうごふん　十五分　fifteen minutes　会L1(s)

じゅうさんぷん　十三分　thirteen minutes　会L1(s)

じゅうじ　十時　ten o'clock　会L1(s)

ジュース　juice　会L12

じゆうせき　自由席　general admission seat　会L10(s)

しゅうでん　終電　last train　会L10(s)

じゅうななふん　十七分　seventeen minutes　会L1(s)

じゅうにがつ　十二月　December　会L4(s)

じゅうにじ　十二時　twelve o'clock　会L1(s)

じゅうにふん　十二分　twelve minutes　会L1(s)

じゅうはちふん/じゅうはっぷん　十八分　eighteen minutes　会L1(s)

しゅうまつ　週末　weekend　会L3

じゅうよっか　十四日　the fourteenth day of a month　会L4(s)

じゅうよんぷん　十四分　fourteen minutes　会L1(s)

じゅうろっぷん　十六分　sixteen minutes　会L1(s)

じゅぎょう　授業　class　会L11

じゅく　塾　cram school　読L7-II

しゅくだい　宿題　homework　会L5, L11(s)

しゅじゅつ　手術　operation　会L12(s)

しゅじん　主人　husband　会L7(s)

じゅっさい　十歳　ten years old　会L1(s)

しゅっしん　出身　coming from　会L11

じゅっぷん　十分　ten minutes　会L1(s)

しゅふ　主婦　housewife　会L1

しゅみ　趣味　hobby　読L11-II

しょうかいする　紹介する　to introduce　会L11

しょうがつ　正月　New Year's　会L11, 読L10-II

じょうしゃけん　乗車券　(boarding) ticket　会L10(s)

じょうず(な)　上手　skillful; good at . . .　会L8

しょうらい　将来　future　会L11

しょくどう　食堂　cafeteria; dining commons　会L7

しり　buttocks　会L7(s)

しりません　知りません　I do not know　会L7

しる　知る　to get to know　会L7

シルバー　silver　会L9(s)

しろ　城　castle　読L5-II

しろい　白い　white　会L9, 会L9(s)

しろくろ　白黒　black and white　会L9(s)

じろじろみる　じろじろ見る　to stare (at)　会L8

～じん　～人　people　会L1

しんかんせん　新幹線　Shinkansen; "Bullet Train"　会L9

しんごう　信号　traffic light　会L6(s)

じんじゃ　神社　shrine　読L11-II

しんせつ(な)　親切　kind　会L7

しんぱいする　心配する　to worry　会L12

しんぶん　新聞　newspaper　会L2

じんるいがく　人類学　anthropology　会L1

あいうえお　かきくけこ　さし**すせそ**　**た**ちつてと　なにぬねの　はひふへほ　まみむめも　やゆよ　らりるれろ　わをん

す

すいようび　水曜日　Wednesday　会 L4, 会 L4(s)
スウェーデン　Sweden　会 L1
スーパー　supermarket　会 L4
すき(な)　好き　fond of; to like　会 L5
スキー　ski　会 L9
すぐ　right away　会 L6
すごく　very　会 L11
すこし　少し　a little　読 L7-Ⅱ
すずしい　涼しい　cool (weather)　会 L10
すてき(な)　素敵　fantastic　会 L12
ストレス　stress　読 L8-Ⅱ
スポーツ　sports　会 L3
すみません　Excuse me.; I am sorry.　会 G
すむ　住む　to live　会 L7
スライド　slide　会 L5(s)
する　to do　会 L3
すわる　座る　to sit down　会 L6

せ

せいかつ　生活　life; living　会 L10
せいけいげか　整形外科　orthopedic surgeon
　　　　　　　　会 L12(s)
せいじ　政治　politics　会 L1, 会 L12
せいせき　成績　grade (on a test, etc.)　会 L12
せいりけん　整理券　vouchers; zone tickets
　　　　　　　　会 L10(s)
せかい　世界　world　会 L10
せがたかい　背が高い　tall　会 L7
せがひくい　背が低い　short (stature)　会 L7
せき　cough　会 L12
せきがでる　せきが出る　to cough　会 L12
せなか　背中　back　会 L7(s)
ぜひ　是非　by all means　会 L9
せまい　狭い　narrow; not spacious　会 L12
せんげつ　先月　last month　会 L4(s), 会 L9
せんじつ　先日　the other day　読 L9-Ⅱ
せんしゅう　先週　last week　会 L4, 会 L4(s)
せんせい　先生　teacher; Professor . . .　会 L1
ぜんぜん＋negative　全然　not at all　会 L3
せんせんしゅう　先々週　the week before last
　　　　　　　　会 L4(s)
せんたくする　洗濯する　to do laundry　会 L8
せんぱつ　先発　departing first　会 L10(s)
せんもん　専門　major　会 L1

そ

そうじする　掃除する　to clean　会 L8
そうです　That's right.　会 L1
そうですね　That's right.; Let me see.　会 L3
そくたつ　速達　special delivery　会 L5(s)
そこ　there　会 L4
そして　and then　会 L11, 読 L9-Ⅱ
その　that . . .　会 L2
そば　near　会 L4
そふ　祖父　(my) grandfather　会 L7(s)
そぼ　祖母　(my) grandmother　会 L7(s)
それ　that one　会 L2
それから　and then　会 L5

た

ダイエットする　to go on a diet　会 L11
たいおんけい　体温計　thermometer　会 L12(s)
だいがく　大学　college; university　会 L1
だいがくいんせい　大学院生　graduate student　会 L1
だいがくせい　大学生　college student　会 L1, 会 L8
だいきらい(な)　大嫌い　to hate　会 L5
だいじょうぶ　大丈夫　It is okay.; Not to worry.;
　　　　　　　　Everything is under control.　会 L5
だいすき(な)　大好き　very fond of; to love　会 L5
たいてい　大抵　usually　会 L3
たいへん(な)　大変　tough (situation)　会 L6, 読 L5-Ⅱ
たかい　高い　expensive　会 L2
だから　so; therefore　会 L4
たくさん　many; a lot　会 L4
〜だけ　just . . .; only . . .　会 L11
ただいま　I'm home.　会 G
たつ　立つ　to stand up　会 L6
たとえば　for example　会 L11(s)
たのしい　楽しい　fun　会 L5
たのしみにする(〜を)　楽しみにする
　　to look forward (to)　読 L7-Ⅱ
たばこをすう　たばこを吸う　to smoke　会 L6
たぶん　多分　probably; maybe　会 L12
たべもの　食べ物　food　会 L5
たべる　食べる　to eat　会 L3
だれ　who　会 L2
たんご　単語　word; vocabulary　会 L9
たんざく　strip of fancy paper　読 L12-Ⅱ
たんじょうび　誕生日　birthday　会 L5
だんな　husband　会 L7(s)

ち

ちいさい　小さい　small　会L5
ちかく　近く　near place　読L11-II
ちかてつ　地下鉄　subway　会L10
ちこくする　遅刻する　to be late (for an appoint-
　　　　　　　　　　　ment)　会L11
ちち　父　(my) father　会L7, 会L7(s)
ちゃ　茶　green tea　会L3
ちゃいろい　茶色い　brown　会L9(s)
ちゅうごく　中国　China　会L1, 会L2
ちゅうしゃ　注射　injection　会L12(s)
ちょっと　a little　会L3

つ

ついたち　一日　the first day of a month　会L4(s)
つかいすてカメラ　使い捨てカメラ
　　disposable camera　会L5(s)
つかう　使う　to use　会L6
つかれている　疲れている　to be tired　読L8-II
つかれる　疲れる　to get tired　会L11
つぎ　次　next　会L6
つぎに　次に　secondly　読L8-II
つぎは～　次は～　next (stop), ...　会L10(s)
つくえ　机　desk　会L2(s), 会L4
つくる　作る　to make　会L8
つける　to turn on　会L6
つごうがわるい　都合が悪い　inconvenient; to have
　　　　　　　　　　a scheduling conflict　会L12
つとめる　勤める　to work for　会L7
つま　妻　wife　会L7(s)
つまらない　boring　会L5
つめたい　冷たい　cold (thing/people)　会L10
つり　fishing　読L11-II
つれてかえる　連れて帰る　to take back　読L12-II
つれてくる　連れてくる　to bring (a person)　会L6

て

て　手　hand　会L7(s)
～で　by (means of transportation); with (a tool)
　　会L10
ていきけん　定期券　commuter's pass　会L10(s)
Tシャツ　T-shirt　会L7
ディスコ　disco　会L8
ていねいないいかた　ていねいな言い方
　　polite expression　会L11(s)

デート　date (romantic, not calendar)　会L3
テープ　tape　会L2
でかける　出かける　to go out　会L5
てがみ　手紙　letter　会L4
できるだけ　as much as possible　会L12
でぐち　出口　exit　会L10(s)
～でしょう　probably; ..., right?　会L12
テスト　test　会L5
てつだう　手伝う　to help　会L6
テニス　tennis　会L3
では、おげんきで　では、お元気で　Take care.
　　　　　　　　　　　　　　読L5-II
デパート　department store　会L4
てぶくろ　手袋　gloves　会L10
でも　but　会L3
てら　寺　temple　会L4
でる　出る　to appear; to attend; to exit　会L9,
　　　　　　　　　　　　　　読L6-I
テレビ　TV　会L2(s), 会L3
テレビゲーム　video game　会L6
てん　天　the heavens; the sky　読L12-II
～てん　～点　... points　会L11
てんき　天気　weather　会L5
でんき　電気　electricity　会L2(s), 会L6
てんきよほう　天気予報　weather forecast　会L8
でんしゃ　電車　train　会L6
でんち　電池　battery　会L5(s)
でんわ　電話　telephone　会L1
でんわをかける　電話をかける　to make a phone
　　　　　　　　　　　　　　call　会L6

と

と　戸　door　読L10-II
～と　together with (a person)　会L4
～ど　～度　... degrees (temperature)　会L12
ドア　door　会L2(s)
どうして　why　会L4
どうぞ(～を)　Here it is.　会L2
どうぞよろしく　Nice to meet you.　会G
どうですか　How about ...?; How is ...?　会L3
どうも　Thank you.　会L2
どうやって　how; by what means　会L10
とお　十　ten　会L9
とおか　十日　the tenth day of a month　会L4(s)
とき　時　when ...; at the time of ...　会L4
ときどき　時々　sometimes　会L3

あいうえお　かきくけこ　さしすせそ　たちつてと　**なにぬねの**　はひふへほ　まみむめも　やゆよ　らりるれろ　わをん

とけい　時計　watch; clock　会L2
どこ　where　会L2
とこや　床屋　barber's　会L10
ところ　所　place　会L8
ところで　by the way　会L9
とし　年　year　読L10-Ⅱ
としょかん　図書館　library　会L2
どちら　which　会L10
とっきゅう　特急　super express　会L10(s)
どっち　which　会L10
とても　very　会L5
となり　隣　next　会L4
どの　which . . .　会L2
どのぐらい　how much; how long　会L10
トマト　tomato　会L8
とまる　泊まる　to stay (at a hotel, etc.)　会L10
ともだち　友だち　friend　会L1
どようび　土曜日　Saturday　会L3, 会L4(s)
ドライブ　drive　会L11
とる　撮る　to take (pictures)　会L4
とる　取る　to take (a class); to get (a grade)　会L11, 読L7-Ⅱ
とる　取る　to take off　読L10-Ⅱ
どれ　which one　会L2
トレーナー　sweat shirt　会L2
とんかつ　pork cutlet　会L2
どんな　what kind of . . .　会L5

ないか　内科　physician　会L12(s)
なか　中　inside　会L4
ながい　長い　long　会L7
なく　泣く　to cry　読L12-Ⅱ
なくす　to lose　会L12
なつ　夏　summer　会L8
〜など　and so forth　読L12-Ⅱ
ななさい　七歳　seven years old　会L1(s)
ななつ　七つ　seven　会L9
ななふん　七分　seven minutes　会L1(s)
なにか　何か　something　会L8
なにも＋negative　何も　not . . . anything　会L7
なのか　七日　the seventh day of a month　会L4(s)
なまえ　名前　name　会L1
ならう　習う　to learn　会L11
なる　to become　会L10
なん/なに　何　what　会L1

に

にかげつまえ　二か月前　two months ago　会L4(s)
にがつ　二月　February　会L4(s)
にぎやか(な)　lively　会L5
にく　肉　meat　会L2
にさい　二歳　two years old　会L1(s)
にさんにち　二三日　for two to three days　会L12
にし　西　west　会L6(s)
にじ　二時　two o'clock　会L1(s)
にじはん　二時半　half past two　会L1
にじゅうよっか　二十四日　the twenty-fourth day of a month　会L4(s)
にじゅうよんまいどり　24枚撮り　24-print roll　会L5(s)
にじゅっぷん　二十分　twenty minutes　会L1(s)
にちようび　日曜日　Sunday　会L3, 会L4(s)
〜について　about; regarding to　読L8-Ⅱ
にっき　日記　diary　読L9-Ⅱ
にふん　二分　two minutes　会L1(s)
にほん　日本　Japan　会L1
にほんご　日本語　Japanese language　会L1
にほんじん　日本人　Japanese people　会L1
にもつ　荷物　baggage　会L6
にょうぼう　女房　wife　会L7(s)
〜に〜をかぶせる　to put (a hat) on a person's head　読L10-Ⅱ
〜にん　〜人　[counter for people]　会L7
にんきがある　人気がある　to be popular　会L9

ね

ネガ　negative　会L5(s)
ねがい　願い　wish　読L12-Ⅱ
ねこ　猫　cat　会L4
ねつがある　熱がある　to have a fever　会L12
ねむい　眠い　sleepy　会L10
ねる　寝る　to sleep; to go to sleep　会L3
〜ねん　〜年　. . . years　会L10
〜ねんせい　〜年生　. . . year student　会L1

ノート　notebook　会L2
〜ので　because . . .　会L12
のど　throat　会L12
のどがかわく　のどが渇く　to become thirsty　会L12
のぼる　登る　to climb　会L11

あいうえお　かきくけこ　さしすせそ　たちつてと　なにぬねの　**は**ひふへほ　まみむめも　やゆよ　らりるれろ　わをん

のみもの　飲み物　drink　会 L5
のむ　飲む　to drink　会 L3
のりかえ　乗り換え　transfer　会 L10(s)
のる　乗る　to ride; to board　会 L5

は　歯　tooth　会 L7(s), 会 L12
パーティー　party　会 L8
バーベキュー　barbecue　会 L8
はい　yes　会 L1
はいいろ　灰色　gray　会 L9(s)
ばいてん　売店　kiosk　会 L10(s)
はいる　入る　to enter　会 L6
はがき　葉書　postcard　会 L5, 会 L5(s)
はく　to put on (items below your waist)　会 L7
はし　chopsticks　会 L8
はじまる　始まる　(something) begins　会 L9
はじめて　初めて　for the first time　会 L12
はじめまして　How do you do?　会 G
はじめる　始める　to begin　会 L8
バス　bus　会 L5
バスてい　バス停　bus stop　会 L4
はたけ　畑　farm　読 L12-II
はたち　二十歳　twenty years old　会 L1(s)
はたらく　働く　to work　会 L11
はたをおる　はたを織る　to weave　読 L12-II
はちがつ　八月　August　会 L4(s)
はちじ　八時　eight o'clock　会 L1(s)
はちふん　八分　eight minutes　会 L1(s)
ばつ　×(wrong)　会 L11(s)
はつおん　発音　pronunciation　会 L11(s)
はつか　二十日　the twentieth day of a month　会 L4(s)
はっさい　八歳　eight years old　会 L1(s)
はっぷん　八分　eight minutes　会 L1(s)
はな　花　flower　会 L12
はな　鼻　nose　会 L7(s)
はなしをする　話をする　to have a talk　読 L9-II
はなす　話す　to speak; to talk　会 L3
パノラマ　panoramic　会 L5(s)
はは　母　(my) mother　会 L7(s)
はやい　早い　early　会 L3
はやい　速い　fast　会 L7
はやく　早く　(do something) early; fast　会 L10
はらう　払う　to pay　会 L10
はる　春　spring　会 L10

はれ　晴れ　sunny weather　会 L12
はん　半　half　会 L1
〜ばん　〜番　number . . .　会 L11(s)
パン　bread　会 L4
ばんごう　番号　number　会 L1
ばんごはん　晩御飯　dinner　会 L3
ハンサム(な)　handsome　会 L5
〜ばんせん　〜番線　track number . . .　会 L10(s)
パンツ　pants　会 L10
バンド　band　読 L11-II
ハンバーガー　hamburger　会 L3

ピアノ　piano　会 L9
ビール　beer　会 L11
ひがし　東　east　会 L6(s)
ひきかえけん　引き換え券　receipt　会 L5(s)
ひく　弾く　to play (a string instrument or piano)　会 L9
ひこうき　飛行機　airplane　会 L5
ひさしぶり　久しぶり　it has been a long time　会 L11
ビジネス　business　会 L1, 会 L2
びじゅつかん　美術館　art museum　会 L11
ひだり　左　left　会 L4
ひだりがわ　左側　left side　会 L6(s)
びっくりする　to be surprised　読 L10-II
ビデオ　video tape; VCR　会 L2(s), 会 L3
ひと　人　person　会 L4
ひとつ　一つ　one　会 L9
ひとつめ　一つ目　first　会 L6(s)
ひとびと　人々　people　読 L12-II
ひとり　一人　one person　会 L7
ひとりで　一人で　alone　会 L4
ひふか　皮膚科　dermatologist　会 L12(s)
ひま(な)　暇　not busy; to have a lot of free time　会 L5
びよういん　美容院　beauty parlor　会 L10
びょういん　病院　hospital　会 L4
びょうき　病気　illness; sickness　会 L9, 会 L12(s)
ひょうじゅんご　標準語　standard Japanese　会 L11(s)
ひるごはん　昼御飯　lunch　会 L3
びん　便　flight　会 L10
ピンク　pink　会 L9(s)

あいうえお　かきくけこ　さしすせそ　たちつてと　なにぬねの　は**ひふへほ**　**まみ**むめも　やゆよ　らりるれろ　わをん

フィルム　film　会L5(s)

ふうしょ　封書　letter　会L5(s)

ふく　服　clothes　会L12

ふたつ　二つ　two　会L9

ふたつめ　二つ目　second　会L6(s)

ふたり　二人　two people　会L7

ふたりずつ　二人ずつ　two people each　会L11(s)

ふつう　普通　local　会L10(s)

ふつか　二日　the second day of a month　会L4(s)

ふつかよい　二日酔い　hangover　会L12

ふとっています　太っています　to be on the heavy side　会L7

ふとる　太る　to gain weight　会L7

ふなびん　船便　surface mail　会L5(s)

ふね　船　ship; boat　会L10

ふゆ　冬　winter　会L8

プリント　print　会L5(s)

ふるい　古い　old (thing)　会L5

プレゼント　present　会L12

ふろ　風呂　bath　会L6

ふろにはいる　風呂に入る　to take a bath　会L6

ぶんか　文化　culture　読L11-Ⅱ

ぶんがく　文学　literature　会L1, 読L7-Ⅱ

ぶんぽう　文法　grammar　会L11(s)

ページ　page　会L6

〜ページ　page number . . .　会L11(s)

へた(な)　下手　clumsy; poor at . . .　会L8

べつに ＋ negative　別に　not . . . in particular　会L7

へや　部屋　room　会L5

ペン　pen　会L2, 会L2(s)

べんきょうする　勉強する　to study　会L3

べんごし　弁護士　lawyer　会L1

へんじ　返事　reply　読L11-Ⅱ

べんとう　弁当　boxed lunch　会L9

べんり(な)　便利　convenient　会L7

ほうげん　方言　dialect　会L11(s)

ぼうし　帽子　hat; cap　会L2

〜ほうめん　〜方面　serving . . . areas　会L10(s)

ホーム　platform　会L10(s)

ホームシック　homesickness　会L12

ホームステイ　homestay; living with a local family　会L8

ほかに　anything else　会L11(s)

ぼく　僕　I (used by men)　会L5

ほけん　保険　insurance　会L5(s)

〜ぼしゅう　〜募集　looking for . . .　読L11-Ⅱ

ホストファミリー　host family　会L11, 読L9-Ⅱ

ホテル　hotel　会L4

ほん　本　book　会L2, 会L2(s)

ほんとうですか　本当ですか　Really?　会L6

ほんや　本屋　bookstore　会L4

ま

まあまあ　okay; so-so　会L11

〜まい　〜枚　[counter for flat objects]　会L5

まいしゅう　毎週　every week　会L8

まいにち　毎日　every day　会L3

まいばん　毎晩　every night　会L3

まえ　前　front　会L4

まがる　曲がる　to turn　会L6(s)

まじめな　serious　読L12-Ⅱ

まず　first of all　読L8-Ⅱ

また　again　読L5-Ⅱ

まだ ＋ negative　not . . . yet　会L8

まち　町　town; city　会L4

まつ　待つ　to wait　会L4

まっすぐ　straight　会L6(s), 読L6-Ⅰ

まつり　祭り　festival　読L11-Ⅱ

〜まで　to (a place); as far as (a place); till (a time)　会L5

〜までに　by . . .　読L12-Ⅱ

まど　窓　window　会L2(s), 会L6

まどぐち　窓口　counter　会L5(s)

まる　○ (correct)　会L11(s)

まんじゅう　sweet bun　読L4-Ⅲ

み

みぎ　右　right　会L4

みぎがわ　右側　right side　会L6(s)

みじかい　短い　short (length)　会L7

みず　水　water　会L3

みずいろ　水色　light blue　会L9(s)

みずうみ　湖　lake　会L11

みせ　店　store　読L4-Ⅲ

みっか　三日　the third day of a month　会L4(s)

あいうえお　かきくけこ　さしすせそ　たちつてと　なにぬねの　はひふへほ　**まみむめも**　**やゆよ**　らりるれろ　わをん

みつける　見つける　to find　読L12-Ⅱ
みっつ　三つ　three　会L9
みどり　緑　green　会L9(s)
みなさん　皆さん　everyone　読L6-Ⅲ
みなみ　南　south　会L6(s)
みみ　耳　ear　会L7(s)
みやげ　土産　souvenir　会L4
みる　見る　to see; to look at; to watch　会L3
みんな　all　会L9, 読L7-Ⅱ
みんなで　all (of the people) together　会L8

むいか　六日　the sixth day of a month　会L4(s)
むかしむかし　昔々　once upon a time　読L10-Ⅱ
むこう　向こう　the other side; over there　読L12-Ⅱ
むずかしい　難しい　difficult　会L5
むすめ　娘　daughter　読L12-Ⅱ
むっつ　六つ　six　会L9
むね　胸　breast　会L7(s)
むらさき　紫　purple　会L9(s)

め　目　eye　会L7, 会L7(s)
めがね　眼鏡　glasses　会L7
メニュー　menu　会L2

もう　already　会L9
もうすぐ　very soon; in a few moments/days　会L12
もくようび　木曜日　Thursday　会L4, 会L4(s)
もしもし　Hello? (used on the phone)　会L4
もち　rice cake　読L10-Ⅱ
もちろん　of course　会L7
もつ　持つ　to carry; to hold　会L6
もっていく　持っていく　to take (something)　会L8
もってくる　持ってくる　to bring (a thing)　会L6
もっと　more　会L11
もの　物　thing (concrete object)　会L12
もらう　to get (from somebody)　会L9

やきまし　焼き増し　reprint　会L5(s)
やきゅう　野球　baseball　会L10
やさい　野菜　vegetable　会L2

やさしい　easy (problem); kind (person)　会L5
やすい　安い　inexpensive; cheap (thing)　会L5
やすみ　休み　holiday; day off; absence　会L5
やすむ　休む　to be absent (from); to rest　会L6
やせています　to be thin　会L7
やせる　to lose weight　会L7
やっつ　八つ　eight　会L9
やま　山　mountain　会L11, 読L5-Ⅱ
やまみち　山道　mountain road　読L10-Ⅱ
やめる　to quit　会L11
やる　to do; to perform　会L5

ゆうびんきょく　郵便局　post office　会L2
ゆうめい(な)　有名　famous　会L8
ゆうめいじん　有名人　celebrity　会L10
ゆき　雪　snow　会L12, 読L10-Ⅱ
ゆっくり　slowly; leisurely; unhurriedly　会L6
ゆび　指　finger　会L7(s)
ゆめ　夢　dream　会L11

ようか　八日　the eighth day of a month　会L4(s)
ようじ　用事　business to take care of　会L12
よかったら　if you like　会L7
よく　often; much　会L3
よじ　四時　four o'clock　会L1(s)
よっか　四日　the fourth day of a month　会L4(s)
よっつ　四つ　four　会L9
よむ　読む　to read　会L3
よやく　予約　reservation　会L10
よる　夜　night　会L6, 読L5-Ⅱ
よんさい　四歳　four years old　会L1(s)
よんぷん　四分　four minutes　会L1(s)

らいがっき　来学期　next semester　会L10
らいげつ　来月　next month　会L4(s), 会L8
らいしゅう　来週　next week　会L4(s), 会L6
らいねん　来年　next year　会L4(s), 会L6

りゅうがくする　留学する　to study abroad　会L11
りゅうがくせい　留学生　international student　会L1
りょう　寮　dormitory　読L9-Ⅱ
りょうり　料理　cooking　読L6-Ⅲ

あいうえお　かきくけこ　さしすせそ　たちつてと　なにぬねの　はひふへほ　まみむめも　やゆよ　**らりるれろ**　わをん

りょうりする　料理する　to cook　会 L8

りょこう　旅行　travel　会 L5

りんご　apple　会 L10

る

ルームメート　roommate　会 L11

れ

れい　例　example　会 L11(s)

れきし　歴史　history　会 L1, 会 L2

レストラン　restaurant　会 L4

れんしゅう　練習　exercise　会 L11(s)

れんしゅうする　練習する　to practice　会 L10

レントゲン　X-ray　会 L12(s)

ろ

ろくがつ　六月　June　会 L4(s)

ろくさい　六歳　six years old　会 L1(s)

ろくじ　六時　six o'clock　会 L1(s)

ろっぷん　六分　six minutes　会 L1(s)

わ

ワイフ　wife　会 L7(s)

わかい　若い　young　会 L9

わかる　to understand　会 L4

わかれる　別れる　to break up; to separate　会 L12

わすれる　忘れる　to forget; to leave behind　会 L6

わたし　私　I　会 L1

わたしたち　私たち　we　読 L12-Ⅱ

わたる　渡る　to cross　会 L6(s)

わるい　悪い　bad　会 L12

A B C D E F G H I J K L M N O P Q R S T U V W X Y Z

さくいん2 English-Japanese

各項目の表示は以下の内容を示す。
Items at the end of each entry indicate the following:
会……　会話・文法編
　　　　(Conversation and Grammar section)
読……　読み書き編
　　　　(Reading and Writing section)
G……　あいさつ (Greetings)
(s)……　課末コラム (Supplement)
Ⅰ・Ⅱ・Ⅲ……問題番号(読み書き編)
　　　　(number of excercise in the
　　　　Reading and Writing section)

A

about　～について　読 L8-Ⅱ
about (approximate measurement)
　～ぐらい　会 L4
absence　やすみ　休み　会 L5
absent (from)　やすむ　休む　会 L6
adult　おとな　大人　読 L12-Ⅱ
aerogramme　エアログラム　会 L5(s)
after . . .　～ご　～後　会 L10
after (an event)　(～の)あと　(～の)後　会 L11, 読 L8-Ⅱ
again　また　読 L5-Ⅱ
air　くうき　空気　会 L8
airmail　こうくうびん　航空便　会 L5(s)
airplane　ひこうき　飛行機　会 L5
alcohol　(お)さけ　(お)酒　会 L3
all　みんな　会 L9, 読 L7-Ⅱ
all (of the people) together　みんなで　会 L8
alone　ひとりで　一人で　会 L4
already　もう　会 L9
always　いつも　会 L12, 読 L6-Ⅲ
A.M.　ごぜん　午前　会 L1
and so forth　～など　読 L12-Ⅱ
and then　それから　会 L5
and then　そして　会 L11, 読 L9-Ⅱ
(get) angry　おこる　怒る　読 L12-Ⅱ
answer　こたえ　答　会 L11(s)
answer　こたえる　答える　読 L8-Ⅱ
anthropology　じんるいがく　人類学　会 L1
antibiotic　こうせいぶっしつ　抗生物質　会 L12(s)
anything else　ほかに　会 L11(s)
apartment　アパート　会 L7
appear　でる　出る　会 L9

apple　りんご　会 L10
April　しがつ　四月　会 L4(s)
art museum　びじゅつかん　美術館　会 L11
as far as (a place)　～まで　会 L5
as much as possible　できるだけ　会 L12
Asian studies　アジアけんきゅう　アジア研究　会 L1
ask　きく　聞く　会 L5
at about　～ごろ　会 L3
at the time of . . .　とき　時　会 L4
attend　でる　出る　会 L9
August　はちがつ　八月　会 L4(s)
Australia　オーストラリア　会 L1, 会 L11

B

back　うしろ　後ろ　会 L4
back　せなか　背中　会 L7(s)
bad　わるい　悪い　会 L12
baggage　にもつ　荷物　会 L6
bag　かばん　会 L2, 会 L2(s)
bamboo hat　かさ　読 L10-Ⅱ
band　バンド　読 L11-Ⅱ
bank　ぎんこう　銀行　会 L2
barbecue　バーベキュー　会 L8
barber's　とこや　床屋　会 L10
baseball　やきゅう　野球　会 L10
bath　(お)ふろ　(お)風呂　会 L6
battery　でんち　電池　会 L5(s)
be on the heavy side　ふとっています　太っています　会 L7
beautiful　きれい(な)　会 L5
beauty parlor　びよういん　美容院　会 L10
because . . .　～から　会 L6
because . . .　～ので　会 L12
become　なる　会 L10
beer　ビール　会 L11
begin　はじめる　始める　会 L8
(something) begins　はじまる　始まる　会 L9
best　いちばん　一番　会 L10
between　あいだ　間　会 L4
bicycle　じてんしゃ　自転車　会 L2
birthday　たんじょうび　誕生日　会 L5
black　くろい　黒い　会 L9, 会 L9(s)
black and white　しろくろ　白黒　会 L9(s)
black board　こくばん　黒板　会 L2(s)
blonde hair　きんぱつ　金髪　会 L9(s)
blue　あおい　青い　会 L9, 会 L9(s)
board　のる　乗る　会 L5

A B C D E F G H I J K L M N O P Q R S T U V W X Y Z

boarding ticket　じょうしゃけん　乗車券　会L10(s)

boat　ふね　船　会L10

book　ほん　本　会L2, 会L2(s)

bookish expression　かたいいいかた　かたい言い方　会L11(s)

bookstore　ほんや　本屋　会L4

boring　つまらない　会L5

borrow　かりる　借りる　会L6

bound for . . .　〜いき　〜行き　会L10(s)

boxed lunch　(お)べんとう　(お)弁当　会L9

boy　おとこのこ　男の子　会L11

boyfriend　かれ　彼　会L12

bread　パン　会L4

break up　わかれる　別れる　会L12

breakfast　あさごはん　朝御飯　会L3

breast　むね　胸　会L7(s)

bright　あたまがいい　頭がいい　会L7

bring (a person)　つれてくる　連れてくる　会L6

bring (a thing)　もってくる　持ってくる　会L6

Britain　イギリス　会L1, 会L2

brothers and sisters　きょうだい　兄弟　会L7

brown　ちゃいろい　茶色い　会L9(s)

Bullet Train　しんかんせん　新幹線　会L9

business　ビジネス　会L1, 会L2

business to take care of　ようじ　用事　会L12

bus　バス　会L5

bus stop　バスてい　バス停　会L4

busy (people/days)　いそがしい　忙しい　会L5

but　でも　会L3

but　が　会L7, 読L5-Ⅱ

buttocks　(お)しり　会L7(s)

buy　かう　買う　会L4

by . . .　〜までに　読L12-Ⅱ

by (means of transportation)　〜で　会L10

by all means　ぜひ　是非　会L9

by the way　ところで　会L9

by what means　どうやって　会L10

━━━━━ Ⓒ ━━━━━

cafe　きっさてん　喫茶店　会L2

cafeteria　しょくどう　食堂　会L7

camera　カメラ　会L8

camp　キャンプ　会L11

cap　ぼうし　帽子　会L2

car　くるま　車　会L7

carry　もつ　持つ　会L6

castle　(お)しろ　(お)城　読L5-Ⅱ

cat　ねこ　猫　会L4

catch a cold　かぜをひく　風邪をひく　会L12

celebrity　ゆうめいじん　有名人　会L10

chair　いす　会L2(s)

cheap (thing)　やすい　安い　会L5

cheerful　あかるい　明るい　読L11-Ⅱ

Cheers! (a toast)　かんぱい　乾杯　会L8

child　こども　子供　会L4

child　おこさん　お子さん　会L7(s)

(my) child　うちのこ　うちの子　会L7(s)

China　ちゅうごく　中国　会L1, 会L2

Chinese character　かんじ　漢字　会L6

chopsticks　はし　会L8

city　まち　町　会L4

class　クラス　会L4

class　じゅぎょう　授業　会L11

clean　きれい(な)　会L5

clean　そうじする　掃除する　会L8

clever　あたまがいい　頭がいい　会L7

climb　のぼる　登る　会L11

clock　とけい　時計　会L2

close (something)　しめる　閉める　会L6

clothes　ふく　服　会L12

cloudy weather　くもり　曇り　会L12

clumsy　へた(な)　下手　会L8

coffee　コーヒー　会L3

cold　かぜ　風邪　会L12

cold (thing/people)　つめたい　冷たい　会L10

cold (weather)　さむい　寒い　会L5

college　だいがく　大学　会L1

college student　だいがくせい　大学生　会L1, 会L8

colloquial expression　くだけたいいかた　くだけた言い方　会L11(s)

color　いろ　色　会L9

come　くる　来る　会L3

coming from　しゅっしん　出身　会L11

commuter's pass　ていきけん　定期券　会L10(s)

company　かいしゃ　会社　会L7

composition　さくぶん　作文　会L9

computer　コンピューター　会L1, 会L2

concert　コンサート　会L9

convenience store　コンビニ　会L7

convenient　べんり(な)　便利　会L7

cook　りょうりする　料理する　会L8

cooking　りょうり　料理　読L6-Ⅲ

cool (weather)　すずしい　涼しい　会L10

corner　かど　角　会L6(s)

correct (○)　まる　会L11(s)

cough　せき　会L12

cough　せきがでる　せきが出る　会L12

counter　まどぐち　窓口　会L5(s)

A B C D E F G H I J K L M N O P Q R S T U V W X Y Z

(counter for flat objects)　～まい　～枚　会L5
(counter for people)　～にん　～人　会L7
country　くに　国　会L7
coupons　かいすうけん　回数券　会L10(s)
cow　うし　牛　読L12-II
cram school　じゅく　塾　読L7-II
credit card　クレジットカード　会L10
cross　わたる　渡る　会L6(s)
cry　なく　泣く　読L12-II
culture　ぶんか　文化　読L11-II
curtain　カーテン　会L2(s)
cut　きる　切る　会L8
cut classes　サボる　会L11
cute　かわいい　会L7

D

dance　おどる　踊る　会L9
date (romantic)　デート　会L3
date/time something is ready
　　しあがり　仕上がり　会L5(s)
daughter　むすめ　娘　読L12-II
day after tomorrow, the　あさって　会L4(s),
　　　　　　　　　　　　　　　会L8
day before yesterday, the　おととい　会L4(s)
day off　やすみ　休み　会L5
deadline　しめきり　会L11(s)
December　じゅうにがつ　十二月　会L4(s)
decide　きめる　決める　会L10
. . . degrees (temperature)　～ど　～度　会L12
delicious　おいしい　会L2
dentist　しか　歯科　会L12(s)
departing first　せんぱつ　先発　会L10(s)
departing second　じはつ　次発　会L10(s)
department store　デパート　会L4
dermatologist　ひふか　皮膚科　会L12(s)
desk　つくえ　机　会L2(s), 会L4
development　げんぞう　現像　会L5(s)
dialect　ほうげん　方言　会L11(s)
diary　にっき　日記　読L9-II
dictionary　じしょ　辞書　会L2, 会L2(s)
die　しぬ　死ぬ　会L6
difficult　むずかしい　難しい　会L5
dining commons　しょくどう　食堂　会L7
dinner　ばんごはん　晩御飯　会L3
disco　ディスコ　会L8
disgusted with　きらい(な)　嫌い　会L5
dislike　きらい(な)　嫌い　会L5
disposable camera　つかいすてカメラ　使い捨
　　　　　　　　　てカメラ　会L5(s)

do　する　会L3
do　やる　会L5
do laundry　せんたくする　洗濯する　会L8
do physical exercises　うんどうする　運動する
　　　　　　　　　　　　　　会L9
doctor　いしゃ　医者　会L1, 会L10
dog　いぬ　犬　会L4
don't look well　げんきがない　元気がない
　　　　　　　　　会L12
door　ドア　会L2(s)
door　と　戸　読L10-II
dormitory　りょう　寮　読L9-II
dream　ゆめ　夢　会L11
drink　のむ　飲む　会L3
drink　のみもの　飲み物　会L5
drive　うんてんする　運転する　会L8
drive　ドライブ　会L11

E

ear　みみ　耳　会L7(s)
early　はやい　早い　会L3
(do something) early　はやく　早く　会L10
east　ひがし　東　会L6(s)
easy　かんたん(な)　簡単　会L10
easy (problem)　やさしい　会L5
eat　たべる　食べる　会L3
economics　けいざい　経済　会L1, 会L2
eight　やっつ　八つ　会L9
eight minutes　はっぷん/はちふん　八分　会L1(s)
eight o'clock　はちじ　八時　会L1(s)
eight years old　はっさい　八歳　会L1(s)
eighteen minutes　じゅうはちふん/じゅうはっぷん
　　　　　　　　　　十八分　会L1(s)
eighth day of a month, the　ようか　八日
　　　　　　　　　　　　　　会L4(s)
electricity　でんき　電気　会L2(s), 会L6
eleven minutes　じゅういっぷん　十一分　会L1(s)
eleven o'clock　じゅういちじ　十一時　会L1(s)
eleven years old　じゅういっさい　十一歳
　　　　　　　　　　会L1(s)
eleventh day of a month, the
　　じゅういちにち　十一日　会L4(s)
(something) ends　おわる　終わる　会L9
energetic　げんき(な)　元気　会L5
English (language)　えいご　英語　会L1
ENT doctor　じびか　耳鼻科　会L12(s)
enter　はいる　入る　会L6
entrance　いりぐち　入口　会L10(s)
erase　けす　消す　会L6

A B C D E F G H I J K L M N O P Q R S T U V W X Y Z

eraser けしゴム 消しゴム 会L2(s)
essay さくぶん 作文 会L9
every day まいにち 毎日 会L3
every night まいばん 毎晩 会L3
every week まいしゅう 毎週 会L8
everyone みなさん 皆さん 読L6-Ⅲ
Everything is under control.
　　だいじょうぶ 大丈夫 会L5
exam しけん 試験 会L9
example れい 例 会L11(s)
excellent food ごちそう 読L9-Ⅱ
Excuse me. すみません 会G
exercise れんしゅう 練習 会L11(s)
exit でる 出る 会L9, 読L6-Ⅰ
exit でぐち 出口 会L10(s)
expensive たかい 高い 会L2
express きゅうこう 急行 会L10(s)
eye め 目 会L7, 会L7(s)

F

face かお 顔 会L7(s), 会L10
fall あき 秋 会L10
family かぞく 家族 会L7
famous ゆうめい(な) 有名 会L8
fantastic すてき(な) 素敵 会L12
farm はたけ 畑 読L12-Ⅱ
fast はやい 速い 会L7
fast はやく 早く 会L10
father おとうさん お父さん 会L1, 会L2,
　　　　　　　　会L7(s)
(my) father ちち 父 会L7, 会L7(s)
February にがつ 二月 会L4(s)
festival まつり 祭り 読L11-Ⅱ
fifteen minutes じゅうごふん 十五分 会L1(s)
fifth day of a month, the いつか 五日 会L4(s)
film フィルム 会L5(s)
find みつける 見つける 読L12-Ⅱ
finger ゆび 指 会L7(s)
first ひとつめ 一つ目 会L6(s)
first car いちばんまえ 一番前 会L10(s)
first day of a month, the ついたち 一日
　　　　　　　　　　会L4(s)
first of all まず 読L8-Ⅱ
first-year student いちねんせい 一年生 会L1
fish さかな 魚 会L2
fishing つり 読L11-Ⅱ
five いつつ 五つ 会L9
five minutes ごふん 五分 会L1(s)
five o'clock ごじ 五時 会L1(s)

five years old ごさい 五歳 会L1(s)
flight びん 便 会L10
flower はな 花 会L12
fond of すき(な) 好き 会L5
food たべもの 食べ物 会L5
foot あし 足 会L7(s), 会L12
for example たとえば 会L11(s)
for . . . months ～かげつ ～か月 会L10
for the first time はじめて 初めて 会L12
for two to three days にさんにち 二三日
　　　　　　　　　　会L12
for . . . weeks ～しゅうかん ～週間 会L10
foreign country がいこく 外国 会L11
forget わすれる 忘れる 会L6
four よっつ 四つ 会L9
four minutes よんぷん 四分 会L1(s)
four o'clock よじ 四時 会L1(s)
four years old よんさい 四歳 会L1(s)
fourteen minutes じゅうよんぷん 十四分
　　　　　　　　　会L1(s)
fourteenth day of a month, the
　　じゅうよっか 十四日 会L4(s)
fourth day of a month, the よっか 四日
　　　　　　　　　　会L4(s)
Friday きんようび 金曜日 会L4, 会L4(s)
friend ともだち 友だち 会L1
frightening こわい 怖い 会L5
from . . . ～から 会L9, 読L7-Ⅱ
front まえ 前 会L4
front end いちばんまえ 一番前 会L10(s)
fun たのしい 楽しい 会L5
future しょうらい 将来 会L11

gain weight ふとる 太る 会L7
game しあい 試合 会L12
gate かいさつ 改札 会L10(s)
general admission seat じゆうせき 自由席
　　　　　　　　　　会L10(s)
get (a grade) とる 取る 会L11
get (from somebody) もらう 会L9
get off おりる 降りる 会L6
get to know しる 知る 会L7
get up おきる 起きる 会L3
Get well soon. おだいじに お大事に 会L12
girl おんなのこ 女の子 会L11
girlfriend かのじょ 彼女 会L12, 読L11-Ⅱ
glasses めがね 眼鏡 会L7
glossy finish こうたくあり 光沢あり 会L5(s)

A B C D E F **G H** I J K L M N O P Q R S T U V W X Y Z

gloves　てぶくろ　手袋　会L10
go　いく　行く　会L3
go back　かえる　帰る　会L3
go on a diet　ダイエットする　会L11
go out　でかける　出かける　会L5
go to sleep　ねる　寝る　会L3
God　かみさま　神さま　読L12-II
gold　きんいろ　金色　会L9(s)
gold　ゴールド　会L9(s)
good　いい　会L3
Good afternoon.　こんにちは　会G
good at . . .　じょうず(な)　上手　会L8
good child　いいこ　いい子　会L9
good deed　いいこと　読L10-II
Good evening.　こんばんは　会G
Good morning.　おはよう/おはようございます
　　　　　　会G
Good night.　おやすみなさい　会G
Good-bye.　さようなら　会G
grade (on a test, etc.)　せいせき　成績　会L12
graduate student　だいがくいんせい　大学院生
　　　　　　会L1
grammar　ぶんぽう　文法　会L11(s)
grandfather　おじいさん　会L7(s)
(my) grandfather　そふ　祖父　会L7(s)
grandmother　おばあさん　会L6, 会L7(s)
(my) grandmother　そぼ　祖母　会L7(s)
gray　グレー　会L9(s)
gray　はいいろ　灰色　会L9(s)
great-looking　かっこいい　会L7
green　グリーン　会L9(s)
green　みどり　緑　会L9(s)
green tea　(お)ちゃ　(お)茶　会L3
guardian deity of children　じぞう　読L10-II
guitar　ギター　会L9

—— Ⓗ ——

hair　かみ　髪　会L7, 会L7(s)
half　はん　半　会L1
half past two　にじはん　二時半　会L1
hamburger　ハンバーガー　会L3
hand　て　手　会L7(s)
handsome　ハンサム(な)　会L5
hangover　ふつかよい　二日酔い　会L12
happy　しあわせな　幸せな　読L10-II
hat　ぼうし　帽子　会L2
hate　だいきらい(な)　大嫌い　会L5
have a fever　ねつがある　熱がある　会L12
have a fight　けんかする　会L11

have a lot of free time　ひま(な)　暇　会L5
have a scheduling conflict
　つごうがわるい　都合が悪い　会L12
have a talk　はなしをする　話をする　読L9-II
head　あたま　頭　会L7(s)
healthy　げんき(な)　元気　会L5
hear　きく　聞く　会L3
heavens, the　てん　天　読L12-II
Hello? (used on the phone)　もしもし　会L4
help　てつだう　手伝う　会L6
here　ここ　会L4
Here it is.　(〜を)どうぞ　会L2
high school　こうこう　高校　会L1
high school student　こうこうせい　高校生
　　　　　　会L1
history　れきし　歴史　会L1, 会L2
hobby　しゅみ　趣味　読L11-II
hold　もつ　持つ　会L6
holiday　やすみ　休み　会L5
home　いえ　家　会L3
home　うち　会L3
homesickness　ホームシック　会L12
homestay　ホームステイ　会L8
homework　しゅくだい　宿題　会L5, 会L11(s)
hospital　びょういん　病院　会L4
host family　ホストファミリー　会L11, 読L9-II
hot (objects)　あつい　熱い　会L5
hot (weather)　あつい　暑い　会L5
hot spring　おんせん　温泉　会L9
hotel　ホテル　会L4
hour　〜じかん　〜時間　会L4
house　いえ　家　会L3
house　うち　会L3
housewife　しゅふ　主婦　会L1
how　どうやって　会L10
How about . . . ?　どうですか　会L3
How do you do?　はじめまして　会G
How is . . . ?　どうですか　会L3
how long　どのぐらい　会L10
how much　いくら　会L2
how much　どのぐらい　会L10
(become) hungry　おなかがすく　会L11
hurry　いそぐ　急ぐ　会L6
hurt　いたい　痛い　会L12
husband　うちのひと　うちの人　会L7(s)
husband　おっと　夫　会L7(s)
husband　(ご)しゅじん　(ご)主人　会L7(s)
husband　だんな　会L7(s)

A B C D E F G H **I** J **K** L M N O P Q R S T U V W X Y Z

I

I わたし 私 会L1
I (used by men) ぼく 僕 会L5
I am sorry. すみません 会G
I do not know しりません 知りません 会L7
I know しっています 知っています 会L7
if that is the case,... じゃあ 会L2
if you like よかったら 会L7
I'll go and come back. いってきます 会G
illness びょうき 病気 会L9, 会L12(s)
I'm home. ただいま 会G
I'm sorry. ごめんなさい 会L4
in a few moments/days もうすぐ 会L12
in the morning ごぜんちゅう 午前中 読L9-Ⅱ
in ... time 〜ご 〜後 会L10
inconvenient つごうがわるい 都合が悪い
　　　　　　　　会L12
inexpensive やすい 安い 会L5
injection ちゅうしゃ 注射 会L12(s)
injury けが 会L12(s)
inside なか 中 会L4
instruct おしえる 教える 会L6
insurance ほけん 保険 会L5(s)
interested (in) きょうみがある 興味がある
　　　　　　　　会L12
interesting おもしろい 面白い 会L5
international relations こくさいかんけい 国際
　　　　　　　　関係 会L1
international student りゅうがくせい 留学生
　　　　　　　　会L1
introduce しょうかいする 紹介する 会L11
(a person) is in ... いる 会L4
it has been a long time ひさしぶり 久しぶり
　　　　　　　　会L11
It is okay. だいじょうぶ 大丈夫 会L5

J

January いちがつ 一月 会L4(s)
Japan にほん 日本 会L1
Japanese language にほんご 日本語 会L1
Japanese people にほんじん 日本人 会L1
jeans ジーンズ 会L2
job しごと 仕事 会L1, 会L8
juice ジュース 会L12
July しちがつ 七月 会L4(s)
June ろくがつ 六月 会L4(s)
just ... 〜だけ 会L11

K

Kabuki かぶき 会L9
kanji かんじ 漢字 会L6
karaoke カラオケ 会L8
kind しんせつ(な) 親切 会L7
kind (person) やさしい 会L5
kiosk ばいてん 売店 会L10(s)
(get to) know しる 知る 会L7
Korea かんこく 韓国 会L1, 会L2

L

lake みずうみ 湖 会L11
language 〜ご 〜語 会L1
language lab LL(エルエル) 会L3
large おおきい 大きい 会L5
last car いちばんうしろ 一番後ろ 会L10(s)
last month せんげつ 先月 会L4(s), 会L9
last train しゅうでん 終電 会L10(s)
last week せんしゅう 先週 会L4, 会L4(s)
last year きょねん 去年 会L4(s)
lastly さいごに 最後に 読L8-Ⅱ
late おそい 遅い 会L10
(do something) late おそく 遅く 会L8, 読L4-Ⅲ
late (for) おそくなる 遅くなる 会L8
late (for an appointment) ちこくする 遅刻す
　　　　　　　　る 会L11
later on あとで 後で 会L6
lawyer べんごし 弁護士 会L1
learn ならう 習う 会L11
leave behind わすれる 忘れる 会L6
left ひだり 左 会L4
left side ひだりがわ 左側 会L6(s)
leg あし 足 会L7(s), 会L12
leisurely ゆっくり 会L6
Let me see. そうですね 会L3
letter てがみ 手紙 会L4
letter ふうしょ 封書 会L5(s)
library としょかん 図書館 会L2
life せいかつ 生活 会L10
light blue みずいろ 水色 会L9(s)
like すき(な) 好き 会L5
line number ... 〜ぎょうめ 〜行目 会L11(s)
listen きく 聞く 会L3
literature ぶんがく 文学 会L1, 読L7-Ⅱ
little, a ちょっと 会L3
little, a すこし 少し 読L7-Ⅱ
little while ago, a さっき 会L4
live すむ 住む 会L7

A B C D E F G H I J K **L M N** O P Q R S T U V W X Y Z

lively　にぎやか（な）　会 L5
living　せいかつ　生活　会 L10
living with a local family　ホームステイ　会 L8
local (train)　ふつう　普通　会 L10(s)
lonely　さびしい　寂しい　会 L9
long　ながい　長い　会 L7
look at　みる　見る　会 L3
look forward (to)　（〜を）たのしみにする　楽しみ
　　　　にする　読 L7-II
look pale　かおがあおい　顔が青い　会 L9(s)
looking for . . .　〜ぼしゅう　〜募集　読 L11-II
lose　なくす　会 L12
lose weight　やせる　会 L7
lot, a　たくさん　会 L4
love　だいすき（な）　大好き　会 L5
lunch　ひるごはん　昼御飯　会 L3

M

magazine　ざっし　雑誌　会 L3
major　せんもん　専門　会 L1
make　つくる　作る　会 L8
make a phone call　でんわをかける　電話をか
　　　　ける　会 L6
man　おとこ　男　読 L11-II
man　おとこのひと　男の人　会 L7
many　たくさん　会 L4
March　さんがつ　三月　会 L4(s)
(get) married　けっこんする　結婚する　会 L7
mat finish　こうたくなし　光沢なし　会 L5(s)
match　しあい　試合　会 L12
May　ごがつ　五月　会 L4(s)
maybe　たぶん　多分　会 L12
meal　ごはん　御飯　会 L4
meaning　いみ　意味　会 L11(s), 会 L12
mean-spirited　いじわる（な）　意地悪　会 L9
meat　にく　肉　会 L2
medicine　くすり　薬　会 L9
meet　あう　会う　会 L4
memorize　おぼえる　覚える　会 L9
menu　メニュー　会 L2
Milky Way, the　あまのがわ　天の川　読 L12-II
Monday　げつようび　月曜日　会 L4, 会 L4(s)
money　（お）かね　（お）金　会 L6
month after next, the　さらいげつ　再来月
　　　　会 L4(s)
more　もっと　会 L11
morning　あさ　朝　会 L3
mother　おかあさん　お母さん　会 L1, 会 L2, 会 L7(s)
(my) mother　はは　母　会 L7(s)

mountain　やま　山　会 L11, 読 L5-II
mountain road　やまみち　山道　読 L10-II
mouth　くち　口　会 L7(s)
movie　えいが　映画　会 L3
Mr./Ms. . . .　〜さん　会 L1
Mr./Ms. . . .　〜さま　〜様　読 L5-II
much　よく　会 L3
Municipal Hospital　しみんびょういん　市民病院
　　　　会 L6
music　おんがく　音楽　会 L3
my place　うち　会 L3

N

name　なまえ　名前　会 L1
narrow　せまい　狭い　会 L12
near　そば　会 L4
near future　こんど　今度　会 L9
near place　ちかく　近く　読 L11-II
neck　くび　首　会 L7(s)
need　いる　会 L8
negative　ネガ　会 L5(s)
neighborhood　きんじょ　近所　読 L11-II
(get) nervous　きんちょうする　緊張する　会 L12
new　あたらしい　新しい　会 L5
New Year's　（お）しょうがつ　（お）正月　会 L11,
　　　　読 L10-II
newspaper　しんぶん　新聞　会 L2
next　となり　隣　会 L4
next　つぎ　次　会 L6
next (stop), . . .　つぎは〜　次は〜　会 L10(s)
next month　らいげつ　来月　会 L4(s), 会 L8
next semester　らいがっき　来学期　会 L10
next week　らいしゅう　来週　会 L4(s), 会 L6
next year　らいねん　来年　会 L4(s), 会 L6
Nice to meet you.　どうぞよろしく　会 G
night　よる　夜　会 L6, 読 L5-II
nine　ここのつ　九つ　会 L9
nine minutes　きゅうふん　九分　会 L1(s)
nine o'clock　くじ　九時　会 L1(s)
nine years old　きゅうさい　九歳　会 L1(s)
nineteen minutes　じゅうきゅうふん　十九分
　　　　会 L1(s)
ninth day of a month, the　ここのか　九日
　　　　会 L4(s)
nonsmoking car　きんえんしゃ　禁煙車　会 L10(s)
north　きた　北　会 L6(s)
nose　はな　鼻　会 L7(s)
not . . . anything　なにも＋negative　何も　会 L7
not at all　ぜんぜん＋negative　全然　会 L3

A B C D E F G H I J K L M **N O P** Q R S T U V W X Y Z

Not at all. いいえ 会G

not busy ひま(な) 暇 会L5

not . . . in particular べつに＋negative 別に 会L7

not much あまり＋negative 会L3

not spacious せまい 狭い 会L12

Not to worry. だいじょうぶ 大丈夫 会L5

not . . . yet まだ＋negative 会L8

notebook ノート 会L2

November じゅういちがつ 十一月 会L4(s)

now いま 今 会L1

no ううん 会L8

No. いいえ 会G

number ばんごう 番号 会L1

number . . . ～ばん ～番 会L11(s)

O

obstetrician and gynecologist さんふじんか 産婦人科 会L12(s)

occupation しごと 仕事 会L1, 会L8

o'clock ～じ ～時 会L1

October じゅうがつ 十月 会L4(s)

of course もちろん 会L7

office worker かいしゃいん 会社員 会L1, 会L8

often よく 会L3

okay まあまあ 会L11

old (thing) ふるい 古い 会L5

old woman おばあさん 会L6, 会L7(s)

older brother おにいさん お兄さん 会L1, 会L7, 会L7(s)

(my) older brother あに 兄 会L7(s)

older sister おねえさん お姉さん 会L1, 会L7, 会L7(s)

(my) older sister あね 姉 会L7, 会L7(s)

once a year いちねんにいちど 一年に一度 読L12-II

once upon a time むかしむかし 昔々 読L10-II

one ひとつ 一つ 会L9

one . . . ある～ 読L12-II

one hour いちじかん 一時間 会L4

one minute いっぷん 一分 会L1(s)

one o'clock いちじ 一時 会L1, 会L1(s)

one person ひとり 一人 会L7

one way かたみち 片道 会L10(s)

one year old いっさい 一歳 会L1(s)

oneself じぶん 自分 読L10-II

on うえ 上 会L4

on foot あるいて 歩いて 会L10

only . . . ～だけ 会L11

open (something) あける 開ける 会L6

operation しゅじゅつ 手術 会L12(s)

ophthalmologist がんか 眼科 会L12(s)

or ～か～ 会L10

orthopedic surgeon せいけいげか 整形外科 会L12(s)

other day, the せんじつ 先日 読L9-II

other side, the むこう 向こう 読L12-II

otorhinolaryngologist じびか 耳鼻科 会L12(s)

outdoor activities アウトドア 読L11-II

over there あそこ 会L2

over there むこう 向こう 読L12-II

overtime work ざんぎょう 残業 読L8-II

own (a pet) かう 飼う 会L11

P

page ページ 会L6

page number . . . ～ページ 会L11(s)

painful いたい 痛い 会L12

panoramic パノラマ 会L5(s)

pants パンツ 会L10

parcel こづつみ 小包 会L5(s)

parenthesis かっこ 会L11(s)

park こうえん 公園 会L4

part-time job アルバイト 会L4

party パーティー 会L8

pay はらう 払う 会L10

pen ペン 会L2, 会L2(s)

pencil えんぴつ 鉛筆 会L2, 会L2(s)

people ～じん ～人 会L1

people ひとびと 人々 読L12-II

perform やる 会L5

person ひと 人 会L4

photograph しゃしん 写真 会L4

physician ないか 内科 会L12(s)

piano ピアノ 会L9

picture しゃしん 写真 会L4

pink ピンク 会L9(s)

pitiful かわいそうな 読L12-II

place ところ 所 会L8

place of origin くに 国 会L7

platform ホーム 会L10(s)

play あそぶ 遊ぶ 会L6

play (a string instrument or piano) ひく 弾く 会L9

. . ., please. (～を)おねがいします 会L2

Please give me . . . (～を)ください 会L2

A B C D E F G H I J K L M N O **P Q R S** T U V W X Y Z

S

A B C D E F G H I J K L M N O P Q R S **S** **T** U V W X Y Z

Shinkansen　しんかんせん　新幹線　会L9
ship　ふね　船　会L10
shirt　シャツ　会L10
shoes　くつ　靴　会L2
shopping　かいもの　買い物　会L4
short (length)　みじかい　短い　会L7
short (stature)　せがひくい　背が低い　会L7
shoulder　かた　肩　会L7(s)
show someone around　あんないする　案内する
　　　　　　　　　　読L9-Ⅱ
shrine　じんじゃ　神社　読L11-Ⅱ
sickness　びょうき　病気　会L9
silver　ぎんいろ　銀色　会L9(s)
silver　シルバー　会L9(s)
simple　かんたん(な)　簡単　会L10
sing　うたう　歌う　会L7
singer　かしゅ　歌手　会L11
sit down　すわる　座る　会L6
six　むっつ　六つ　会L9
six minutes　ろっぷん　六分　会L1(s)
six o'clock　ろくじ　六時　会L1(s)
six years old　ろくさい　六歳　会L1(s)
sixteen minutes　じゅうろっぷん　十六分　会L1(s)
sixth day of a month, the　むいか　六日　会L4(s)
ski　スキー　会L9
skillful　じょうず(な)　上手　会L8
sky, the　てん　天　読L12-Ⅱ
sleep　ねる　寝る　会L3
sleepy　ねむい　眠い　会L10
slide　スライド　会L5(s)
slow　おそい　遅い　会L10
slowly　ゆっくり　会L6
small　ちいさい　小さい　会L5
smart　あたまがいい　頭がいい　会L7
smoke　たばこをすう　たばこを吸う　会L6
snack　(お)かし　(お)菓子　会L11
snow　ゆき　雪　会L12, 読L10-Ⅱ
so　だから　会L4
soccer　サッカー　会L10
something　なにか　何か　会L8
sometimes　ときどき　時々　会L3
song　うた　歌　会L7
so-so　まあまあ　会L11
south　みなみ　南　会L6(s)
souvenir　(お)みやげ　(お)土産　会L4
spa　おんせん　温泉　会L9
speak　はなす　話す　会L3
special delivery　そくたつ　速達　会L5(s)
spend time pleasantly　あそぶ　遊ぶ　会L6

sports　スポーツ　会L3
spring　はる　春　会L10
stairs　かいだん　階段　会L10(s)
stand up　たつ　立つ　会L6
standard Japanese　ひょうじゅんご　標準語
　　　　　　　　　　　　　会L11(s)
stare (at)　じろじろみる　じろじろ見る　会L8
station　えき　駅　会L10, 読L6-Ⅰ
stay (at a hotel, etc.)　とまる　泊まる　会L10
stays at . . .　いる　会L4
stomach　おなか　会L7(s), L12
store　みせ　店　読L4-Ⅲ
straight　まっすぐ　会L6(s), 読L6-Ⅰ
stress　ストレス　読L8-Ⅱ
strip of fancy paper　たんざく　読L12-Ⅱ
student　がくせい　学生　会L1
student discount　がくわり　学割　会L10(s)
study　べんきょうする　勉強する　会L3
study abroad　りゅうがくする　留学する　会L11
subway　ちかてつ　地下鉄　会L10
summer　なつ　夏　会L8
Sunday　にちようび　日曜日　会L3, 会L4(s)
sunny weather　はれ　晴れ　会L12
super express　とっきゅう　特急　会L10(s)
supermarket　スーパー　会L4
surface mail　ふなびん　船便　会L5(s)
surfing　サーフィン　会L5
surgeon　げか　外科　会L12(s)
(be) surprised　びっくりする　読L10-Ⅱ
sweat shirt　トレーナー　会L2
Sweden　スウェーデン　会L1
sweet　あまい　甘い　会L12
sweet bun　(お)まんじゅう　読L4-Ⅲ
sweets　(お)かし　(お)菓子　会L11
swim　およぐ　泳ぐ　会L5

tail end　いちばんうしろ　一番後ろ　会L10(s)
take (a class)　とる　取る　会L11, 読L7-Ⅱ
take (amount of time/money)　かかる　会L10
take (pictures)　とる　撮る　会L4
take (something)　もっていく　持っていく
　　　　　　　　　　会L8
take a bath　(お)ふろにはいる　(お)風呂に入る
　　　　　　　　　　会L6
take a walk　さんぽする　散歩する　会L9
take back　つれてかえる　連れて帰る　読L12-Ⅱ
Take care.　では、おげんきで　では、お元気で
　　　　　　　　　　読L5-Ⅱ

A B C D E F G H I J K L M N O P Q R S **T** U V W X Y Z

take care of oneself　からだにきをつける
　体に気をつける　読L7-Ⅱ
take medicine　くすりをのむ　薬を飲む　会L9
take off　とる　取る　読L10-Ⅱ
talk　はなす　話す　会L3
tall　せがたかい　背が高い　会L7
tape　テープ　会L2
teach　おしえる　教える　会L6
teacher　せんせい　先生　会L1
telephone　でんわ　電話　会L1
tell a lie　うそをつく　会L11
temperature (weather)　きおん　気温　会L12
temple　（お）てら　（お）寺　会L4
ten　とお　十　会L9
ten minutes　じゅっぷん　十分　会L1(s)
ten o'clock　じゅうじ　十時　会L1(s)
ten years old　じゅっさい　十歳　会L1(s)
tennis　テニス　会L3
tenth day of a month, the　とおか　十日
　　　　　　　　　　　　　　会L4(s)

test　テスト　会L5
textbook　きょうかしょ　教科書　会L6
Thank you.　ありがとう/ありがとうございます　会G
Thank you.　どうも　会L2
Thank you for the meal. (after eating)
　ごちそうさま　会G
Thank you for the meal. (before eating)
　いただきます　会G
that . . .　その　会L2
that . . . (over there)　あの　会L2
that one　それ　会L2
that one (over there)　あれ　会L2
That would be fine.　けっこうです　結構です
　　　　　　　　　　　　会L6
That wouldn't be necessary.
　けっこうです　結構です　会L6
That's right.　そうです　会L1
That's right.　そうですね　会L3
That's too bad.　ざんねんですね　残念ですね
　　　　　　　　　　　　会L8
then . . .　じゃあ　会L2
there　そこ　会L4
there are many . . .　おおい　多い　会L12
there is . . .　ある　会L4
therefore　だから　会L4
thermometer　たいおんけい　体温計　会L12(s)
these days　このごろ　会L10
thin　やせています　会L7
thing (concrete object)　もの　物　会L12

think　おもう　思う　会L8
third day of a month, the　みっか　三日　会L4(s)
(become) thirsty　のどがかわく　のどが渇く
　　　　　　　　　　　　会L12
thirteen minutes　じゅうさんぷん　十三分　会L1(s)
thirty minutes　さんじゅっぷん　三十分　会L1(s)
this . . .　この　会L2
this month　こんげつ　今月　会L4(s), 会L8
this morning　けさ　今朝　会L8
this one　これ　会L2
this person (polite)　こちら　会L11
this semester　こんがっき　今学期　会L11
this week　こんしゅう　今週　会L4(s), 会L6
this year　ことし　今年　会L4(s), 会L10
three　みっつ　三つ　会L9
three minutes　さんぷん　三分　会L1(s)
three o'clock　さんじ　三時　会L1(s)
three years old　さんさい　三歳　会L1(s)
throat　のど　会L12
Thursday　もくようび　木曜日　会L4, 会L4(s)
ticket　きっぷ　切符　会L5
(boarding) ticket　じょうしゃけん　乗車券　会10(s)
ticket vending area　きっぷうりば　切符売り場
　　　　　　　　　　　　会L10(s)
till (a time)　～まで　会L5
(be) tired　つかれている　疲れている　読L8-Ⅱ
(get) tired　つかれる　疲れる　会L11
to (a place)　～まで　会L5
today　きょう　今日　会L3, 会L4(s)
together　いっしょに　一緒に　会L5
together with (a person)　～と　会L4
tomato　トマト　会L8
tomorrow　あした　会L3, 会L4(s)
tonight　こんばん　今晩　会L3
tooth　は　歯　会L7(s), 会L12
tough (situation)　たいへん（な）　大変
　　　　　　　　　　　　会L6, 読L5-Ⅱ
town　まち　町　会L4
toy　おもちゃ　会L11
track number . . .　～ばんせん　～番線　会L10(s)
traffic light　しんごう　信号　会L6(s)
train　でんしゃ　電車　会L6
transfer　のりかえ　乗り換え　会L10(s)
travel　りょこう　旅行　会L5
T-shirt　Tシャツ　会L7
Tuesday　かようび　火曜日　会L4, 会L4(s)
turn　まがる　曲がる　会L6(s)
turn off　けす　消す　会L6
turn on　つける　会L6

TV　テレビ　会L2(s), 会L3

twelve minutes　じゅうにふん　十二分　会L1(s)

twelve o'clock　じゅうにじ　十二時　会L1(s)

twentieth day of a month, the　はつか　二十日
　　　　　　　　　　　　　　　　会L4(s)

twenty minutes　にじゅっぷん　二十分　会L1(s)

twenty years old　はたち　二十歳　会L1(s)

twenty-four-print
　　にじゅうよんまいどり　24枚撮り　会L5(s)

twenty-fourth day of a month, the
　　にじゅうよっか　二十四日　会L4(s)

two　ふたつ　二つ　会L9

two minutes　にふん　二分　会L1(s)

two months ago　にかげつまえ　二か月前
　　　　　　　　　　　　　　　会L4(s)

two o'clock　にじ　二時　会L1(s)

two people　ふたり　二人　会L7

two people each　ふたりずつ　二人ずつ
　　　　　　　　　　　　　　会L11(s)

two years old　にさい　二歳　会L1(s)

uh-huh　うん　会L8

uh-uh　ううん　会L8

um . . .　あの　会L1

umbrella　かさ　傘　会L2

under　した　下　会L4

understand　わかる　会L4

unhurriedly　ゆっくり　会L6

university　だいがく　大学　会L1

U.S.A.　アメリカ　会L1, 会L2

use　つかう　使う　会L6

usually　たいてい　大抵　会L3

various　いろいろな　読L9-Ⅱ

VCR　ビデオ　会L2(s), 会L3

vegetable　やさい　野菜　会L2

very　とても　会L5

very　すごく　会L11

very fond of　だいすき(な)　大好き　会L5

very soon　もうすぐ　会L12

video game　テレビゲーム　会L6

video tape　ビデオ　会L2(s), 会L3

vocabulary　たんご　単語　会L9

voice　こえ　声　読L10-Ⅱ

vouchers　せいりけん　整理券　会L10(s)

wait　まつ　待つ　会L4

wallet　さいふ　財布　会L2

warm　あたたかい　暖かい　会L10

wash　あらう　洗う　会L8

watch　とけい　時計　会L2

watch　みる　見る　会L3

water　みず　水　会L3

we　わたしたち　私たち　読L12-Ⅱ

weather　てんき　天気　会L5

weather forecast　てんきよほう　天気予報
　　　　　　　　　　　　　　　会L8

weave　はたをおる　はたを織る　読L12-Ⅱ

Wednesday　すいようび　水曜日　会L4, 会L4(s)

week after next, the　さらいしゅう　再来週
　　　　　　　　　　　　　　　会L4(s)

week before last, the　せんせんしゅう　先々週
　　　　　　　　　　　　　　　会L4(s)

weekend　しゅうまつ　週末　会L3

Welcome (to our store)　いらっしゃいませ　会L2

Welcome home.　おかえりなさい　会G

west　にし　西　会L6(s)

what　なん/なに　何　会L1

what kind of . . .　どんな　会L5

when　いつ　会L3

when . . .　とき　時　会L4

where　どこ　会L2

which　どちら/どっち　会L10

which . . .　どの　会L2

which one　どれ　会L2

white　しろい　白い　会L9, 会L9(s)

who　だれ　会L2

why　どうして　会L4

wife　おくさん　奥さん　会L7(s)

wife　かない　家内　会L7(s)

wife　かみさん　会L7(s)

wife　つま　妻　会L7(s)

wife　にょうぼう　女房　会L7(s)

wife　ワイフ　会L7(s)

window　まど　窓　会L2(s), 会L6

winter　ふゆ　冬　会L8

wish　ねがい　願い　読L12-Ⅱ

with (a tool)　～で　会L10

woman　おんな　女　読L11-Ⅱ

woman　おんなのひと　女の人　会L7

word　たんご　単語　会L9

work　しごと　仕事　会L1, 会L8

work　はたらく　働く　会L11

A B C D E F G H I J K L M N O P Q R S T U V **W X Y Z**

数 かず　Ｎｕｍｂｅｒｓ

	regular				h → p	h → p/b	p	k
1	いち				いっp	いっp	（いっ）	いっ
2	に							
3	さん				p	b		
4	よん	し	よ	よ	p			
5	ご							
6	ろく				ろっp	ろっp	（ろっ）	ろっ
7	なな	しち	しち					
8	はち				（はっp）	はっp	（はっ）	はっ
9	きゅう	く	く					
10	じゅう				じゅっp	じゅっp	じゅっ	じゅっ
how many	なん				p	b		
	～ドル dollars　～円えん yen　～枚まい sheets　～度ど degrees　～十じゅう ten　～万まん ten thousand	～月がつ month	～時じ o'clock　～時間じかん hours	～年ねん year　～年間ねんかん years　～人にん people	～分ふん minute　～分間ふんかん minutes	～本ほん sticks　～杯はい cups　～匹ひき animals　～百ひゃく hundred	～ページ page　～ポンド pounds	～か月げつ months　～課か lesson　～回かい times　～個こ small items

This chart shows how sounds in numbers (1-10) and counters change according to their combination.

1. *Hiragana* indicate the sound changes in numbers, and alphabets show the changes in the initial consonant of counters.
2. ( ) means that the change is optional.
3. An empty box means no sound change occurs.

k → g	s	s → z	t	special vocabulary for numbers			
いっ	いっ	いっ	いっ	ひとつ	ついたち	ひとり	1
				ふたつ	ふつか	ふたり	2
g		z		みっつ	みっか		3
				よっつ	よっか		4
				いつつ	いつか		5
ろっ				むっつ	むいか		6
				ななつ	なのか		7
はっ	はっ	はっ	はっ	やっつ	ようか		8
				ここのつ	ここのか		9
じゅっ	じゅっ	じゅっ	じゅっ	とお	とおか		10
g		z		いくつ			how many
～階 かい floor ～軒 けん houses	～セント cents ～週間 しゅうかん weeks ～冊 さつ books ～歳 さい years of age	～足 そく shoes ～千 せん thousand	～通 つう letters ～丁目 ちょうめ street address	small items years of age cf. はたち (20 years old)	date cf. じゅうよっか (14) はつか(20) にじゅう よっか(24) なんにち (how many)	people cf. ～人 にん (three or more people)	

活用表 Conjugation Chart
かつ ようひょう

verb types	dictionary forms	long forms (*masu*) (L. 3)	*te*-forms (L. 6)	short past (L. 9)	short present neg. (L. 8)	short past neg. (L. 9)
irr.	す<u>る</u>	します	して	した	しない	しなかった
irr.	く<u>る</u>	きます	きて	きた	こない	こなかった
ru	たべ<u>る</u>	〜ます	〜て	〜た	〜ない	〜なかった
u	か<u>う</u>	〜います	〜って	〜った	〜わない	〜わなかった
u	ま<u>つ</u>	〜ちます	〜って	〜った	〜たない	〜たなかった
u	と<u>る</u>	〜ります	〜って	〜った	〜らない	〜らなかった
u	あ<u>る</u>	〜ります	〜って	〜った	*ない	*なかった
u	よ<u>む</u>	〜みます	〜んで	〜んだ	〜まない	〜まなかった
u	あそ<u>ぶ</u>	〜びます	〜んで	〜んだ	〜ばない	〜ばなかった
u	し<u>ぬ</u>	〜にます	〜んで	〜んだ	〜なない	〜ななかった
u	か<u>く</u>	〜きます	〜いて	〜いた	〜かない	〜かなかった
u	い<u>く</u>	〜きます	*〜って	*〜った	〜かない	〜かなかった
u	いそ<u>ぐ</u>	〜ぎます	〜いで	〜いだ	〜がない	〜がなかった
u	はな<u>す</u>	〜します	〜して	〜した	〜さない	〜さなかった

The forms with * are exceptions.